PUBLISHED IN THE UNITED STATES of AMERICA IN 1985
by RIZZOLI INTERNATIONAL PUBLICATIONS, Inc.,
597 FIFTH AVENUE, New York NY 10017
© JMG PARIS
All rights reserved
No part of this publication may be reproduced in any manner whatsoever without permission in writing
from Rizzoli International Publications, inc.
ISBN 0-8478-5410-8
Printed and bound in France

This volume is affectionately dedicated to Mr and Mrs Fedja Anzelewski.

ALTDORFER AND FANTASTIC REALISM
IN GERMAN ART

Edited by Jacqueline & Maurice Guillaud
Guillaud Editions - Paris
15, rue des Beaux-Arts - 75006 PARIS
Distributed by Rizzoli - New-York *R*

Above all else, we should like to thank Professor Fedja Anzelewski for the help and unfailing attention which he gave us during the course of our research as well as during the preparation of this volume, and also as scientific curator of our Exhibition at the Centre Culturel du Marais, from April 3 to July 15, 1984.

We should also like to thank for their invaluable assistance Doctor Wolfgang Pfeiffer, Director of the Museen der Stadt Regensburg, as well as Madame Laure Beaumont, Director of the Cabinet des Estampes of the Bibliothèque Nationale, Paris, and the Directors and Curators of the following Museums: Berlin, Staatliche Museen Preussischer Kulturbesitz, Kupferstichkabinett.
Braunschweig, Herzog Anton Ulrich-Museum.
Cambridge, The Fitzwilliam Museum.
Copenhagen, Musée Royal des Beaux Arts, Cabinet des Estampes
Dusseldorf, Kunstmuseum.
Grenoble, Musée de Grenoble
Hamburg, Kunsthalle.
London, University College.
Oxford, The Ashmolean Museum.
Paris, Bibliothèque Nationale, Cabinet des Estampes.
Plymouth, City Museum and Art Gallery.
Regensburg, Stadt Museen Regensburg.
Rotterdam, Musée Boymans.
Seitenstetten, Library of the Benedictine Convent.
Stuttgart, Staatsgalerie, Graphische Sammlung.
Vienna, Bibliothek und Kupferstichkabinett der Akademie der Bildenden Künste.

as well as the staffs of the following museums:
Basel, Cabinet des Estampes de la Collection Publique des Beaux Arts.
Besançon, Bibliothèque Municipale.
Bremen, Kunsthalle.
Budapest, Musée des Beaux Arts.
Erlangen, Graphische Sammlung, Universitäts-Bibliothek.
Frankfurt, Städelsches Kunstinstitut.
Kassel, Gemäldegalerie.
Lille, Musée des Beaux Arts.
London, The National Gallery.
Munich, Bayerische Staatsgemäldesammlungen.
Munich, Bibliothek der Stadt.
Nuremberg, Germanisches Nationalmuseum.
Vienna, Albertina.
Vienna, Kunsthistorisches Museum.
for photographs of paintings and engravings.
Our gratitude goes especially to Madame Gisela Goldberg, Mr. Wolfgang Pfeiffer, Mr Pierre Vaisse and Fr. Benedikt Wagner whose close cooperation was particularly valuable and who wrote essays for this catalogue.

Our thanks also to the scientific staff in Berlin who, in collaboration with Professor Anzelewski, helped to write the technical descriptions of the works in this catalogue: M.B. Brinkmann, Frau Dr. R. Braig, Mr. M. Roth.

A special word of gratitude is due to Mlle Hébert whose enormous work on the occasion of the publication of the inventory of the engravings of the Northern Schools in the collection of the Bibliothèque Nationale was of great assistance to us during the preparation of the exhibition. Our thanks also to those in charge of the Réserve des Estampes of the Bibliothèque Nationale, Mlle Barbin, Mme Lambert and Mlle Gardey.

We express our sincere appreciation to all those who helped us, among whom:
The Abbot of Seitenstetten, Austria - Mr Jörg P. Anders Berlin, Germany - Mr James Barber, Plymouth - Mr W.A.L. Beeren, Rotterdam - Mr André Bouchy, Paris - Mr E. Fischer, Copenhagen - Mr Garlick, Oxford - Mr Pierre Gaudibert, Grenoble - Mme Ulrike Gauss, Stuttgart - Mr F.-W. Heckmanns, Dusseldorf - Mr Ch von Heusinger, Braunschweig - Mr Jürgen Hinrichs, Munich - Mr M. Jaffé, Cambridge - Mme Jenni, Vienna - Mme Jestaz, Paris - Mme Lightbwon, London - Mme F. Mölzer, Paris - Mr W. Pfeiffer, Regensburg - Mr Karl Rahberger, St Florian - Mr Schaar, Hamburg - Mr Violland, Paris.
A special word of thanks to the translators, Elizabeth Bronfen, Gill Gladstone, Felice Haskell, Michael Walsh and Paul Willenbrock.

Our thanks are also due to the Austrian Institute at the Austrian Embassy, Paris and to the Goethe Institut, Paris.

Lastly, we should like to express our warmest thanks to Mr Jörg von Uthmann, Cultural Counsellor at the Embassy of the Federal Republic of Germany, for his assistance in compiling the catalog.

1 - The dead lansquenet - Cat. 1

TABLE OF CONTENTS

In this work, towards which several specialists have contributed, under the scientific direction of Mr. Fedja Anzelewski, it was our intention to group together most of the artists who during this period of German art at the beginning of the 16th century, could be said to belong to the "Danube School". It is for this reason that, along with Altdorfer, the uncontested master of this "School" and whose work has been here almost integrally reproduced, we have chosen to include the early works of Lukas Cranach the Elder, as well as a wide selection from the art of Wolf Huber and other masters who were either their contemporaries or immediate successors.
In the case of each artist the adopted order of works is:

Drawings, engravings, paintings.

For the first time and with special authorisation from the Libraries of Besançon and Munich, we have decided to present as a centerpiece a wide selection of pages from Maximilian's Prayerbook, decorated with the incomparable drawings executed by the masters of the Danube School (Altdorfer, Cranach the Elder, Jörg Breu and others). M.G.

2 - Weeping willows in an alpine landscape - Cat. 2

Scientific Curator: Professor Fedja Anzelewski

General Curators: Jacqueline and Maurice Guillaud

The Exhibition was designed and arranged by Jacqueline and Maurice Guillaud.

3 - Woodcutter in a Landscape - A. Altdorfer
c. 1522 - Hand-coloured pen-and-ink drawing - 210×136 mm - Berlin K., SMPK.

Albrecht Altdorfer and the question of "the Danube School"

In German art history, Albrecht Altdorfer, who worked as a painter, designer and architect in Regensburg in the early part of the 16th century, is intimately connected with the idea of a "Danube School of Painting"[1]. In general, the name "Danube School" refers to the art of those regions bordering both sides of the Danube between Vienna and Regensburg. Basically, this geographical area corresponds to those parts of the country once populated by the Bavarians[2]. Thus, the art of the Danube School is considered to be a special Bavarian form of artistic expression.

Recently, scholars have maintained that the style typical of the Danube School can also be found in art works that were produced contemporaneously in neighboring regions. Thus, Franz Winzinger considers Tyrol and the Salzburg[3] region, and Anton Legner considers Carinthia and Styria[4] to be part of the Danube School. F. Dworschak sees the influence of the Danubian style at work in the Friuli[5] and Ruppert Feuchtmüller in Hungary and Transylvania[6].

The term "Danube School", originally coined to point out and characterize a unity of style that can be found in the artistic works occuring in a comparatively precisely delineated geographical area, today no longer covers the entire area to which these stylistic features are meant to apply. The Salzburg region, Tyrol, Carinthia and Styria, in short, the entire eastern part of the Alps and the Danube Basin cannot be considered a part of the Danube region without misrepresenting the geography of art. But the stylistic term "Danube School" is too narrowly conceived in more respects than this.

However, the discussion about the Danube School is in danger of developing into a mere verbal battle, since no definition for what is meant by the style of this school has so far been formulated, at least no definition that can claim to have general validity. We must, therefore, try to describe the phenomenon of this art movement in the hope of clarifying its distinctive characteristic features to such an extent that a sufficiently stable rudimentary definition can be determined, on which further remarks, as well as an understanding of this exhibition, can be based.

Someone who has encountered the works of one or several Masters of the Danube School is left with strong impressions of scenic landscapes depicting bizarre mountains and gigantic trees. In these pictures man seems to become one with surrounding Nature. At times these landscapes contain something primeval, as though the radiant sunrises ans sunsets and the dramatic cloud configurations were taking place above an earth as yet untouched by human beings. Often man's existence is betrayed only indirectly through the buildings he has erected although, due to their ruinous appearance, they frequently evoke the impression of assimilating themselves with Nature. This overemphasis on Nature in comparison with the depiction of man, at a time when not only in European painting, but also in different German landscapes, the human figure stood at the center of artisitic endeavors, is unusual and can thus be considered one of the most remarkable features of the art of the Danube School.

However, this peculiarity is far more pronounced in the drawings of Altdorfer and Huber — to name only the most prominent artists of this group — than in the paintings and graphic arts of the Danube Masters (a difference which is also apparent in the exhibition). Landscape depictions without accessory decorations began with Albrecht Altdorfer's landscape etchings shortly before 1520, while the first paintings of this kind were created by him around 1528.

In the years after 1500, when the first works which can be ascribed to the Danube School appeared, artistic production was still dominated by panels depicting a Christian theme, whether in the form of altarpieces or in the form of devotional paintings for use during private prayers. Alongside religious art, profane paintings such as portraits or representations of mythology or allegory were assigned an extremely minor role. Common to all these areas of artistic representation was, however, the fact that they placed the human figure in the center of interest, so that it consequently stood at the center of the artistic endeavor as well. For these obvious reasons the artists of the Danube School were unable to do without the depiction of human figures, just like the Masters of other provinces.

Yet the human depictions of this art group only rarely assume individual character traits. In the roundish heads of the female figures, the eyes, the nose and the mouth are only formally hinted at and the body disappears to a large extent under a mass of clothes. The arrangement of the surface of the garments into bulging folds and a system of parallel and radial folds, hides the figures' bodies rather than illustrating the functions of the limbs, as would be expected at the time of the Renaissance. Even the men, whose differently styled clothes tend to allow the movements of the limbs to be seen more clearly, the

shapes of their bodies are obfuscated by the stylishly puffed pants and sleeves, the slits, as well as the knee-length doublets. The painters of the Danube School used garments but not the bodies of their figures to illustrate movment and expression.

This peculiarity of the art of the Danube School, which the late Franz Winzinger correctly called highly anticlassical, allows one to understand why portraiture played a very subordinate role in the artistic area influenced by this style. No other German landscape painting has preserved fewer portraits than the Danube School. This further elucidates how such an approach is foreign to the aspirations of the Renaissance. The program for German painting of this epoch, as formulated by Dürer, postulated that in addition to religious themes portraiture was to be the most important artistic task.[7]

The special position occupied by the Danube School can, however, be grasped not only in respect to subject matter and formal questions, but also, and primarily, in a very distinctive style and in a preference for certain applied techniques.

Scholars have repeatedly emphasized the picturesque character of the Danube style. The absoluteness and generality of such an observation, however, tends to foster misconceptions. One cannot call the art of the Danube School picturesque in the way one would the Dutch School of the 17th century. Apart from the fact that the paintings of the southeastern German painters of the Dürer period were at times quite colorful, the linear element in a painting played a major part in this art school. The significance of the line as a means of expression is, of course, more striking in the drawings than in the paintings.

The Masters of the Danube School preferred to use color-pigmented paper, on which they would sketch their compositions in black lines, using a very fine pen or a very pointed brush made of marten hair. These were then artistically finished off by an application of opaque white paint, which was not, as is usually the case, applied in whole layers but, as we find in Dürer's brush drawings, in consecutive strokes.

While Dürer used the technique of brush drawing on color-pigmented paper only for comparatively large format drawings and only for specific purposes (portraits, figures and drapery sketches, made in preparation for paintings),[8] the drawings of the Danube School are surprising because of their often quite modest format and their pictorial unity. Very few sketches and sketches made in preparation for larger works have been preserved (Fig. 230) and only in the work of Wolf Huber can many be found.

The use of the brush drawing technique for completed composition appears, however, to be a peculiarity of the generation of Dürer's students and their peers, as for example Hans Baldung, Hans Leu, Nikolaus Manuel Deutsch. By means of the three-step toning process, in which the color-pigmented drawing surface constituted the second phase, these drawings acquired a certain picturesque effect, although they were, in fact, distinctly graphic art works. Their picturesque effect made them suitable for preparatory sketches as well as pictorially conceived representations.

But a far greater significance is attached to the linear element in the drawings of the Danube School than is generally assumed. The execution of the drawn line in Dürer's classical drawing style, which was greatly influenced by the technique of copper plate engraving, is such that each line serves a precise description of the form of an object, with the aim of depicting it as plastically and spatially as possible, and thus attaching only a very limited intrinsic value to the line itself. Within this, as I would like to call it, system of ordered lines, even a fragment or a detail is understood as a part of a meaningful whole. For the artist of the Danube School the line had a value of its own, with which he could play freely. Thus, the often recurring spiral line, to give an example, could assume a variety of meanings. It could depict clouds or smoke, foliage, vegetation, or worn and cracked tree barks, or might simply be hachures, indicating curvature.

Parallel or vertical lines were used to indicate garment folds but were equally used to signify the shaded side of the face of a rock, as in Altdorfer's painting "Samson's Battle with the Lion" (fig. 26). They only derive their meaning from the compositional whole, because they indicate rather than describe a certain object. Due to its great generosity, this play of lines gains the quality of non-representational ornamentation, wherein lies its appeal to present-day viewers.

One can hardly imagine a greater contrast than that between Dürer's ordered line and the unbounded, freely wandering execution of the line of the Masters surrounding Albrecht Altdorfer. Winzinger has correctly spoken of an anti-classical movement in connection with this art school.

In contrast to Altdorfer's drawings on color pigmented paper, comparatively few of his pen-and-ink drawings on non-pigmented paper have been preserved. These are usually preparations for other works, such as the sketch for the engraving "Venus Punishes Cupid" (fig. 108) or the piece "Church Interior" (fig. 47), which is a sketch for the interior space of the Munich "Birth of Mary". In this drawing, as in others, Altdorfer uses a wash consisting of gray watercolor, in order to give greater relief to his depictions through the opposition of light and dark. Pen-and-ink drawings are far more numerous in the work of Wolf Huber than in that of any other Master, whereas he used the technique of chiaruscuro on colour-pigmented paper (generally tile red), in particular for studies of heads.

5 - The Virgin Mary of Regensburg - A. Altdorfer - 1518 - Pen-and-ink - Berlin, K., SMPK.

The stylistic peculiarities of the artists of the Danube region, which I have shown in their drawings, can be seen in their paintings as well. They appear most prominently in the depiction of a Battle, painted on a tabletop (fig. 236). Although this may be an extreme example of the treatment of drawn lines in a painting, it is by no means an exception.

The intrinsic value of the lineament resulted in no more importance being attached to the depiction of the human figure, which for the Renaissance was the primary concern of art, than to the depiction of Nature and the architecture surrounding the figures. Thus, neither a philosophical idea nor a particularly strongly developed feeling for nature among the Bavarian artists led to the frequently described phenomenon of unity in their artistic style, but rather solely the artistic temperament of a group of artists. This realization forces one to reconsider how one is to assess the art-historical construction of a Danube School and its Bavarian nature.

It has already been pointed out that the term "Danube School" is open to discussion. Having seen that intellectual connections, as has hitherto been outlined, did not exist in that form, one must ask whether something like a Danube School ever existed. And what role, if any, the so often cited Bavarian element played in it. If one looks at the "fathers" of the Danube style, as Otto Benesch has described them[9], one discovers that of the three painters named by him, namely Lukas Cranach the Elder, Jörg Breu the Elder and Albrecht Altdorfer, only the last was a Bavarian in the strict sense of the word, because one assumes that he was born and raised in Regensburg. Cranach came from Kronach, a small town in the northern part of Franconia, and Breu came from an artisan family from the Swabian city of Augsburg.

Altdorfer and Breu[10] were probably born around 1480, while Cranach was some eight years older. What these painters have in common is something highly superficial and more or less accidental. Around the year 1500 all three spent some time in Austria[11]. Both Cranach and Breu, the latter of whom worked exclusively as a painter in this region, were at the time in the midst of their "storm and stress" period. This is extraordinary for Cranach, since he was already 30 in 1520, the year he created his first known works, paintings and woodcuts (fig. 259).

Although it is proven that Jörg Breu was in Krems-on-the-Danube in 1500, he had already returned to his home town Augsburg by 1502. In his altarpieces in the Carthusian monastery Aggsbach, dated 1501 and for the Cistercian monastery Zwettl[12], done in the year 1502, he emerges as a painter who, under the influence of the painter Jan Polack (from Crakow but working in Munich), heightened to expressivity the style of Rueland Früauf the Elder or the Masters from Großgemein. It further appears that he met the painter's apprentice PW from Cologne here,[13] who also influenced him.[14] Jörg Breu was an artist with more of a receptive than a creative disposition, and prone to assimilate and rework the influences of his various surroundings.

His personal manner could hardly have been strong enough to create a new style. Only the Franconian Cranach was strong enough to leave a lasting influence on the artistic creations in southeastern Germany. One need only compare the head of John the Baptist in the drawing in Lille (fig. 256), of 1490, with the figure of the same saint in the portal of the church in Kronach[15], to recognize that his art was still deeply rooted in the late Gothic sense of form.[16] In the two Berlin sketches for a depiction of the theives (cat. 172 fig. 258) at the Crucifixion one can recognize the same influences. These obviously appear to be influenced by works of Bavarian origin, for example by the Crucifixion by the so-called Gabriel Mäleßkircher (Master of the Tegernsee Tabula magna).

The relationship between the art of the early Cranach[17] and these works of Bavarian provenance having been clarified, it is no longer difficult to recognize the late Gothic tendencies in the burly figures of the two woodcuts depicting the Crucifixion (fig. 257-258). In the "St. Stephen" (fig. 261)[18] this connection to the older art is clearly visible in Cranach's recourse to the woodcut of Erhard Reuwich, from the "Peregrinationes in terram sanctam" (Mainz 1486)[19]. His stocky proportions, similar to those in other works done by Cranach in his Viennese period, are both indebted to the Bavarian sense of style and express a sense of body that belonged to the new century, a sense of body related to that of the Renaissance. In no other artist does one notice so markedly the tension between an exaggerated late gothic expressivity, discharging itself in a seething desire for movment, and the aspiration towards a calm Renaissance-like monumentality. The combination of these two heterogeneous elements with a drawing technique emphasizing the intrinsic value of the line, as described above, results in that fantasy or romanticism which constitutes the particular charm of this art, bt which at the same time has led to the many misinterpretations of the "Danube style".

It is possible that Albrecht Altdorfer learned the craft of illuminated painting from his father, prior to devoting himself to panel painting and graphics. Around 1500 he created fifteen woodcuts of small and minute format[20] for the Mondsee monastery in the Salzkammergut, but then his tracks are lost until 1506. The Berlin drawing of 1504, "Lovers in a Landscape" (fig. 6) is all the more significant in that it is all that remains of his activity during those years. It shows that the young artist had studied the work of his older colleague. Not only the first drawings that can be attributed to him, but also his first copperplate engravings reveal this examination and attempt to grapple with

7 - Two Young Women - A. Altdorfer - 1506 - Pen-and-ink - 172×123 mm - Berlin, K., SMPK.

8 - St Nicholas calms the tempest - Cat. 5

Cranach's style of figure drawing and his way of depicting landscapes[21].

Of course the young artist could not have learned exclusively from Cranach. Neither Cranach's art nor Altdörfer's can be conceived of without Dürer's graphics, especially his series of woodcuts, entitled "Apocalypse", and the first prints of the "Great Passion". In these large format prints, graphic methods had for the first time been utilised to illustrate, with artistic perfection, the interplay between the human figure and space, that is, both the interior and the landscape. Their effect on contemporary artists, especially on the younger ones, must indeed have been overwhelming. In fact, it seems that the graphic arts played a vital role in Altdorfer's development.

The influence of Italian copperplate engravings and niello prints, as has been repeatedly noted by Winzinger[22], seems also to have occured in this period of Cranach's development. It is more difficult, however, to establish with certainty that his encounter (also suggested by Winzinger) with the art of Michael Pacher[23], which most probably took place in Salzburg, where the last and most monumental work of the Tyrolian woodcutter and painter stood, fell into the period of this trip to the Mondsee. The encounter can be proven only after his second trip to Austria.

From 1507 on Altdorfer finally developed his own unmistakable style. While he preferred to depict nude figures with a mythological or allegorical meaning in his first copperplate engravings, and always placed them in front of a neutral background, a visible change occurred in this period. Especially in the drawings, spatial relations begin to play a more pronounced role. The execution of the drawn line, which was still somewhat timid and limited to a small area, becomes freer and more eloquent, in short, more expressive.

Most probably in connection with the commission from the prior Peter Maurer of St. Florian for a large Sebastian altar, Altdorfer undertook a journey down the Danube. The drawings "The Danube at Sarmingstein" of 1511 in Budapest and "Alpine landscape with willows" (fig. 2) bespeak of this trip. These are obviously landscapes painted from Nature. And yet, despite the exact rendition of each topographical situation, these drawings are the opposite of vedutas. They contain an aggressive quality. The willows appear to be more like evil, fantastic animals than like plants.

Faced with this conception of Nature, one is immediately reminded of fairy tales or even prehistoric myths, of a time when plants could speak or, as was the case with Orpheus, move about. Nature represented here something against whose huge demonic powers man must fight for his survival. People living today confronted with the problem of how to avoid a definitive destruction of Nature,

that is of our water, our air, our plants, and animals, can hardly imagine how immensely difficult it was for the people of the 16th century to master the force of Nature. During this age, the majority of human beings, among them many educated persons, were convinced of the real existence of witches, who had the power to misuse demonic forces for their own, usually evil, purposes. In the work of Marsilio Ficino (1433-1499), the founder of Florentinian Neoplatonism and a philosopher still esteemed in Germany, one can read about all the horrible powers people at that time thought demons were capable of[24]. In Cranach's Stephen woodcut one finds fiends of this kind harrying the first Christian martyrs. One can hardly find a more significant testimony to the fear of demons at that time than this print, where Cranach has replaced the joyful children climbing up and down little trees with infernal monsters.

A person's life around 1500 was determined on the one hand by a still very concrete and real threat posed by Nature, along with a belief in spirits and demons, and on the other hand by the Christian hope for redemption and eternal life. Only when one realizes this, can one comprehend the fantastic elements in the works of Altdorfer and his contemporaries. The trees depicted in many of Altdorfer's drawings embody the same threat which emanates fro the evil spirits in Cranach's woodcuts. As though endowed with enormous tentacles, they seem to grasp at any person moving about in their vicinity. This is a Nature which is both hostile to man, yet of which he is also a part, for according to Ficino, man partakes both of God and of Nature.

Altdorfer's work reflects these teachings of Ficino with extraordinary accuracy, although it cannot fully be proven, as it can for Dürer, that the Master from Regensburg was familiar with the neoplatonic philosophy of Ficino. Works such as the small Berlin painting "The Satyr Family" of 1507 (fig. 198), the Munich panel "St. George's Battle with the Dragon" done 1510 (fig. 197) and "The Dead Mercenary" depict, each in their own way, the creature-like essence of man, depict his inextricable bonds to Nature. The Satyrs in the Berlin painting are forces of Nature which have taken on human shape. The Mercenary of the drawing depicts the biblical words, "ashes to ashes, dust to dust", in a highly poetic form. And the painting of the battle with the dragon informs us that even saints are subject to Nature. Only the dramatic lighting accompanies the drama of Christ's passion and the martyrdom of the saints.

The night scenes from the St.Florian altar "Prayer at the Mount of Olives" and "The Arrest of Christ" (fig. 204 - 205) do not, however, stand isolated from the rest of German art of that time. Grünewald's "Resurrection of Christ" from the Isenheimer: altar is only the zenith within his work, and, as has been pointed out by Panof-

9 - Two Mercenaries and a Pair of Lovers - Cat. 6

10 - Lovers in a Wheat Field - A. Altdorfer - 1508 - Pen-and-ink - 221×149 mm - Basel, Offentliche Kunstsammlung.

sky, Dürer for his part included light as an element in the organization of his copperplate engravings and woodcuts from the years 1510-1515. One must, however, go further and include Dutch and Italian painting as well, for there the painting of nocturnal scenes was also developed in this period, as for example in Jan Gossaert's painting "Christ at the Mount of Olives", dated 1512. It was also around 1519 that Raphael painted the "Liberation of Peter" in Rome for the Vatican Stanzas. Altdorfer's artistic importance, it is necessary to emphasize this simultaneity. But the similarity between the painter from Regensburg and Dutch Painting is not just limited to a mutual preference

parable sense of style in Altdorfer on the one hand, and the three Dutch painters Jan Gossaert, Jan Mostaert and Joachim Patenier, all roughly the same age, on the other[25]. All three originated in the late Gothic tradition and in their work tried to reconcile this tradition with the new tendencies in art. In all four cases the result was a certain manneristic tendency, which very quickly, that is to say around 1520, resulted in a very pronounced Mannerism in the Netherlands, while Altdorfer did not follow manneristic conceptions of form until the last years of his creative life, having gone through a phase in which he tried to approach the classical norms. Thus, a figure like the

for scenes with nocturnal lighting. Leaving all individual differences aside one can ascertain an approximately com-

Ethiopian king in the Frankfurt "Adoration of the Three Magi", made around 1530/35, can most certainly be com-

11 - Young Woman on Horseback, Hawking. - A. Altdorfer - c. 1508 - Pen-and-ink - 142×139 mm - Berlin, K., SMPK.

pared to corresponding figures in Dutch painting. Moreover, Altdorfer and other Masters of the Danube School are not as isolated within the realm of German art either, as is often suggested. The element of the fantastic, which has been pointed out several times, as well as their Mannerism, which only partially corresponds with the fantastic element, were already known for quite some time to German painting. In his pioneering work, writing as early as 192..., Wilhelm Pinder exhaustively described late gothic Mannerism in German sculpture[26]. In the field of painting, representatives of this style can be found, above all in painters from Cologne, such as the Master of the Ursula legend, whose "Dream of St. Ursula" unites all the above named characteristic traits-the fantastic element, the light symbolism, and formal Mannerism. Jörg Ratgeb is another artist who displays obvious late Gothic manneristic traits. Within the southwestern part of Germany, the Master HL, a woodcarver and copperplate engraver, who did the drawing for the woodcut (fig. 334 to 337), also belongs to this group. One has tried to identify him as the sculptor Hans Leinberger[27], who was a native of Bavaria, and of late, with the woodcutter Hans Loy[28] from Ulm. Without wanting to take sides, obvious stylistic similarities between the works of the Master HL and the woodcut works of Austrian artists like the Master Mauer and the woodcutter who did the sculptures for the shrine of the altar in Zwetl (today Adamsthal by Brünn) are so striking that one can assume there to have been some contact between them. Lately elements of the Danube School style have been discovered in the work of Hans Baldung Grien[29]. In the case of the Swiss artists Urs Graf, Nikolaus Manuel Deutsch[30] and especially Han Leu the Elder[31], one occasionally finds an extraordinary similarity between their manner of drawing and the generous execution of the drawn line typical of the Danube School, so that the question avises as to whether one is not perhaps dealing here with a phenomenon typical of Alpine regions. The two Crucifixion panels by Mathis Nithart Gothart in Basel and Washington also contain peculiarities of style which are generally attributed in the Danube School.

The second great artist of southeastern German art is Wolf Huber. He was born the son of the artist Hans Huber in Feldkirchen in the Vorarlberg and was probably the same age as Altdorfer. It is most likely that he received his first training from his father. Because the name Huber, though not uncommon, is already mentioned in the annals of Feldkirchen in 1424 and one finds representatives of this name throughout the century, it is assumed that Huber comes from an old-established family. This means he was not a Bavarian, but rather Alemannian. Nothing is known about his further development until the year 1510[32]. According to the Nuremberg drawing dated 1510, he was at that time in the Salzkammergut, drawing the landscape of the Mondsee with the Schafberg. Shortly after this, he

sketched the town Urfahr, on the banks of the Danube across from Linz. Both works are so sparingly drawn that they cannot be compared with Altdorfer's way of using drawing techniques. All expressivity seems foreign to Huber. And yet the way in which he condenses the form of the willows to their outlines, without drawing anything inside these contours suggests a sense of form and creative power in no way inferior to Cranach and Altdorfer. The ability to summarize a form, using an almost formalistic conciseness, continues to be one of Huber's typical traits right through to his last works, such as "The Prayer at the Mount of Olives" (fig. 306) dated 1545/50. Even when he tries to heighten the artistic effect by offering a more detailed rendition of that drawn inside the contours of an object or by a wash of the drawing, a clarity and transparency of composition is almost always preserved.

In his landscape drawings as in the compositional sketches and the portrait sketches, however, a certain expressivity increases in the course of his development. In the landscapes (the sites for which in most cases have been found), one can see how the small-scale, tightly-curled forms of the drawn space inside the outlines are increased and assume a position which creates a dynamic tension with the generously drawn cloud configurations and light rays, found only in his drawings. Thus, light is also an intrinsic element in Huber's work[33].

A comparison between the way Altdorfer and Huber depict willows, which were a particularly popular motif of this art group, clarifies the difference between these two artists in a way which is more useful than any verbal description. This can be done by contrasting Altdorfer's drawing from the Viennese Academy (fig. 2) and Huber's drawing, dated 1529 from Erlangen. In the drawing by the Regensburg artist one finds a landscape depicting two trees, which seem like strange creatures; in the drawing of the Passau court painter we find a composition governed by one tree. But the hollow willow has become a monument of expressive calligraphy. Although both artists are far removed from a naturalistic manner of artistic practice, they are so in very different ways. To describe their varying temperaments, one might call Altdorfer expressive, free, footloose to the point of incomprehensibility, and see Huber, on the other hand, concerned with clarity and the beauty of the drawn line, even when extremely expressive. Even though many of his drawings were done in geographical areas bordering on the Danube in Austria, one cannot count him as a member of the Danube School in a narrow sense of the word.

After working one to two years in the southeastern part of germany, during which they most probably formatively influenced the artistic style of a large area, Lukas Cranach and Jörg Breu left the Danube region. While Breu totally reassimilated himself to his native tradition, Cranach transferred at least some of the artistic achievements of his

12 - The Deposition from the Cross - A. Altdorfer c. 1508/09 - Pen-and-ink - 220×139 mm Frankfurt, Städelisches Kunstinstitut.

13 - Christ on the Mount of Olives - A. Altdorfer - 1509 - Pen-and-ink - 210×157 mm - Berlin, K., SMPK.

Viennese years to central and northern Germany. He was followed by Erhard Altdorfer, Albrecht's younger brother, who finally worked as a court painter to the Duke of Mecklenburg from 1512 until his death in 1561/62. In his main work, the illustrations for the Lübeck Bible, done 1533/34, the style of the so-called Danube School lives on in an unbroken form.

The case of the painter Georg Lemberger, originally from lower Bavaria is similar. He seems to have followed

became a citizen of Leipzig, where he continued to work as a painter and wood-engraver until his early death in 1532. To the end of his life, he also remained true to the style of the Danube School.

One of the most striking examples for the expansion of the Danube style is the portrait relief of the Bishop of Ermland, by Tiedemann Giese, who comes from a family from Danzig. The work was attributed to Hans Schenck, called Scheutzlich, an artist working primarily for the

the Palatine Count Philipp to Thuringia, when the latter was appointed Bishop of Naumburg in 1517. In 1523 he

court of Duke Albrecht of Prussia. In the catalogue for the exhibition "The Art of the Danube Scholl", Anton Legner

14 - Saint Margaret Standing on the Devil - A. Altdorfer - 1509 - Pen-and-ink - 159×104 mm - Berlin, K., SMPK.

wrote: "More decivie, however, is the fact that the pictorial conception as a whole of this relief can only be explained in conjunction with the phenomenon of a Danube style".[34]

If the term "Danube School" is applied in such an extended sense, however, it is totally drained of its original meaning.

To summarize the observations made so far one can say that all those elements which, according to common opinion, distinguish the character of the "Danube School" can be found concurrently in other areas as well. Since these elements were common in areas far beyond the borders of what was then called the Holy Roman Empire of German Nations, one can hardly consider this style to be a regionally limited, specifically Bavarian-Austrian art movement. Rather we are concerned here with the appearance of a dispute, noticeable in many part of Europe, between the expressive, late gothic tradition of art and the new artistic conceptions of the Renaissance from Italy. Only in Germany, however, did sculpture and painting, as well as graphics and drawings, have such a decisive part in this process.

The solutions found by painters and sculptors in the areas extending from Udine[35] in the South, to Lübeck and Danzig (now Gdansk) in the North and from Vienna in the East to Antwerp in the West are in many cases surprisingly similar. The resemblance lies particularly in the fact that for all the artists, late gothic expressivity has priority over the realism demanded by the Italian predecessors.

One of the most significant examples of this artistic dispute is the monument in honor of Archbishop Uriel of Gemmingen in the cathedral of Mainz, which was made by Hans Backoffen between 1515 and 1517. The frame, composed of pilasters, capitals depicting warriors and semicircular arches imitating classical style has been combined, in a unique and unequaled way, with baldachins of late gothic tracery. The presentation of the figures' garments, especially the thick tubular folds, remind one of Hans Leinberger's use of garments. The sculptorial conception of the heads, is reminiscent of the sculptures of the Altar of Mauer. [36]

In the area of the "Danube Style" a similarly obvious example of this artistic dispute can be found only at a much later date, namely in a work of architecture, the church of the "Beautiful Mary" in Regensburg. Although von Baldaß considers this church to be one of the earliest architectural structures of the German Renaissance[37], its detail work, rose windows, tracery and tower ornamentation is as late gothic as the baldachins of Backoffen. In the woodcut by Michael Ostendorfer (fig. 332 to 334) the dynamically rich combination of these two styles is far more clearly noticeable than in the reduced form in which it is applied in the architectural structure.

This problem by no means emerges as clearly for the painters of the "Danube School". If one, however, looks at Altdorfer's Altar in St. Florian, bearing this dispute in mind, one discovers even here a co-existence of the old and the new. The often very slender, highly active figures of late gothic origin form an extraordinary, albeit usually, unnoticed contrast to the sumptuous architectural forms, which imitate classical style. Altdorfer's study of Italian art manifests itself at an even earlier period in his graphic arts. Thus even in their dramatic conception, the copperplate engravings from the years 1506/07 reveal aspects of this artistic exchange. It is almost touching to see how the artist is concerned again and again with depicting the recumbent, highly foreshortened figure as in the dead Christ by Mantegna.

Naturally, this course of events is too general adequately to explain the peculiarities of the style of the "Danube School". On the other hand, the course of events delineated above should not be forgotten, so as not to run the risk of overemphasizing the already mentioned anticlassical stance of this art style.

The first tendency in this art movement is characterized by an emphasis on the vividness of the figures, an inclination towards a block-like unity and a certain heaviness. Overall, the attempt at expression is slight. An endeavor to depict the figures in spatial relationships is very limited. As regards the depiction of interior spaces, the artist is usually content with formal intimation without any ambition at perspective. A rendition of landscape is all but unknown. Even as able a painter as the Master of Großgmain, working in Passau, continues to depict space at the turn of the 15th century in a way which corresponds, when compared with other European areas, to a sense of space common at the first third of the century.

The other stylistic trend in this movement produced compositions with many, usually small figures in copious scenic surroundings, but only rarely in interior spaces. The most important representative of the trend, which was influenced by Dutch painting, was the Master of the Schottenstift, who worked in Vienna.

For Bavaria proper, the oft-noted expressivity of Bavarian-Austrian art, especially in connection with the "Danube Style", is associated with this latter conception of art. This can be seen, for example, in the paintings of the Master of the Tabula magna (Gabriel Mäleßkirchner). The expression of his figures is often uncouth, coarse and dramatic. In the austrian provinces, the expressive style is also represented by a painter of this artistic trend, who is known as the Master of the Martyrdom of the Saints. In this respect Jan Polack, who presumably came from Poland but was working in Munich from 1479 on deserves a special position. Many have seen in this strongly emotive style, with its leanings towards expressivity, one of the starting points for the "Danube style".

The significance of Jan Polack's painting for the emergence of the "Danube Style" (hitherto presumed by art historians) adds another component of non-Bavarian art to the already mentioned influences. This new realization forces one, however, to reexamine the influence that each individual artist and art province had on the southern German area.

If one judges him by his earliest work, the Crucifixion in the Viennese Schottenkloster, the Franconian Lukas Cranach seems to have had a nobile if dainty style, related to that of the above-mentioned second group of artists. In his encounter with Bavarian-Austrian art, the vividness of a painter like Mäleßkircher seems at first to have impressed him. Then, during his work in Vienna, he seems to have been impressed by the block-like heaviness of the other stylistic trend. Cranach's style in those years, to which the artists in the southeastern area attached themselves, developed out of the combination of Franconian flexibility with a coarse Bavarian expressivity and increasingly, also, with a liking for closed cubic form.[38]

One must not, however, see Cranach as an isolated problem. His role in the emergence of the "Danube style" is not nearly as unique as it is usually claimed to be. As is generally known, the Babenbergers were not only the ruling house in medieval Austria before the Habsburg family succeeded to the throne but also a Franconian family. Throughout the Middle Ages, the Franconian bishopric Bamberg which derives its name from the Babenberg family, had rich estates in Austria and Bamberg.

It seems that throughout the Middle Ages the cultural relations between Franconia and Austria (to be more precise the area of Poznán, West Prussia and Upper Silesia which were then subsumed under the name Ostmark) remained constant. Two examples from the 15th century produce evidence for these uninterrupted cultural relations. In the High Altar of Maria Laach in Lower Austria (north of Aggsbach) we find a depiction of the Crucifixion, which is modelled on similar works by Hans Pleydenwurff (+1472), an artist working in Bamberg and Nuremburg. In the gallery of klosterneuburg convent near Vienna hangs one of the rare depictions of the Erection of the Cross. It is unquestionably a copy of the triptych, created in the joint workshop of Wolgemut and Pleydenwurff, and is now hanging in the Städelmuseum in Frankfurt[39]. Such examples could easily be multiplied[40]. As has thus been shown, Lukas Cranach was only following an old tradition, by going to Vienna in the last years of the 15th century.

With him, however, the cultural exchange that had been in existence for centuries did not end. One aspect of old German art history, which still remains obscure, is an analysis of those elements of the "Danube Style" which can be found in the entourages of Michael Wolgemut and Albrecht Dürer. Gisela Goldberg has resolved this difficult question for the Schwabach High Altar, created in the Wolgemut workshop[41]. The second example of elements from the Danube region can be found in the Schreier Altar, executed around 1506/7 in Dürer's workshop[42]. Since the "Danube style" was only just beginning to in these years, one can hardly assume that southeast German art had a retroactive effect on Franconia.

The two artists who brought the "Danube Style" to perfection were again Franconians, Augustin Hirschvogel and Hans Lautensach, both working in Nuremburg. In their graphic works (fig. 345 to 368) they closely followed Altdorfer's landscape etchings (fig. 156 to 163) and thus, through their own drawings, carried the "Danube style" smoothly over into the epoch of Mannerism. It seems almost symptomatic that both Masters finally moved to Austria. This compilation of observations should serve as evidence that one can hardly evaluate the significance of Franconia for the "Danube Style" highly enough.

The influence which artists coming from the Alemannic region might have had on the "Danube School" cannot be defined as clearly as is possible for the Franconians. Today the role which Jörg Breu's paintings played in the materialization of the "Danube Style" is repeatedly being questioned. At least one no longer ascribes the Zwettler Altar to this artist.[43] Indeed, it appears that his work in this region, despite the other large altars, was all too brief to have left a lasting influence on the art of the Danube area. On the other hand, one also finds only minimal traces of the stylistic generosity of those years in his later creative work.

From the early Twenties onwards, Wolf Huber, originally from Feldkirch, in Vorarlberg, was working in the service of the bishops of Passau. Although, as Schindler emphasized, Passau was one of the artistic centers of the Danube area, one can find only a few stylistic traits of the "Danube School" in the work of Huber. Nevertheless he is considered, after Altdorfer, to be the leading representative of the "Danube School". Apparently he did not, however, have any noticeable influence on the work of his contemporaries. Just as he looked upon himself as a court painter for the bishop and thus independent of the painters' guild in Passau, he must be seen, within the context of the "Danube School" as an outsider. He cannot be compared with any of the other artists, and most certainly cannot be mistaken for one of them.

Hans Leu from Zurich is the only Swiss artist who had direct contact with the artists of the "Danube School" (fig. 324 to 328). His relationship to the art of the Danube region is clearly one of an artist who received essential impulses for his own work there. Even later on, after his return to Switzerland, this influence is noticeable in his understanding of landscape.

In the case of his Swiss compatriots, the goldsmith and graphic artist Urs Graf of Basel (fig. 371 to 373) and the painter and poet Nikolaus Manuel Deutsch of Bern (fig. 369-370) the discovered similarities to the "Danube Style" cannot be explained solely by a catchword like "alpine". This term was meant to express the idea that the mountain landscape was not just a geographically, but also an artistically binding element.

That this assumption is not accurate even in the fact that the artists of the Confederacy and the Masters of the "Danube School" work with an entirely different understanding of the human figure. In contrast to the "Danube School", the Swiss art works show a clear predominance of the figurative aspect. Furthermore, in the western alpine regions artists preferred a large, slim and well-proportioned figural type. For these artists garments do not serve the purpose of hiding the body, but rather ac-

School". Within the composition as a whole, the human body always remains the dominating element; interior spaces and landscapes always represent the background for figures in movement. Common to both the Swiss and the Bavarian depictions of landscape, however, is the looseness of the painting and drawing techniques. The observation of this similarity is probably responsible for starting the idea of a close tie between these two regional areas. In the Swiss art circle this loose way of treating landscapes stands in clear contrast to the care with which the depiction of figures was handled.

Also common to both the Masters in Switzerland and in the Danube area was a certain inclination towards imaginative exaggeration. With Nikolaus Manuel Deutsch this manifests itself in his landscapes, with Urs Graf in

28

centuate the flexibility of the limbs of the usually athletic men and the well-developed women.

Corresponding to the different sense of the human body, the relationship of the figure to the landscape in Swiss art is entirely different from the art of the "Danube

often bizarre compositions. The very generous execution of the drawn line in the drawings of the Swiss Masters appears to be another common bond between the two groups. One must not overlook the fact, however, that even in quickly executed sketches by the Swiss artists an

15 - St Genoveva - Cat. 7

16 - Saint Margaret and Saint Barbara - A. Altdorfer - c. 1509
Pen-and-ink - 190×138 mm - Frankfurt, Städelesches Kunstinstitut.

unmistakeable regularity in the positions of the line remains dominant. In this respect, the Swiss Masters resemble other artists of Alemannic origins. Thus, the compositional sketches of for example, Hans Burgkmair, now in Stockholm,[44] assume an intermediate position between the drawings of the Swiss and those of the "Danube School". With the former they share their transparent clarity, with the latter, their loose penstroke. The preference for depicting trees with hanging beards made of braids, which can be observed in the Swiss as well as the Bavarian artists, can certainly be understood as a borrowing from the graphic arts of the "Danube School".

Also working in the Alemannic area, in Breisach and Niederrottweil on the Upper Rhine, was the woodcarver, engraver and woodcut draftsman known, from his signature, as Master HL from Breisach. Of all the German artists of these decades who were working outside the Bavarian-Austrian artistic landscape, he is unquestionably the one most closely related to the "Danube Style". An attempt has, therefore, been made to identify him as the well-known woodcutter Hans Leinberger from Landshut,[45] although this nominal designation has not won general acceptance. Recently Schindler has tried to connect the signature of the unknown artist with Hans Loy from Ulm.[46] Unfortunately this attempt is also not very helpful, since up to now, Hans Loy is himself an artist about whom little is known. The strongly pronounced sense of vividness, even in the graphic art of this highly individual artist, clearly distinguishes him from the style of other artists of the southeastern area. Yet he remains unknown and his relationship to the "Danube School" is obscure.

Of the alpine regions bordering Switzerland on the east, the Salzkammergut is generally considered to belong to the central area of the "Danube Style". The least one can say is that the big altars by Michael Pacher in St. Wolfgang and Salzburg must, in themselves, have had an effect on the younger artists. In contrast to this, the Vorarlberg, Tyrol, Carinthia and Styria tend to be more dependent on the influence of the Danube region than the other way around. In his prosaic, reserved and somewhat old-fashioned manner of depiction, the court painter of Emperor Maximilian, Jörg Kolderer from Innsbruck was not significant enough to make an impression on artists like Cranach or Altdorfer. In so far as traces of the "Danube Style" are distinguishable in Tyrol, they would be found in the works of the Franconian Bartholemäuss Till (Dill), son of the great woodcut-engraver Tilmann Riemenschneider, or in the works that were created under his influence. The occurrence of stylistically related works in Styria and Carinthia along with regions beyond the German-speaking area, like Carniola, Hungary and Bohemia (now Cechy), should not be counted as part of the "Danube Style". We believe these similarities to be stylistic affinities or even stylistic influences.

We have established that in the first third of the 16th century stylistic phenomena similar to the "Danube School" can be found in Saxony, Franconia, at the Middle and Upper Rhine as well as in Switzerland, in the eastern alpine area and beyond. Furthermore, we have established that artistic forms of expression can be found in the art of the Lower Rhine, in the work of the artist Erhard Altdorfer (fig. 246-255) in Mecklenburg and in the northeastern part of Germany as far as Danzing (now Gdansk), that are closer to the "Danube Style" than, for example to Dürer's art. This discovery forces one either to drop the terms "Danube School" and "Danube Style"[47] altogether, or to redefine them. From the extensive dissemination of this stylistic trend, which has been termed "fantastic realism" above, we can deduce that it must have been the dominant one. In contrast, classic realism,[48] as represented by Dürer and Burgkmaier, may have served as a model and inspiration for the younger artists, but was never their general fate.

If, within of the context of what has just been described, one wants, nevertheless, to save the generally adopted terms "Danube School" and "Danube Style" for German art history, it will not suffice to limit them to the area where this style originally had validity and authority. Rather, one must consider two aspects. Firstly, the "Danube Style" is, in fact, only a variant of the "fantastic realism" common throughout Germany at that time, namely as it manifested itself in Bavaria, in the Austrian provinces, and in Lower and Upper Austria. Secondly, this variant is not genuinely Bavarian, but rather developed under the influence of foreign regional styles, of which the Franconian style seems to have been the most important component.[49]

The central artist in the area of the "Danube School" was Albrecht Altdorfer. Although such a statement may seem platitudinous, the significance of Altdorfer in this area must be particularly emphasized. For it is obvious that he was the first to combine the stylistic innovations, introduced into the Danube region by Cranach and Breu at the beginning of the century, with the traditional regional style. Very early on, that is at the lates in 1506, Altdorfer studied the form and content of Italian art. The earliest example of this study is the drawing in the Berlin Kupferstichkabinett (fig. 7) of two women dressed in the manner of classical antiquity, with a fruit basket. Similarly, his first copperplate engravings, miniature-like works done the same year, imitate the classical antique style. Their format suggests that their models must have been Italian niello works, a kind of art Altdorfer prefered to use as a model for his own engravings even in later years. The influence of Jacopo de' Barbari's copperplate engravings on the graphic work of Albrecht Altdorfer cannot be proven with as much certainty as it can for his brother Erhard.[50]

Regardless of whether, as copperplate engraver, he was dependent on the Venetian Master or not, he was more or less unable to make the specific quality of his art, namely the unbounded line, perceptible in his copperplate engravings. The technique of engraving presupposes a maximum regularity in the execution of the drawn line. This con-

his life the artist turned toward the new technique of etching on iron plates. For the etching needle puts up far less resistance to the drawing hand than does the burin, a graving tool, with which the engraver makes furrows in the metal.

One would have thought that Albrecht Altdorfer would

straint, conditioned by the equipment necessary for engraving, may well have been the reason why early on in

also have used the possibilities for free artistic design offered by the woodcut-engraving technique. Yet only the

17 - Saint Andrew - A. Altdorfer - c. 1509/10 - Pen-and-ink - 161×116 mm - Berlin, K., SMPK.

"St. Christopher" made 1513 (cat. 60) shows a fully personal style. While the other woodcuts are in general freer in their formal design than the copperplate engravings, Altdorfer nevertheless used a disciplined and regular line in all those prints where he was working with richly graded tone values. While drawing on woodcuts, he also had to take into consideration the technical conditions posed by the material used, in this case the possibilities of cutting

18 - Saint Christopher - A. Altdorfer - c. 1509/10 - Pen-and-ink - 179×144 mm - Vienna, Albertina.

19 - The Family of Savages - A. Altdorfer - c. 1510 - Pen-and-ink - 193×140 mm - Vienna, Albertina.

wood.
Thus a generosity within Altdorfer's artistic creation can

chiefly be found in his drawings and paintings. However, this generosity reveals itself to a lesser degree in the pain-

20 - The Sacrifice of Abraham - A. Altdorfer - c. 1510 - Pen-and-ink - 190×155 mm - Vienna, Albertina.

tings, as these were dependent on patrons and painting technique. Interestingly enough, a recent infrared reflectographic examination of the Berlin painting "Serenity during the Flight" (1510), revealed that the sketch beneath the color layer was designed in a far richer and freer manner than can be distinguished in the final execution of the painting.

In Altdorfer's paintings freedom of artistic design reveals

21 - The Adoration of the Magi - A. Altdorfer - c. 1512 - Pen-and-ink - 185×135 mm - Vienna, Albertina.

itself less in the formal aspect than in the boldness with which he disregarded the iconographic tradition of religious painting, and, favoring a depiction of the surroundings and the atmosphere, allowed the thematically dominating figures to assume an inferior role. This boldness reveals itself as early as the period between 1510 and 1515, at a time when Dürer was developing his classical style. The rendition "St. George's Battle with the Dragon" (1510) now in Munich, is far more a landscape painting than a picture of a saint. Possibly even more extraordinary is the Berlin "Birth of Christ", done around 1513. Here the major scene has been crowded into one of the corners of a ruined architectural structure, which itself dominates the composition. A similar tendency is suggested in the Berlin drawing (fig. 42) by the body of the dead Pyramus, who has almost become a part of surrounding Nature. This is not, as one might suspect, artistic inability, but rather a more or less conscious wish to depart from earlier and contemporary manners of artistic depiction. This departure quite clearly anticipates the conception of art that became common in the second half of the century. Within Altdorfer's work, the Munich "Alexander's Victory" (1529) can be seen as the last example of this kind of treatment.

It is typical that without exception, these pictures were executed in a small or minute format, which could only have been intended for private worship. They are not only characteristic of the artist's training as a book illustrator but seem also to comply with a certain personal predilection. Neither as a graphic artist nor as a designer did Altdorfer, in general, go much beyond the format of a post card.[51] Even "Alexander's Battle", despite its large format, is the work of a miniaturist. Only an artist who was used to working on a small scale could paint the host of little figures in a picture in such a way that a considerable number appear as individuals. The fury of the battle is embedded into a landscape, which merges the entire eastern Mediterranean and the coast of North Africa into one fantastic panorama. The sun and the moon, indicating the duration of the battle, give the whole depiction a cosmic dimension.

Seen from this zenith of Altdorfer's art, the previously mentioned smaller panels seem like preliminary stages within the entire work of the artist. Yet they must also be seen as decisive steps in the development of an independent landscape depiction, with or without figures employed as accessory decorations. A similar development can be found in the graphic works of Hans Lautensack and, within the larger context of European art history, in the landscape etchings by Pieter Bruegel the Elder.

Within Altdorfer's creative work there is, however, a second line of development. In these works the figural element stands entirely in the foreground. One is thus inclined to assume that here his already mentioned interest in classical subjectmatter was combined with the requirements posed by the large format altar paintings.

This second line of development can be traced from the Berlin drawing "Two Women with Fruit Basket", dated 1506, to the painting "The Holy Family at the Well" (1510), and to the large altars. This stylistic tendency is integral for Altdorfer's mural paintings (Cat. 162 fig. 186 bis) and finally ends with the late, already manneristic paintings.

Among his drawings, the eleven prints depicting the Apostles most of which bear the date 1517 (fig. 29 to 40), belong to the group emphasizing the individual figure. Due to a certain monumentality, they stand alone within Altdorfer's work. Only two of the Apostles, Andrew and Jacob the Elder, are placed in front of a scenic background. All the other depictions have only a neutral priming, varying between green and reddish-brown, for a background. These eleven prints are almost model examples of Altdorfer's drawing abilities. While the renditions of St. Philippus, Thomas Jakobus the younger and Simon reveal a comparatively regular line, the depiction of the Prince of the Apostles, Peter, is infused with a somewhat unstable and nervous quality, due to the irregular application of white highlighting. (see the essay by P. Benedikt Wagner).

Altdorfer's drawings which include architectural structures assume a special position within his work as a whole, since they are executed in a technique otherwise rarely encountered, namely as pen-and-ink drawings, in part also with washes. They convey an approximate idea of Altdorfer's architectural accomplishments. According to these drawings, he adhered to the spacial arrangements of the French gothic cathedral, as may can be found in the cathedral in Regensburg. The detail work of the architectural parts, however, already indicates Renaissance forms. The sketch for the painting "The Birth of Mary" now in Munich, is particularly characteristic of a combination of varying stylistic elements. The entire collection of these drawings is another example of his artistic dispute with the Renaissance. These drawings probably belong to the period when Altdorfer was preoccupied with studying the building of the Church of Mary the Beautiful in Regensburg. An example of a pure Renaissance building is to be found in the rendition of Susanna's palace in the Düsseldorf sketch for the painting "Susanna in the Bath", which was done around 1526. It is probable that Altdorfer used such copperplate engravings as Franscesco Roselli's[52] "Solomon and the Queen of Sheba" as models for his own work. The utilization of copperplate engravings as models does not speak against a trip to Trent, which Winzinger, following Nicolò Rasmo, thinks might have taken place around 1532.[53] Altdorfer must have seen more, however, than the most southern Germanic bishopric, for in the buildings rendered in the painting, Lombardian and Venetian impressions have been merged into a highly im-

22 - The Death Jump of Marcus Curtius - Cat. 8

aginative whole, doing honor to the architectural understanding of the artist. Incidentally, both the drawing and the matching painting, now in Munich, are yet another testimony of his minute manner of working.

As is the case with Albrecht Dürer, the pieces done by Albrecht Altdorfer for the Emperor Maximilian assume a special position in his creative work. His contribution to

The colossal commission to complete the "Triumphal Procession" in the form of coloured pen-and-ink drawings, based on the sketched drawings by the imperial court painter Jörg Kölderer, must have been an extremely fascinating assignment for the trained book illustrator. But the 109 large prints on parchment exceeded the working-power of a single man, especially since Maximilian insisted

the artistic plans of the imperial leader include works for the "Triumphal Procession" and part of the illustrations for the "Prayer Book".

on a rapid execution of the work. It is thus not surprising that Altdorfer engaged a number of younger artists as co-workers, who, from the year 1513-1515, were busy fulfill-

23 - Saint George Felling the Dragon - A. Altdorfer - 1512
Pen-and-ink - 156×111 mm - Berlin, K., SMPK.

24 - Battle between a Knight and a Mercenary - Cat. 9

ing this assignment. In direct connection with this work, the transference of the standard-bearers on horse-back and of the train of followers onto woodcuts was carried out. The execution of the cutting work was assigned to someone else. Even in the woodcut engravings the various groups making up the train of followers reveal the unmistakeable signature of Altdorfer himself. For the standard-bearers it is difficult to differentiate between Altdorfer's personal work and that done by the co-workers of his work shop, because the person responsible for the woodcut strove for the largest possible uniformity, and thus obscured the peculiarities of each individual drawer.

Of all the artists involved in the illustrations for Emperor Maximilian's prayer book (pp. 279-322) Altdorfer was most successful in his attempt to adapt himself to Dürer's margin-illustrations, which had been set as the artistic standard. The twenty-five pages decorated by him with pen-and-ink drawings in colored ink, reveal not only decorative skill but also the same kind of humorous candor as the pages illustrated by Dürer. In any case, he proves himself, in his designs for the book ornamentation, to be superior not only to his own coworkers, but also to Hans Baldung and Jörg Breu, and even in most cases to Lukas Cranach. Again, his original training in his father's workshop makes itself felt.

The fact that Altdorfer carried out the imperial assignment in collaboration with several helpers once more leads back to the problem of the emergence of a "Danube School". For the miniatures of the "Triumphal Procession", Franz Winzinger distinguishes the hands of five to six co-workers[54]. Of these, Georg Lemberger is the only artist whose name is known. It is possible that he left for central Germany soon after completion of his work; at least his presence there can be proven from 1517 on. After Lukas Cranach and Erhard Altdorfer he is the third artist to carry the stylistic peculiarities of the School to the north. Yet, that this style should have acclimatized itself and resonance in Wittenburg and Schwerin as well as in Leipzig, is hardly conceivable otherwise than in that it found related artistic tendencies in each respective area.

The second artist from this group whose works are known beyond his activity in Altdorfer's workshop is the Master of the Historia Friderici et Maximiliani, who is named after 46 illustrations with the same signature, describing the life of the two Emperors[55]. The manuscript, composed by Maximilian's secretary, Joseph Grünpeck, was decorated by the Master of the Historia 1514/15 with colored pen-and-ink drawings that were intended to be the model for a later printed edition. On account of his major work as a painter, the High Altar in the Heiligblut church in Pulkau (North Austria), he is occasionally called Master of Pulkau. This painter and drawer, whose works are often confused with those of

Altdorfer, is possibly the most characteristic representative of the "Danube style". In his manner of drawing and painting, he clearly continues the work of the young Albrecht Altdorfer[56] and at times exaggerates his style to the point of caricature, as, for example, in "The Outing on Horseback". In the drawing "Landscape with Watermill" on the other hand, he shows himself to be a sensitive observer, capable of expressing scenic countryside with delicate lines. Fritz Dworschak's[57] suggestion that this artist might be identified as Niklas Breu, brother of Jörg Breu, has not been generally accepted. Thus, although the most interesting among Austrian artists of his day this artist, remains anonymous, despite the fact that he has a clearly recognizable artistic identity.

If one considers the influence of Cranach on Altdorfer and the dependence of the Master of the Historia on the latter, the anonymous Austrian artist appears as a spiritual heir of the Franconian. His Pulkau Altar even suggests direct dependence[58]. The art of Georg Lemberger should probably be understood in a similar manner, with the reserve that, because of the greater geographical proximity, it is quite likely that Cranach had a far more intensive and direct influence on his later work.

Without wanting to generalize the findings made in the course of this discussion, it can, nevertheless, be said that the most significant Bavarian and Austrian artists, traditionally considered as part of the "Danube School", received their artistic schooling from close personal contacts. This connection once more underlines the central position which must be attributed to Altdorfer among the artists of southeastern Germany. It can, therefore, be no coincidence that not just Lemberger and the Master of the Historia, but also painters like the Master from Mühldorf (monogramist JW, Wilhelm Weinholt?) seem to have taken as their point of departure Altdorfer's work from the years 1508-1512. All these mostly anonymous painters apparently strove to attain the same generosity in their painted and drawn style as Altdorfer had, although with few exceptions they remained entrenched in provincial imitations. Their works never reach that well-balanced combination of formally fantastic and realistic rendition, which lends Altdorfer's creative work its greatness and unique significance.

Fedja Anzelewski

1. Herbert Schindler: "Albrecht Altdorfer und die Anfänge des Donaustils", in, *Ostbairische Grenzmarken* 23, 1981, p. 60 f. See also the essay by Pierre Vaisse.
2. The Bavarians were formed of a coalition between Germanic tribes, the Celts, the Romans and the Slavs. The area in which they settled extended, since the 6th century, from the Lech in the West to the Enns in the East, but in the course of the Middle Ages spread as far as the Viennese forest.
3. Franz Winzinger: "Zur Malerei der Donauschule", in *Die Kunst der Donauschule* (Exhibition in St. Florian and Linz), 1965, p. 22.
4. Anton Legner: "Plastik", in *Die Kunst der Donauschule,* p. 270.
5. Fritz Dworschak: "Kärnten and Friaul", in *Die Kunst der Donauschule,* p. 169 ff.
6. Rupert Feuchtmüller: "Ungarn", in *Die Kunst der Donauschule,* p. 148 ff.
7. Albrecht Dürer, Written bequests. Edited by Hans Rupprich, Vol. 2, 1966, p. 109, lines 49-52.
8. Compare, for example W. 380-409, 434-436 and 448-465. The purpose for which the prints of the Green Passion were created is still unknown.
9. Otto Benesch: "Altdorfer und der 'Donaustil'", in Beiträge zur *Geschichte der deutschen Kunst,* edited by E. Buchner and K. Feuchtmayer, Vol. 2, 1928, p. 268-271.
10. Buchner hassuggested, that Breu must have been born around 1475, since he became an apprentice to Ulrich Apt already in 1493, but it seems that in this Buchner presumes modern conditions. It is not so long ago, that apprentices to crafts-men began their training at the age of fourteen. In Breu's age boys were generally apprenticed between the ages of ten and fourteen years. See E. Buchner: "Der ältere Breu als Maler", in: *Beiträge zur Geschichte der deutschen Kunst,* Vol. 2, 1928, p. 272.
11. With this is meant the present state of Austria. The Archbishopric of Salzburg, however, only belongs to Austria under public law since the decision of the Deputation of the German Estates in 1803.
12. Herbert Schindler: "Albrecht Altdorfer und die Anfänge des Donaustils", in *Ostbairische Grenzmarken, Passauer Jahrbuch für Geschichte, Kunst und Volkskunde* 23, 1981, p. 68. Schindler attributes the Zwettler Altar to an anonymous artist from Krems, who is to have had relations to the Kreichbaum work shop in Passau. According to Schindler's opinion, Passau is more likely to have been the center, in which the "Danube Style" was formed than Vienna.
13. Compare F. Anzelewsky: "Der Meister des Aachener Altars und der Monogrammist PW", in *Studien aus dem Berliner Kupferstichkabinett,* Berlin 1966, p. 16-20. idem. "Zum Problem des Meisters des Aachener Altars", in *Wallraf-Richartz-Jahrbuch* 30, 1968, p. 185-200. idem, "Der Meister des Aachener Altars und der Monogrammist PW", in Kunstgeschichtliche Gesellschaft zu Berlin, minutes of proceedings N.F. 16. 1968, p. 14 f.
14. Schindler, *Donauschule,* p. 69. He attributes the sculptures to the same sculptor who carved the central panel of the High Altar in Zwettel.
15. Alfred Schädler: *Die fränkische Galerie.* Zweigmuseum des Bayerischen Nationalmuseum. Vest Rosenberg Kronach, Munich 1983, p. 42-45. It seems hardly advisable to go as far as Schädler and see in the sculpture of John the Baptist, in the church portal in Kronach, the work of Cranach.
16. Schindler, *Donauschule,* p. 69, suggests that in Vienna, Cranach experienced the new art of the "Danube style" as a great event.
17. Schindler, *Donauschule,* p. 69, believes this woodcut-engraving to be the work of one of the artists from Passau, in the vicinity of the Kriechbaum workshop and suggests that Cranach received his stimulation from him.
18. Compare Friedrich Winkler: "Ein Titelblatt und seine Wandlungen", in *Zeitschrift für Kunstwissenschaft* 15, 1961, p. 156 ff.
19. Schindler, *Donauschule,* p. 69, attributes the entire early work of Cranach, with the exception of the Berlin "Serenity during the Flight", dated 1504, to an unknown artist. Thus one again a *Dop-*

25 - Christ in Limbo - Cat. 10

26 - Samson's Battle with the Lion - Cat. 11

27 - The Mouth of Truth - A. Altdorfer - 1512 - Pen-and-ink - 219×155 mm - Berlin, K., SMPK.

28 - St Catherine Refuses the Worship of Idols - Cat. 12

pelgänger is introduced, as was once the case with the young Dürer.

20. The woodcuts (Wz 1-13) are pasted as decoration into a book now in the Bavarian State Library in Munich. Two prints (Wz 1 and 7) carry Altdorfer's monogram.

21. Compae also Dieter Koepplin's characterisation of the course of events involved in the emergence in the "Danube style", quoted by Gisela Goldberg, "Die Gemälde des Schwabacher Hochaltars", in Der Schwabacher Hochaltar — Internationales Kolloquim anläßlich der Restaurierung (Arbeitscheft 11. Bayerisches Landesamt für Denkmalspflege), Munich 1982, p. 85.

22. Franz Winzinger: *Albrecht Altdorfer. Zeichnungen, Gesamtausgabe,* Munich, 1952, p. 109 f. idem: *Albrecht Altdorfer. Graphik,* Munich, 1963, p. 132-136.

23. Winzinger 1963, p. 13. His claim that "The Birth of Christ", done 1507, now in Bremen, was modeled on a piece by Pacher is not convincing.

24. Masilia Ficino: *Opera omnia* (Riprod. in fototipia 1. ristampa), Turin 1959, p. 1935.

25. Compare Lucas van Leyden-grafiek (Exhibition in Amsterdam), 1978, Ill. on p. 98/99.

26. Wilhelm Pinder: *Die deutsche Plastik vom angehenden Mittelalter bis zum Ende der Renaissance,* Vol. 2, Potsdam 1929, p. 451-482. Compare also Michael J. Liebmann: *Die deutsche Plastik 1350-1550,* Leipzig 1982, p. 380-393. He also recognizes a survival of gothic woodcarving in both artists and thus calls his chapter "Das Ende der Tradition der Altarbaukunst und der Holzschnitzerei" (the end of the tradition of altar architecture and wood-carving).

27. Max Lossnitzer: "Hans Leinberger. Nachbildungen seiner Kupferstiche und Holzchnite", *Graphische Gesellschaft* XVIII., Berlin, 1913.

28. Herbert Schindler: *Der Meister HL = Hans Loy? Werk und Wiederentdeckung.* Königstein i. T., 1981.

29. Gerd von der Osten: *Hans Baldung Grien, Gemälde und Dokumente,* Berlin, 1983, p. 21.

30. Compare Alan Shestack and Charles Talbot: *The Danube School* (Exhibition at Yale University), 1969, nr. 119 and 121. The authors believe that Urs Graf and Nikolaus Manuel Deutsch's formal affinity with the "Danube School" can be attributed to influences through the graphic arts.

31. Hans Ley the younger is possibly the only Swiss painter of that time who had contact with Altdorfer.

32. A meeting with Cranach in Vienna around 1500, such as Winzinger postulates, can not be proven. Compare Winzinger, 1979, p. 19.

33. Light as a major compositional factor or as an element used to convey mood can be found in painting since Hugo van der Goes. Geertgen tot Sint Jans and Jan Joest von Kalkar adopted this usage of light. Within the graphic arts one should also remember the prints forming the Joseph-Sequence by Lucas Van Leyden, dated 1512 (B. 21).

34. *Die Kunst der Donauschule,* 1965, Nr. 699.

35. Compare "Nicolo Rasmo: Donaustil und italienische Renaissance", in *Werden und Wandlung. Studien zur Kunst der Donauschule,* Linz, 1967, p. 115-136.

36. The combination of the classic Renaissance form and the late gothic tracery framing the wings of the later Wettenhausener altar, made 1523 by Martin Schaffner from Ulm, strikes one as beign rather inorganic. Munich, Alte Pinalkothek.

37. Ludwig von Baldass: *Albrecht Altdorfer,* Vienna, 1941, p. 14.

38. Schindler: *Donaustil,* p. 68, decidedly questions Cranach's role. At

least he questions that Cranach made the "Stephanus" from 1502. See p. 69.

39. Kurt Bauch: "Dürers Lehrjahre", in *Städel-Jahrbuch* 7/8, 1932, Ill. 74 and 75.

40. Betty Kurth: "Über den Einfuß der Wolgemut-Werkstatt in Öster-reich und im angrenzenden Süddeutschland", in *Jahrbuch der K.K. Zentralkommission für Denkmalspflege* 1916, p. 79-100.

41. Goldberg 1982, p. 83-91. The author thinks it is possible that elements of the "Danube style" are of Franconian origin. Already Herman Voß: *Der Ursprung des Donaustiles*, Leipzig 1907, p. 53.

42. *Meister um Albrecht Dürer* Exhibition in Nuremburg), 1961, p. 148 ff..

43. Schindler: *Donaustil,* p. 68.

44. Per Bjurström: *German Drawings.* Nationalmuseum, Stockholm 1972, Nr. 27 and 29.

45. Lossnitzer, Berlin, 1913. Apart from Hans Leinberger the following names have been found for the monogramist: Hans Leu (Passavant and Nagler), Hans Loy from Freiburg i.B. (Münzel, H.A. Schmid and Schindler 1981), the curate Hans Löhelin from Breisach (P. Alberts) and Johannes Setzer von Lauchheim (v.d. Osten). None of these attempts at identifying the artist are convincing.

46. Schindler: *Der Meister HL=Hans Loy?,* Königstein i.T., 1981.

47. Cf. Anton Legner's presentation "Zum Wert und Unwert des Begriffes 'Donaustil'", in *Werden und Wandlung. Studian zur Kunst der Donauschule,* Linz 1967, p. 148-152.

48. I have coined this formulation along with the corresponding phrase, "fantastic realism" in imitation of the term "pathetic realism", which Winkler found as a description for the style of Dürer's "Apocalypse". Compare F. Winkler: *Albrecht Dürer, Leben und Werk,* Berlin 1957, p. 105.

49. Already Hermann Voß, 1907, p. 53, recognized that artistic ideas coming from outside must have played a decisive role in the emergence of the "Danube style". Already in his discussion the term "Danube School" becomes obfuscated, since he counts the Upper Rhine area, Upper Swabia and Tyrol as part of the area of this school.

50. Compare Schindler, *Donauschule,* p. 67. He holds the opinion that both brothers imitated Barbari's engravings.

51. Only the colored woodcut engraving "'The Beautiful Mary' of Regensburg", dated 1519/20 (Wz 89), printed from 4-6 wood cuts, with the dimensions of 34×24.5 cm and 23 etchings of the preparatory sketch for "Susanna in the Bath" with 33×27.5 cm and the drawing for the frescos of the imperical bath in Regensburg are larger than is usually the case with Altdorfer.

52. See Winzinger 1975, Ill. Appendix 43 and 44.

53. Winzinger 1975, p. 55 f. and Ill. Appendix 47 and 48.

54. Winzinger 1973, Kommentatband p. 28-32. In fifth place he simply refers to other co-workers, to be dealt with in summary.

55. Otto Benesch and Erwin Auer: *Die Historia Friderici et Maximiliani,* Berlin 1957.

56. See Peter Haim: "Die Landschaftszeichnungen des Wolf Huber", in *Münchener Jahrbuch d. Bildenden Kunst* N. F. 7, 1930, p. 65

57. Fritz Dworschak: "Die Meister des Heiligblut-Altars in Pulkau. Regesten Rechnungen und Exkurse", in *Die Gotik in Niederöster-reich,* Vienna, 1963, p. 155 f. and 164 ff. idem. "Der Meister der Historia (Niclas Preu), Niederösterreich und die Nachbargebiete", in *Die Kunst der Donauschule* (Exhibition in St. Florian and Linz) 1965, p. 96-98.

58. Benesch/Auer 1957, Ill. 29 and 30.

Albrecht Altdorfer, german painter, architect, draughtsman and engraver in copper and wood, was born at Regensburg about 1480. He is believed to have been the son of Ulrich Altdorfer, an illuminator residing there. In 1500-1501 he worked at the Monastery of Mondsee in the province of Salzburg.

He became a citizen of Regensburg in 1505. Very soon, he became reasonably well-off and got important commissions such as the painting of the altarpiece for the monastery of St. Florian in Upper Austria in 1509. He made drawings for Maximilian's Prayer Book in 1515 and he worked on the Triumphal Arch and the Triumphal Procession of the Emperor Maximilian I. In 1517, he was the owner of a second house. He was elected a member of the Outer Council

in 1519 and of the Inner Council in 1526.

At the same date, he became official architect of the city.

The city's wine cellars, the slaughterhouse and the tower of the city hall were built according to his designs.

Albrecht Altdorfer died at Regensburg on February 12, 1538. He was buried in the churchyard of the old Augustinan cloister whose curator he had been since 1534. R.B.

29 - St Andrew - Cat 13

The Apostles of Seitenstetten
by Albrecht Altdorfer

I. Description

a) General description.

The Apostles series is today composed of eleven edgeless leaves[1], all rather roughly cut by hand. With one exception[2], they are all more or less rectangular in shape. Altdorfer used different kinds of paper. He therefore did not draw the apostles on a single sheet of paper and subse-

The type of paper used by Altdorfer was, in part, very fine and several leaves have had to be strengthened with modern paper. All are in a good state of conservation and most are in very good condition. At present, they are all (most of them with folds) in passe-partout frames of 47,2×35,2 cm. Pen-and-ink studies are to be found on the verso of a number of the leaves[3].

Altdorfer drew on each leaf a full-length pen-and-ink portrait of an apostle, with white highlights. None of the sheets is signed but most bear the date 1517 in the upper half[4].

quently cut each one out separately. For although they were all drawn on a grey-brown background, the shades vary. For St. John the Lesser, the background is clearly grey-brown and for St. Matthew brown-yellow.

Altdorfer has depicted each apostle with the usual iconographical attributes[5]. It is no longer possible to discern the order in which they were drawn and it is for this reason that we present them here in the traditional

30 - St James the Elder - Cat 14

order[6]:

b) Detailed description

St Peter (with a key), dated, 128×97 mm (cat. 15 fig. 31)
St Andrew (with an x-shaped cross), undated, 143×101 mm, (cat. 13, fig. 29).
St James the Greater (as a pilgrim, holding staff and shell), dated, 139×99 mm (cat. 14, fig. 30)
St John the Evangelist (with chalice, patten and palla) dated, 132×87 mm (cat. 16, fig. 32)
St Thomas (with a lance) dated, 143×99mm (cat. 18, fig. 34)
St James the Lesser (with a fulling mill and a woollen bag) dated, 143×108 mm (cat. 19, fig. 35)
St Phillip (with a staff surmounted by a cross) dated, 138×102 mm (cat. 17, fig. 33)

St Matthias (with an axe) undated, 128×72 mm (cat. 21, fig. 37)

II. Their Career prior to Seitenstetten

It has long been known with great certainty how these works came into the possession of the convent of Seitenstetten in Lower Austria[7]. A codex, originally composed of 55 sheets, is contained in the archives of the Benedictine convent. To the binding, a liturgical score of the early 15th century, a paper bearing the following inscription has been glued: "Hierin gar schöne Conterfet Keyser, König, Fürsten, Obristen[8]:... Stückh dabei auch die Apostl und St[9]:... vom Maller Aldorf getuscht in 13 Stückhen zufinden." (Contains beautiful portraits of

St Bartholomew (with a scalpel), undated, 124×86 mm (cat. 23, fig. 39)
St Matthew (as a tax-gatherer with an abacus) undated, 128×90 mm (cat. 22, fig. 38)
St Simon (with a saw), dated, 143×95 mm (cat. 20, fig. 36)

Emperors, Kings, Princes, Military Dignitaries to the number of..., as well as the Apostles and St... to the number of 13, drawn by the painter Aldorf). At the present time, the collection contains no more than 32 gouache portraits on paper of Emperors, Kings, high-ranking

31 - St Peter - Cat 15

32 - St John the Evangelist - Cat 16

51

military persons, reformers and ministers of the reformed church which were taken in part from an earlier collection and reassembled by a collector around 1570. Such collections of portraits of famous people were highly treasured in the 16th and 17th centuries[10].

The collection in question, however, originally contained other works of value. On sheets 3, 4 and 5, the collector stuck a hand-colored pen-and-ink drawing by Bernhard Strigel *Christ and his Apostles*, which he cut into three on account of its oblong shape which prevented it from fitting

whose name he seriously distorted. St Florian, mentioned in the title, is lost, as is one of the apostles[12]. A drawing of a saint dated 1518 in a similar style was also added[13]. Lastly, the collector also included two self-portraits in wedding apparel by the painter Hans Burgkmair from Augsburg[14].

The origin of the collection is known, thanks to an inscription at the beginning of the book on the inside cover: "Dieses Buch ist mir von meinen H. Bruder Leopold Joseph Schaukegl Stadt-Syndicus in Welß Verehrt worden

into the collection[11]. After the gouache portraits, the collector stuck on 13 drawings by Albrecht Altdorfer which he evidently considered to be very precious since he referred to them by name in the title. It is, however, no longer possible to say how he knew that they were by Altdorfer,

1765. P. Joseph Schaukegl Benedictinus Seitenstettensis Cammerer.' (This book was given to me by my brother Leopold Joseph Schaukegl, trustee of the city of Welß 1765. Father Joseph Schaukegl, Treasurer of the Bendictines of Seitenstetten). But this reverend father was not

33 - St Phillip - Cat 17

merely the convent treasurer, he was also a great connoisseur of art. Thus one can understand why his brother, who was a trustee in Wels and therefore a sort of director of the Chancellory, gave him such a gift. For very few people can have been in a position to appreciate the value of the album during the roccoco period.

Fritz Dworschak[15] concluded from the inscription by Father Schaukegl that this precious collection had formerly been in his possession and he supposed that the portraits had also been gathered together in Wels[16]. In view of the fact that Emperor Maxmilian the First died in Wels in 1519,

with certainty, but they are highly probable, for not only Bernhard Strigl[17] and Hans Burgmair[18] but also Albrecht Altdorfer[19], at exactly this time, in 1517, were in contact with Maxmilian and an anonymous drawing of a saint had been made in 1518, that is to say shortly before the Emperor's death.

III. Their place and importance in the history of art

Around 1500, the apostles were a very fashionable subject in artistic circles. The statues of apostles which decorated the walls, pillars and railings of the choirs in late Gothic churches were highly appreciated. The apostles in the

Dworschak presumes that all of the precious drawings in the collection came from the Emperor's estate and had remained in Wels.

Dworschak's suppositions cannot, of course, be proven

chapel of Blutenburg[20] castle near Munich were probably executed before 1500. They are endowed with the usual attributes but have little individual character. The statues of the apostles by Lorenz Luchsperger in the Cathedral of

35 - St James the Younger - Cat 19

Wiener Neustadt are, by comparison, much more mobile in their attitudes[21]. The apostles by Peter Vischer which were used to decorate the reliquary of Saint Sebald in Nuremberg[22] prefigure the Renaissance and the period of Altdorfer's apostles.

In the domain of the graphic arts, Martin Schongauer had already depicted the apostles in a series of twelve copperplate engravings[33] around 1475. All of the apostles are standing on a partly grassy hillock. They are differentiated from each other by the usual attributes and more often than

album dates from this period.

Two series by Lucas Cranach from this period are extant. Around 1512, Cranach did a series of 14 woodcuts depicting Christ and his Apostles. The apostles are already far too individual and have knotted outlines. They all wear tunics with parallel pleats and one in particular has a very puffed-out garment. This work exemplifies a conscious shift away from the sculptural calm of the Apostles of Blutenburg and of Schongauer's copperplate engravings. But here also the landscape is only cursorily sketched in, while on either side

not are wearing tunics with parallel pleats and puffed-out capes which may have inspired Altdorfer.

The number of representations of the twelve apostles made between 1510 and 1520 is very great. It is possible that the *Christ and his Apostles* by Bernhard Strigel in the Wels

of the figures, a Renaissance vegetable ornament serves to fill out the space[24]. In his studies for altarpieces between 1515 and 1520[25], Lucas Cranach placed the apostles in front of an outline of architectural features or of landscape.

Altdorder sought to spiritualise the representation of the

36 - St Simon - Cat 20

apostles. The ravaged faces of Lucas Cranach give way to characters endowed with individuality. The best-known of these are Dürer's *Four Temperaments*, of 1526. However, in his studies for the altar of Heller in 1508, the brush drawings with white highlights on green or blue paper already showed highly individualised faces which were intended to depict the apostles[26]. In 1514, Dürer began a series of copperplate engravings[27] and returned to the same theme between 1522 and 1526[28]. In his engravings, Dürer most often placed the apostles in front of a landscape or of a cursorily sketched architectural feature and the figure's physiognomies are more type-cast, whereas the sketches for paintings do give the impression of true character studies. In 1519, Hans Baldung known as Grien, depicted Christ and

37 - St Matthias - Cat. 21

the apostles in two series of woodcuts; in the larger of the two, the figures are big and heavy, with impressively pleated clothing and large haloes which take up a great deal of space[29]; in the smaller series, the haloes have been eliminated as superfluous but a landscape has been partially sketched in[30]. Altdorfer drew his apostles on a dark background which immediately distinguishes them from the mass-produced woodcuts and copperplate engravings of the time and gives them their unique and original character. He used two techniques to give the figures volume. On each leaf, he started with a light source located in the left-hand foreground, just outside the composition, which strikes the figure obliquely. Those features which come into contact with the light are given white highlights, applied with a brush, and the areas in shadow are treated in pen and black ink. This is particularly elegant in drawings such as St Thomas, where part of the clothing streams in the breeze or, as is the case with St Peter's key, when an attribute emerges from the shadows and is thus highlighted in white.

Moreover, he adds a constant variation to the theme[31]: St James the Greater and St Matthew move towards the left, St Philipp is seen with his back turned, the others are turned sideways, to right or left, and the effect thus obtained from the oblique incidental light from off-left is greater. But it is not merely the position of the body in general that varies from figure to figure; the position of the head, hands and feet (in view of their size, variations in the feet are particularly visible) also changes. Similarly, the tunic with its parallel pleats and the streaming or ruffled cape are different in each case. But here the cape does not have the hard triangular pleats of the late, flamboyant, Gothic style as is mostly the case in the work of Hans Baldung known as Grien, and as Dürer preferred them, albeit in a midler form; here the lines are soft and supple, as they would be later on in the Baroque period when they would also be far more differentiated and variable. In these works, Altdorfer was opening the way to the final phase of the Gothic style of the Danube School, which has very properly been called Baroque Gothic[32]. It is, of course, true that the lines of a pen-and-ink or brush drawing are far more supple than those of an engraving or woodcut. But Altdorfer's mastery is evident in the way he uses the possibilities offered by hand drawing.

He also proves himself in these drawings, as in his paintings, to be a master of landscape and atmosphere. A series of strong, rapid white lines create the impression that St John is walking in a field of high grass, while a few white highlit patches suggest that St Peter is standing on a flat bank by the water's edge. St James the Greater, striding singlemindedly forward, is associated with a pathway, a footbridge and a village nestling in a mountain landscape, all of which is merely sketched in. In St Andrew, the horizontal white lines above a mountain and the clouds outlined in white recall the lowering clouds in a flamboyant crepuscular sky in the Mount of Olives canvas in the Altarpiece of the Passion in the Monastery of St Florian. Whereas in his paintings, he depicted partially fantastic landscapes in an epic style and with a wealth of detail, in his apostle series, in the manner of a lyric poet, he used a few clear lines on a dark background to create a context and an atmosphre charged with meaning in which he placed the apostles. Thanks to this facility which enabled him, in a few lines, to conjure up a landscape and an atmosphere, Altdorfer also appears in his apostles as one of the great masters of the Danube School whose strength lay precisely in the representation of the relation between man and landscape, between the scene in the foreground and the surrounding atmosphere.

IV. The Conceptual Content

But in spite of all, the outline of the apostles is in the foreground. This leads to the difficult, thorny question as to whether these figures have retained any religious character. Andrew, James the Lesser, Phillip, Bartholomew and Matthias have no halo and in the others it is not especially emphasised. Were the apostles no more than a pretext for Altdorfer to pursue his study of the noble man in another form so as to widen and test his artistic range, just as composers were to do 300 years later with favourite themes and variations upon them[33]? Gerd Tolzien even went so far as to assert that, for Altdorfer, the scenes of the Passion in the Altarpiece in the Monastery of St Florian were nothing other than "a welcome opportunity to display the full range of his artistic gifts". In reality, he was not "so naïvely pious as these pathetic scenes might at first lead one to imagine". The Apostle Peter supplies the best answer. He has a far more marked personality than any of the others. In his left hand, he is holding a simple key, as if he did not know quite what to do with it. Similarly, the gesture of the right hand seems awkward and clumsy, but his venerable old man's face is turned towards the invisible light that illuminates his entire silhouette, unlike any of the other apostles. He is, so to speak, all ears and eyes for the celestial light beaming in upon him. As soon as he has understood God's message, his hand will grow firm and show the path to the Infant Church. It is clear from this analysis that the technique of white highlight on a dark background that Altdorfer used in his drawings in order to depict various saints has a religious and metaphysical significance: the brilliance of the Eternal transforms the saints into figures of light who stand out against the dark background of their time. The piety that emanates from these drawings is indeed a muted piety and does not seek to assert itself but it would be unjust to attempt to reduce these figures to the purely human level.

P. Benedikt Wagner

38 - St Matthew - Cat 22

1. Paul and Judas Thaddeus are missing.

2. The upper part of the leaf depicting the apostle Bartholomew has been cut into a semi-circular shape.

3. The leaves depicting Matthew, Phillip and Thomas.

4. Andrew, Matthew, Bartholomew and Matthias are undated.

5. With one exception, Matthew is depicted with the taxgatherer's abacus and not the usual halberd.

6. Hanna L. Becker, *Die Handzeichnungen Albrecht Altdorfer's, Münchener Beiträge zur Kunstgeschichte*, vol I, Munich 1938, p. 118-120, n° 59-69, claims, it is true, that her classification corresponds to the classification in the Seitenstetten collection of which she speaks. Furthermore, on the back of each leaf is a hand-written number of recent origin which, in all logic, should give the order in which they had been in the Wels album at the time were cut out. If this supposition is correct, James the Lesser should be placed before St Thomas in Hanna L. Becker's classification. But in view of the fact that the portraits in the Wels album have not been classified in any pre-established order, it is not possible to deduce any information about the order in which the apostles were

7. Cf. Fritz Dworschak "Ein Welser Stammbuch der Zeit um 1575" in *9 Jahrbuch des Musealvereines Wels*, 1962-1963.

8. The number of portraits is missing.

9. The name St. Florian is written in pencil.

10. A series of such albums, including our *Stammbuch eines Welser Thurnermeisters* was exhibited in Linz castle in 1976. Cf. the catalogue of the exhibition *Der oberösterreichische Bauernkrieg 1625*, Linz 1976, pp. 1-143, n° 630. The album was also exhibited in Wels in 1983. Cf. the catalogue of the exhibition *Tausend Jahre Oberösterreich - Das Werden eines Landes*, Wels 1983, vol 2, p. 404, n° w 78.

11. Since 1952, the Strigel drawing has been in the Graphische Sammlung, Albertina Vienna.

12. If the title speaks of "13 Stückhen" by Altdorfer, this means that St Florian was included and that the album must also originally have contained twelve drawings of apostles by Altdorfer.

13. Pen and ink and brush in grey-black ink with white highlights on a red background. The silhouette is, however, much stiffer and the treatment of the clothing less elegant than in Altdorfer's work. After a dagger

drawn from the way in which they were classified in the Wels album. The Apostles were exhibited in Munich in 1938 (and probably cut out of the Wels album at this time). Cf. the catalogue *Albrecht Altdorfer und sein Kreis*, Munich 1938, pp. 36, n° 105-115. They were also exhibited in St Florian in 1965: *Die Kunst der Donauschule 1490-1540*, catalogue of the exhibition St Florian-Linz 1965, pp. 54, n° 76-86.

was plunged into the saint's breast, Thieme-Becker in *Allgemeines Lexikon der Bildenden Künste*, claimed that the painter of this work is the Master of Our Lady of Sorrows of Seitenstetten. This work is also in the Albertina in Vienna. It was exhibited in Munich in 1938: the catalogue of the exhibition *Albrecht Altdorfer und sein Kreis*, p. 146, n° 667.

40 - Saint Thomas - A. Altdorfer - 1517 - Pen-and-ink - 202×135 mm - Berlin, K., SMPK.

14. Cf Heinrich Röttinger, *Burgkmair im Hochzeitkleide,* Münchener Jahrbuch der Bildenden Kunst, 1908 2. Halbband, p. 48-52. These two drawings are also in the Vienna Albertina.

15. Dworschak (as in note 7 above) p. 173; and Roland Wiechesmüller, *P. Joseph Schaukegl, Priester, Künstler und Gelehrter,* in *Studien und Mitteilungen zur Geschichte des Benediktin erordens,* 89 Vol., Ottobeuren 1978, pp. 384.

16. It is for this reason that, after Dworschak, it has generally been described as the Wels album. The collector must have been protestant, since only protestant religious figures have been included. In view of the inscription at the bottom of page 42 "thurner Stamungspeuch" the collector of the portraits must have been Keeper of the Keys and therefore must have occupied the position of Chief of Harmony in the City Council.

17. Between 1515 and 1518, Bernhard Strigel painted portraits of Emperor Maxmilian I, of Charles V, of the imperial family and also a portrait for an altar which the Emperor gave as a gift to the Bishop of Vienna, Georg Slatkonia: Thieme-Becker (see note 13), vol 32, Leipzig 1938, p. 188.

18. Hans Burgkmair the Elder made woodcuts for the triumphal chariot of the Emperor Maxmilian between 1512 and 1518: Thieme-Becker, vol 5, Leipzig 1911, pp. 254.

19. 38 woodcuts of the triumphal chariot of the Emperor Maxmilian I dating from 1517 have been attributed to Altdorfer: *Die Kunst der Donauschule* (see note 6) pp. 67.

20. Zum Meister der Blutenburger Apostel "Thieme-Becker, vol. 37, p. 50.

21. Karl Oettinger, *Altdeutscher Bildschnitzer der Ostmark*, Vienna 1939, plates 50-52 and 54-59; p. 15. Oettinger supposes that, while he was working on the statues of the apostles, around 1490-1501, Lorenz Luchsperger changed direction artistically and moved from "Late Gothic" to figures with individual characters in whom the religious element is scarcely to be seen.

22. Between 1508 and 1519, Peter Vischer the Elder and his son made the reliquary of Saint Sebald in the style of the Renaissance, whereas the apostles and their idealisation recall more Gothically inspired models. Cf. Reclams Kunstführer, Deutschland I, 1970, p. 677.

23. Marianne Bernhard, *Martin Schongauer und sein Kreis,* Munich, 1980, p. 78-83. St Matthias is missing from the Apostles of the Schongauer series.

24. Johannes Jahn, *Lucas Cranach d. A., Das gesamte graphische Werk,* Herrsching, undated (after 1972), p. 246-261.

25. Idem, p. 60-69, pen-and-ink drawings.

26. Wolfgang Hütt, *Albrecht Dürer, Das gesamte graphische Werk,* Herrsching, undated (after 1972), vol. I, hand drawing. p. 509-516.

27. Idem, vol. II Etchings, pp. 1910.

28. Idem, vol I, p. 1012-1022 (hand drawings) and vol II, p. 1912-1914, engravings.

29. Marianne Berhard, *Hans Baldung Grien,* Munich, 1978, p. 330-343.

30. Idem, pp. 344.

31. Cf. Hanna L. Becker, *Die Handzeichnungen Albrecht Altdorfers,* Munich, 1938, p. 33.

32. Ludwig von Baldass, *Albrecht Altdorfer,* 2nd edition, Vienna, 1941, comes to the conclusion that Altdorfer prefigured many aspects of the art of 1600 and subsequently. (p. 220).

33. Altdorfer cannot really have felt that he was involved in a demonstration of his artistic capacities in the Apostle series, since he merely dated it and did not sign it (unlike the Budapest St Barbara, the style of which is very similar, also executed in 1517 and signed). For St Barbara, cf. Hanna Luise Becker, pp. 106, n° 24 and reproduction on plate 26.

34. Article on Albrecht Altdorfer in the "Kindlers Malereilexikon" Munich 1976, vol I, p. 78. Ludwig von Baldass (see note 32) explains on page 212 that Altdorfer had been tempted by a "conception which was purely secular, since it was based solely on man". Dürer is first and foremost a painter of meditation, whereas Altdorfer is not deeply and fundamentally religious (idem pp. 207).

The Apostles of the Abbey of Seitenstetten
1517
Library of the Benedictine Convent of Seitenstetten
(Lower Austria)

29 - St Andrew - Cat 13
Pen and black ink, white highlights, grey-brown background.
143×101 mm. Wz 50.

30 - St James the Elder - Cat 14
Pen and black ink, white highlights, grey-brown background.
139×99 mm. Wz 51.

31 - St Peter - Cat 15
Pen and black ink, white highlights, grey-brown background.
128×97 mm. Wz 49.

32 - St John the Evangelist - Cat 16

Pen and black ink, white highlights, grey-brown background.
132×87 mm. Wz 48

33 - St Phillip - Cat 17

Pen and black ink, white highlights, yellow-brown background.
138×102 mm. Wz 52.

34 - St Thomas - Cat 18

Pen and black ink, white highlights, reddish background.
143×99 mm. Wz 53.

35 - St James the Younger - Cat 19

Pen and black ink, white highlights, dark brown-red background.
143×108 mm. Wz 54.

36 - St Simon - Cat 20

Pen and black ink, white highlights, brown background.
143×95 mm. Wz 55.

37 - St Matthias - Cat. 21

Pen and black ink, white highlights, brown background.
Undated.
128×90 mm. Wz 57.

38 - St Matthew - Cat 22

Pen and black ink, white highlights, yellow-green background.
Undated
128×90 mm. Wz 57.

39 - St Bartholomew - Cat. 23

Pen and black ink, white highlights, brown background.
Undated, c. 1517
Upper edges rounded off.
124×86 mm. Wz 58.

This series of Apostles reveals a break in Altdorfer's style characterised on the one hand by large forms and on the other, as Winzinger has pointed out, by a new attitude to the body. It is this also which explains the diversity of the pictorial treatment. Winzinger insists, for instance, on the disproportionate feet of the figures which are painted in a very detailed way. Only Saints Andrew and James the Elder are placed in a featureless landscape. Six of the Apostles have a halo; one, Judas, is missing. There is no way of knowing what the raison-d'être of the series may have been. The Apostles were originally contained in a book in the convent library. F.A.

Winzinger 1952, n° 48-58.

41 - Footsoldier with Lance - A. Altdorfer - c. 1517
Pen-and-ink - 185×127 mm - Erlangen, Universitäts-Bibliothek.

42 - Pyramus and Thisbe - A. Altdorfer - c. 1513
Pen-and-ink - 134×106 mm - Erlangen, Universitäts-Bibliothek.

43 - Sketch of Castle and Five Heads - A. Altdorfer
c. 1515 - Pen-and-ink - 148×115 mm - Vienna, Albertina.

44 - Ship in Full Sail - A. Altdorfer - c. 1515
Pen-and-ink - 172×126 mm - Erlangen, Universitäts - Bibliothek.

1 - The dead lansquenet - Cat. 1
Pen and black ink drawing, with white highlighting on a blue paper background.
c. 1511.
213×156 mm.
Berlin, Kupferstichkabinett, SMPK Inv. n° KdZ 83.

A dead man dressed as lansquenet, a dagger in his chest, is lying stretched out on the ground. He is surrounded by tall conifer trees, dense thicket and foliage. To the right is a deep vault overrun with bracken, which seems not to have been trodden by human foot for some time. This is probably a portrayal of the love story between Pyramus and Thisbe. According to Ovid, the young lovers had arranged a nocturnal rendez-vous under the full moon at the tomb of the legendary king Ninus. Thisbe, arriving there first, was chased by a lioness. Pyramus discovers her blood-stained veil and stabs himself, supposing that she has been kil-led by some wild animal. Thisbe finds her lover dying and follows him in death.
With regards to this extremely popular subject — which Altdorfer trea-ted in two further drawings, an engraving and a woodcut, — the most striking aspect is the blue background of night and the white highlights which effectively bring out, in the cold light of the moon, the two dead bodies and the plants. R.B.

Friedländer and Block, 1921, p. 4 — Winzinger, 1952, n° 27 — Oettinger, in: *Hubert und Altdorfer*, 1959, p. 43 ff. — Cat. *Kunst der Donauschule*, 1965, n° 66

2 - Weeping willows in an alpine landscape - Cat. 2
Pen and black ink.
Signed. c. 1511.
197×141 mm. Wz. 29.
Vienna, Academy of Fine Arts, (Inv. n° 2518).

This drawing is a remarkable example of the way in which Altdorfer gives life to his landscapes and expresses his profound vision of nature. The fantastic willow in the foreground, leaning over to the side, empha-sizes the unreal character of his landscape. The two willows take root in the mass constitued by the large forests and the steep rocky slopes, and reduce the distance between the foreground and background to almost nothing. This effect is above all produced by the strong broad lines which are almost evenly rendered in all parts of the drawing. In Altdorfer's work it is to a large extent the lines which convey the expres-sion and create the atmosphere and these change completely depending on the picture. (cf the two etchings of the large spruces) (Cat. 157 to 163). R.B.

Winzinger, 1952, n° 29 - Cat. *Kunst der Donauschule*. 1965, n° 68.

45 - Christ bearing the cross - A. Altdorfer - c. 1512 - Pen and lavis 250×201 mm - Erlangen, Universitäts-Bibliothek.

Albrecht Altorfer von Regenspurg

46 - Interior of a Church - Cat. 24

47 - Church Interior - A. Altdorfer - c. 1518/20 - Hand coloured pen-and-ink drawing
212×138 mm - Erlangen, Universitäts-Bibliothek.

48 - Two Footsoldiers - A. Altdorfer (attribution) - c. 1515/20 - Pen-and-ink - 204×155 mm - Vienna, Albertina.

4 - St. Christopher - Cat. 3

Pen in black, heightened in white, on blue-pigmented paper.
With monogram and dated 1510.
214×143 mm. Wz. 22.
Hamburger Kunsthalle (Inv. n° 22 887).

St. Christopher stands out powerfully and giant-like from the low-lying landscape, which is outlined with a few sparse strokes. Since the 12th century, depictions of the larger than life-sized giant with a child on his shoulders and usually a tree trunk in his hands are common. Typical of the Danube School and especially of Altdorfer is the low-lying landscape, which accentuates the foreground. R.B.

Winzinger, 1952, n° 22. - Winzinger, 1963, n° 111.

6 - Lovers in a Landscape - Cat. 4

Pen in black.
With a date mark (1) 504 and an inscription,
"Lucas Cran...", drawn by an unknown hand.
282 × 205 mm. Berlin, Kupferstichkabinett, SMPK. Kdz 2671.

A young couple is sitting under a group of trees in the foreground of a landscape. Far away, on a steep range of rocks, separated by a river, lies a village.
This drawing, which was for a long time considered to be a part of the work done by Lucas Cranach the Elder during his stay in Vienna, was first attributed to Albrecht Altdorfer by Winkler, who based his judgement on the manner in which the date has been inscribed on the upper right-hand corner of the drawing. Since then, art historians have differed in their opinions as to the degree to which Altdorfer imitated Cranach. One group maintains that this drawing is a copy of a drawing done by Cranach, while the other points out that the motif of a pair of lovers placed in a landscape is influenced by Dürer and the way Cranach depicted landscapes in his early work.
A certain degree of uncertainty in the drawing style, as for example in the position of the youth's leg, indicates that at the time when he made the drawing, Altdorfer was still a student, who used other painters as models for his own work without, however, copying them. One particularly revealing aspect of this drawing, done one year before Altdorfer settled down in Regensburg, is his early encounter with the work of Cranach, whose late works contains the first examples of those characteristics now attributed to the Danube School of painting.
R.B.

F. Winkler, in : *Berliner Museen 55,* 1934, p. 2, - Winzinger, 1963, p. 130. - Cat. *Kunst der Donauschule,* 1965, n° 30. - F. Anzelewski, in: Cat. *Dürer und seine Zeit,* 1967/68, n° 126.

8 - St Nicholas calms the tempest - Cat. 5

Pen in black, heightened in white, on brown-pigmented paper.
With a monogram and dated 1508.
190×148 mm. Wz. 5
Oxford, Ashmolean Museum.

The expressive force of the young Altdorfer is appropriate to the subject matter of this drawing. The tumult of the elements corresponds to the drawing style employed to depict formless clouds hanging low in the sky and a turbulently swelling mass of water, which seems almost to crush the ship. The frightening condition of the vehicle is expressed by the slanting position of the board, mast, yard and sails of the ship. But the upright figure of St. Nicholas from Myra, whom the sailors called upon in their distress promises rescue, so that the devil clings onto the basket of the falling mast in vain. F.A.
Winzinger 1952, n° 5.

9 - Two Mercenaries and a Pair of Lovers - Cat. 6

Pen in black, heightened in white, on reddish-brown-pigmented paper.
With monogram and dated 1508.
176×137 mm.
Copenhagen, Statens Museum for Kunst.

The drawing in Copenhagen, to which little attention is paid by art historians, represents a varaint of the theme "Lovers out of Doors", executed for the first time by Altdorfer in the Berlin drawing of 1504 in imitation of Cranach.
He drew this subject two more times, in the year 1508 (Wz. 11 and 12) yet in both of these drawings the mercenaries are missing. One might interpret the drawing in question as depicting the mercenaries eavesdropping on the pair of lovers.
In his early crative period, Altdorfer preferred stocky figures with a block-like heaviness. As is the case with the Berlin drawing, the date is almost hidden on the left edge among the grass. F.A.

Becker 151. - Winzinger 1952, n° 7.

15 - St Genoveva - Cat. 7

Pen in black, heightened in white, on brown-pigmented paper.
Bevelled on all four edges.
c. 1909.
116×80 mm.
Berlin, Kupferstichkabinett, SMPK. KdZ 17661.

The woman, wearing a long coat, is carrying a candle in one hand and has a crown on her head. Both are symbols with which St. Genoveva, patroness of the city of Paris, is frequently depicted. According to the legend, she moved to Paris after having consecrated her life to God and there committed countless benevolent miracles. Her burning candle was repeatedly extinguished by the wind, understood to have been a manifestation of the devil, but always caught fire again, spontaneously, whenever the girl took the candle into her hand.
The conspicuously small head of St. Genoveva indicates that this drawing belongs to the early work of Altdorfer (cf. cat. 26).
This drawing serves as a particularly good depiction of the drawing style of this master, who was less interested in a consistent execution of the drawn pen line than in the total artistic effect produced by the work. This artistic impression is considerably accentuated by the brush application of white heightening. R.B.

Winzinger, 1952, n° 16. - Oettinger, 1959, p. 15 ff.

22 - The Death Jump of Marcus Curtius - Cat. 8

Pen in black, heightened in white, on olive-green-pigmented paper. With the date 1512.
195×144 mm.
Brunswick. Herzog Anton Ulrich-Museum. Inv. n° Z. 2.

A Roman folk-legend recounts that in 362 B.C., in the forum, at a spot which was later called *Curtius lacus,* a deep chasm formed and that the population feared the entire city would sink. An oracle demanded for the most valuable property to be thrown into the gorge in order to make it close up again. Thereupon the Roman youth Marcus Curtius, who interpreted the demanded property to mean heroic courage, thrust himself, along with his horse and his armour, into the chasm. The opening immediately disappeared.
Altdorfer drew this episode twice. In the drawing in Dessau he strove to designate the original locality of the event more closely by depicting the Colosseum. In the drawing in question, however, the scene has been transferred to a German city. Only the monumental pillars to the right suggest any Italian traits. M.R.

Winzinger, 1952, n° 31. - Cat. *Kunst der Donauschule,* 1965, n° 69.

24 - Battle between a Knight and a Mercenary. - Cat. 9
Pen in black, heightened in white, on brown-pigmented paper.
With the date 1512.
219×157 mm. Wz. 30.
Rotterdam, Museum Boymans (MB 248).

25 - Christ in Limbo - Cat. 10
Pen in dark brown, heightened in white, on brown-pigmented paper.
Monogram and dated 1512.
195×147 mm. Wz. 37.
Oxford, The Ashmolean Museum.

Christ is standing with the banner of victory at the gates of hell, after his own interment. He has just released Adam and Eve, along with other persons, although the devil, enraged, is racing though the air. Baldass was the first to recognize that Altdorfer used Mantegnas' copperplate engraving (B. 5) as inspiration for this drawing. Under the influence of Italian art, the proportions of Altdorfer's figures have also changed from his earlier works. They are now more slender and their movements more skillfully captured. Only the figure of Eve indicates Altdorfer's attempt to grapple with the depiction of the nude human body. F.A.

L. Baldass : *Albrecht Altdorfer. Studien über die Entwicklungfaktoren im Werk des Künstlers. Vienna 1923; p. 40 - Winzinger 1952 n° 37.*

26 - Samson's Battle with the Lion - Cat. 11
Pen in brown, heightened in white, on gray-yellow-pigmented paper.
c. 1512.
216×155 mm.
Berlin, Kupferstichkabinett, SMPK.

The story of Samson (Richter 13-16) who conquered the lion was a theme which was most popular in the late Middle Ages. Its portrayal was understood as a symbol for the virtue of fortitude and as typological of how evil was overcome due to the death of Christ and his resurrection. Altdorfer, who examines the problem of reproducing the human figure here, has juxtaposed the biblical scene with a landscape of Alpine foothills, which to a large extent determines the effect of this print. This motif, inspired by the artist's native environment, along with the folkloristic atmosphere are major characteristics that can be found throughout the entire art of the Danube School. R.B.

Friedländer and Bock, 1921, p. 4 and p. 372. — Winzinger, 1952, n° 34 — Oettinger, 1959, p. 48 — Stange 1964, p. 75 and 111. 113. — Cat. *Dürer und seine zeit,* 1967/68, n° 129.

28 - St Catherine Refuses the Worship of Idols - Cat. 12
Pen in black, heightened in white, on dark-brown-pigmented paper.
With a fake Dürer monogram and dated 1512.
211×142 mm. Wz. 42
Copenhagen, Statens Museum for Kunst.

Despite the subsequent addition of the Dürer monogram and the date 1512 by an unknown hand, the attribution of this drawing to Albrecht Altdorfer is most probably accurate. Winzinger correctly points out the vivid execution of the drawn line as a clear indication of Altdorfer's authorship.
Of the various interpretations given to this drawing Winzinger's reference to the legend of St. Catherine is probably the most applicable. The Christian woman Catherine, whom the Roman Emperor Maxentius was prepared to save from a condemnation to death if she showed herself willing to worship the ancestral Roman gods, once more, preferred to sacrifice her life in order to remain faithful to Christian belief. This story fits the figures in the drawing, which depicts Catherine who has dropped to her knees and a man, beseechingly pointing at an idol on a pillar. The general interest during Altdorfer's time in detailed depictions of the lives of Christian martyrs and saints also speaks in favor of this interpretation. F.A.
Winzinger 1952, n° 42.

46 - Interior of a Church - Cat. 24
Pen in brown, gray wash.
c. 1520/25.
On the upper left is an inscription by an unknown hand : "Albrecht Altdorfer of Regensburg".
183×200 mm.
Berlin, Kupferstichkabinett, SMPK. KdZ 11920.

This drawing is an architectural study for the painting *The Birth of Mary with a Roundel of Angels,* now in the Alte Pinakothek in Munich. The incised and drawn in guidelines indicate Altdorfer's attempt to grapple with the problems of perspective construction. Several sections, however, suggest that he was also interested in a picturesque rendition of the church interior, for which he used a gray wash, applied with a brush, as well as in the architectural and ornamental details. It is most probable that the pilgrimage church for the *Beautiful Mary,* located in his home city, served as the source of inspiration. This supposition is particularly plausible because art historians assume that Altdorfer was acquainted with the sketches for this church, done in 1519 by the architect Hans Huber from Regensburg. R.B.

Cat. *Dürer and seine Zeit,* 1967/68, n° 132.

49 - Serenity during the Flight. - Cat. 25
c. 1512/15
Pen in black, heightened on white, brownish-pigmented paper.
205×155 mm. Wz. 156
London University College.

Hind, *Catalogue of the Drawings in the University College London,* 1930, p. 12.

49 - Serenity during the Flight. - Cat. 25

108 - Venus punishes Cupid - Cat. 26
Pen in black.
With monogram and dated 1508.
97×66 mm.
Berlin, Kupferstichkabinett, SMPK. KdZ 4184.

The goddess Venus, dressed in contemporary clothing, is standing on a hill, which is only outlined. She is holding her son Cupid by the hand, who in turn seemingly attempts to get away from her and is covering his face with his hands in shame. His symbols, the bow and arrows, are lying on the ground. The satirical, mystical novel by the classical writer Apulejus, *The Golden Donkey,* which was particularily popular in the Renaissance, relates the love story between Cupid and the king's daughter Psyche. Since the beauty of the girl roused the envy of the goddess Venus, she ordered her son to stir up in the princess amorous feelings for the lowest of all human creatures. Instead, however, Cupid fell in love with the girl and kidnapped her. Angered, Venus scolded her son and pursued Psyche with her vengence. Finally Zeus intervened and married the two lovers.
This drawing represents a sketch for a copperplate engraving by Albrecht Altdorfer, which is in the Bibliothèque Nationale in Paris (2312 Ec. 2, a rés). R.B.

Friedländer and Bock, 1921, p. 4 — Winzinger, 1952 n° 9. — Cat. *Kunst der Donauschule,* 1965 n° 60.

230 - Suzanne and the old men - Cat. 162 Bis
Pen and dark brown ink, with a black lead frame
c. 1526.
332×274 mm.
Düsseldorf, Kunstmuseum, Graphische Sammlung.

This drawing, of unusual dimensions for Altdorfer, constitutes, with its black lead frame, a sketch of the picture at Munich which he executed towards 1526. For the painting, however, the composition was modified. The palace, which takes up a little more than half the space in the sketch, has been brought forward towards the left and now occupies 2/3 of the picture. The building itself has been "embellished" by two annexes in the form of turrets, to the right and left. In this way, the main action — Suzanna at her bath — takes on a greater importance; the secondary scenes — the court and the stoning of the two seducers — take up more room.
It is only from the second half of the 15th century that artists began to deal with the subject fo Suzanna at her bath (based on an apocryphal text from the Bible). The artists of the Middle Ages — unlike those who were painting at the end of the classical period — did not portray this legend, which was interpreted as being the triumph of chastity. However, in German pictoral art, the theme of Suzanna is illustrated almost at the same moment as the story of David and Bathsheba (II Samuel, 11). Although as a general rule the public of this time was not shocked by the representation of erotic scenes, in both protrayals the bath is interpreted as a foot bath, as is also the case in Altdorfer. F.A.

Ille Budde, Katalog der Handzeichnungen der Kunstakademie Düsseldorf, Düsseldorf 1930, p. 143. — Winzinger, 1952, n° 111. — Winzinger 1975, n° 59.

75

50 - Joshua and Caleb bring the Fruits of the Promised Land - Cat. 27   50 Bis - Abraham's Sacrifice - Cat. 28

51-52 - Slaughter of the Children at Bethlehem. - Cat. 29-30

Woodcut. Whit monogram and dated 1511.
194×146 mm. B. 46, H. 46, Wz. 15
Berlin, Kupferstichkabinett, SMPK. Inv. n° 380-4.

This woodcut depicts the New Testament story, in which King Herod ordered all male babies in Bethlehem to be murdered. Altdorfer places the event in front of a partially destroyed building, in whose architectural style gothic and renaissance forms are merged. Soldiers are tearing babies away from their mothers, who in turn flee, seeking shelter on the steps of the building. On of the soldiers, leaning on his sword in an affected manner, watches the horrible deed. Functioning as a sign of admonition, a sword standing upright points with the corpse of a child toward heaven. In the clouds one can see the souls of the children.

This depiction is one of the earliest woodcuts done by Altdorfer, a medium he began working in around 1511. Typical of these early works is the very slight distinction made between light and shadow, due to which the forms seem to flow into each other. In this drawing Altdorfer seems to have been particularly interested in the human figure, which he represents in many different positions, using above all foreshortening. A comparision with the woodcut sequence *Fall and Redemption of the Human Race* (cf. Cat. 39-56), executed some two years later shows how quickly Altdorfer learned to master such technical problems. R.B.

Winzinger, 1963, n° 15. — Catalogue *Kunst der Donauschule*, 1965, n° 97. — Catalogue *The Danube School*, 1969/70, n° 20.

51-52 - Slaughter of the Children at Bethlehem. - Cat. 29-30

B.60.   EC N. 1514

53 - The Judgement of Paris - Cat. 31

53 -   The Judgement of Paris - Cat. 31
Woodcut.
With monogram and dated 1511.
198×158 mm. B. 60 H. 75, Wz. 16.
Paris, Bibliothèque Nationale, Cabinet des Estampes,
ECN/1514.

The Greek mythological story of the judgement of Paris, a story which
was rich in consequences, inspired Homer's *Illiad*. It is considered to
be one of the main pictorial themes which, by offering new
possibilities of depiction, enriched the art north of the Alps after
enriched reception of the humanistic ideas and forms of the Italian
Renaissance. Thus, the Paris story, in which the hero is to settle the
dispute between the goddesses Hera, Athena and Aphrodite, as to
which is the most beautiful of the three, served as a new artistic examination of the female nude, which could be rendered in three different positions. This was most probably the reason why Altdorfer
chose to treat the subject of the judgement of Paris, since his early
work, especially, to which the woodcut in question belongs, indicates
an intense struggle with the problem of rendering the human body.
Hera, Athena and Aphrodite are standing in front of a group of trees
whose tops disappear in a huge cloudlike configuration. Illuminated by
a bright light, they reveal the unclad charm of their bodies. The
messenger of the gods, Hermes, is pointing at the women, and calls on
Paris to make a choice. The chosen goddess is to receive a golden ball,
which Eris, goddess of discord, is holding in her hand. Her offer of this
prize of victory had originally started the dispute. By incorporating
this mythological scene into a landscape of fantastic configurations,
Altdorfer imbues this depiction with a fairy-tale-like, charmes mood —
a characteristic trait of the Danube style. R.B.

Winzinger, 1963, n° 16. — Catalogue *The Danube School*, 1969/70,
n° 21.

54 - Pair of Lovers - Cat. 32
Woodcut.
With name sign and date 1511.
135×100 mm. B. 63, H. 88, Wz. 17.
Paris, Bibliothèque Nationale, Cabinet des Estampes ECN 1518.

This depiction of a pair of lovers in a forest is considered to be one of
the earliest woodcuts executed by Albrecht Altdorfer.
In comparison with works done at a later date, this depiction lacks pictorial depth and a vividness in the rendition of the figures, similar to
the depiction of the "Slaughter of the Children at Bethlehem" (cf. cat.
29-30). The slight differentiation of the contours and the dense series
of little strokes allow the foreground and background to flow into each
other. Yet one can already discern Altdorfer's tendency to limit
himself to a few motives within each depiction, a tendency which is
quite clearly expressed in such works as the neatly composed woodcut
sequence, *The Fall and Redemption of the Human Race*, executed soon
after this woodcut.
The motif of a pair of lovers sitting in a landscape, already to be found
in Dürer, appears in a very early pen drawing of a pair of lovers, done
in 1504, which was first attributed to Lucas Cranach, now, however,
recognized as a drawing by Altdorfer. R.B.

Winzinger, 1963, n° 17. — Cat. *Kunst der Donauschule*, 1965, n° 98.

54 - Pair of lovers - Cat. 32

55 - The Beheading of John the Baptist - Cat. 33
Woodcut.
With monogram and dated 1512.
204×155 mm. B. 52, H. 54, Wz. 19.
Regensburg, Museen der Stadt Regensburg.

The martyrdom of John takes place in the ruined porch of a mighty gothic palace. The executioner, leaning forward, has completed his work and is now placing the head of the Baptist on the silver plate belonging to Salome. Deeply moved, spectators watch the event.
The artitectural frame of the scene heightens the forcefulness of the depiction. The pointed tower and the covered arch concentrate the view onto the executioner. On the right, the fragments of a vault construction behind the five figures repeats their slight flection and thus heightens the framing effect.
Probably under the influence of Michael Pacher's altar in St. Wolfgang, Altdorfer lines up the figures on the edge one behind the other and thus directs the view into the spatial depth toward a landscape with mountains, forests and houses. M.R.

Winzinger, 1963, n° 19. — Cat. *The Danube School*, 1969/70, n° 22.

55 - The Beheading of John the Baptist - Cat. 33

56 - The Resurrection of Christ - Cat. 34
Woodcut.
With monogram and date 1512.
232×181 mm., B. 47, H. 49, Wz. 20.
Brunswick, Herzog Anton Ulrich-Museum.

Brightly illuminated, Christ, holding a banner of victory is hovering in a Mandorla, surrounded by clouds and praying angels. Underneath this zone lies the opened grave, around which more angels and in part still sleeping guards are grouped.
In this woodcut Altdorfer attempts for the first time to give the woodcut a pictorial effect. Different types of hachures come together, forming surface qualities of differing density and lightness. Here, Altdorfer surpasses Dürer's Resurrection, executed in 1510 (B. 15), since in that drawing the single line, as for example in the shroud wrapped around Christ, still has a meaning of its own. A connection between the two spaces of action on earth and in heaven is also abandoned in favor of the hovering effect of the Mandorla. The beams from the various sources of light (the rising sun, the langern, the oil lamps) support this impression. M.R.

Winzinger, 1963, n° 20. — Koepplin, 1967, p. 94-101. — Cat. *The Danube School*, 1969/70, n° 23.

57 - The Annunciation to Mary - Cat. 35
Woodcut.
With monogram and date 1513.
125×98 mm., B. 44, H. 44, Wz. 21.
Paris, Bibliothèque Nationale, Cabinet des Estampes ECN 1501.

In this woodcut Altdorfer renders the theme of the Annunciation to Mary in a completely new and original pictorial form. Due to his monumentality, the angel Gabriel, seen from the back, draws the attention of the viewer onto himself. Wrapped in a wide flowing coat, this figure with heavily outspread wings, is illuminated by gleaming light, falling over its back, head and hand and directing the viewer's gaze toward the small, delicate figure of Mary. She is sitting, with folded hands and her head bent down in humility, in a room depicted in such a way as to suggest great depth. Above her hovers the dove representing the Holy Ghost, which is surrounded by beams of light. Winzinger connects this woodcut with a sketch for the woodcut of the Lamentation of Christ (Munich). The similarity in format and manner have led him to suspect that Altdorfer executed both woodcuts as part of a sequence depicting the Passion of Christ but that he abandonned this project in favor of the smaller format woodcut cycle, *Fall and Redemption of the Human Race* (cf. cat. 39-56). R.B.

Winzinger, 1963, n° 21. — Cat. *Kunst der Donauschule*, 1965, n° 101. — Cat. *The Danube School*, 1969/70, n° 25.

58 - Pyramus and Thisbe - Cat. 36

Woodcut.
With monogram and dated 1513.
119×100 mm. B. 61, H. 76, Wz. 22.
Regensburg, Museen der Stadt Regensburg.

The scene of the action, the grave of Nimus, is depicted as a cut sepulchre with a massive tombstone and a tree next to it and thus serves as a foil for the theme. Pyramus lies with a dagger in his breast on a gigantic squared stone, the veil of his lover at his feet. Full of sorrow, Thisbe leans with folded hands over him.

As in the woodcut *Jael and Sisera* (Cat. 37), Altdorfer uses the theme in order to grapple with the problem of space, which he tries to solve by depicting foreshortened figures. A complementary sketch belonging to this woodcut has been preserved in Erlangen. This drawing, indicates the numerous corrections Altdorfer undertook before he solved the problem of form and found a suitable construction, which he then used for the final woodcut. M.R.

Winzinger, 1963, n° 22.

59 - Jael and Sisera - Cat. 37

Woodcut.
With monogram, c. 1513
122×95 mm. B. 43, H. 43, Wz. 23.
Regensburg, Museen der Stadt Regensburg.

This woodcut treats a them from the Old Testament. Sisera was the commander-in-chief of the army of the king of Canaan Jabin, who repressed the Israelites for twenty years (Judges 4,2-3). After the defeat of his army in a decisive battle against the Jews, Sisera escaped as the only survivor. He reached the tent of Jael, who pretended she would protect him. Once he had fallen asleep, however, she took a tent peg and drove it into Sisera's temple (Judges 4,21).

Altdorfer has transfered the scene from Jael's tent to the city wall. The exhausted Sisera has fallen asleep on the ground and Jael raises her hand to deliver the fatal blow.

The theme gives the artist the possibility of depicting an extremely foreshortened lying figure, which reminds one of Mantegna's painting *The Dead Christ*. Such foreshortening appears frequently in the work of Altdorfer at this time, for example in the woodcut *Pyramus and Thisbe* (cat. 36). It seems to be the result of Altdorfer's artistic confrontation with the work of Pacher and Mantegna. M.R.

Winzinger, 1963, n° 23. — Cat. *The Danube School*, 1969/70, n° 27.

60 - St. Christopher - Cat. 38

Woodcut.
With monogram and date 1513.
165×118 mm. B. 53, H. 56, Wz. 24.
Brunswig, Herzog Anton Ulrich-Museum.

St. Christopher, patron of travellers, made it his task to help people cross a certain large river by carrying them across on his back. One day a child asked to be carried across. On the way, however, the burden seemed to become increasingly heavier until Christopher threatened to drown in the river. Then the child spoke to him, saying he had carried more than the world, since he who had created the world had been his burden. He dipped the giant into the water and baptized him.

The depiction of St Christopher, leaning on a dried up bough and carrying Christ across the water had been a popular theme since the 12th century. Altdorfer treated this motif in three drawings, two copperplate engravings and one other woodcut. Among these works the woodcut in question, which expresses Altdorfer's versatility is certainly artistically the most important.

In the majority of his woodcuts, Altdorfer was concerned with spatial depth and pictorial expression. Here, however, due to the use of sparing and generous lines which are comparable to the penstroke in some of his drawings, he has created a very individual, two-dimensional effect. R.B.

Winzinger, 1963, n° 24. — Cat. *The Danube School*, 1969/70, n° 26.

59 - Jael and Sisera - Cat. 37

60 - St. Christopher - Cat. 38

61 to 102 - The Sequence "Fall and Redemption of the Human Race" - Cat. 39 to 80

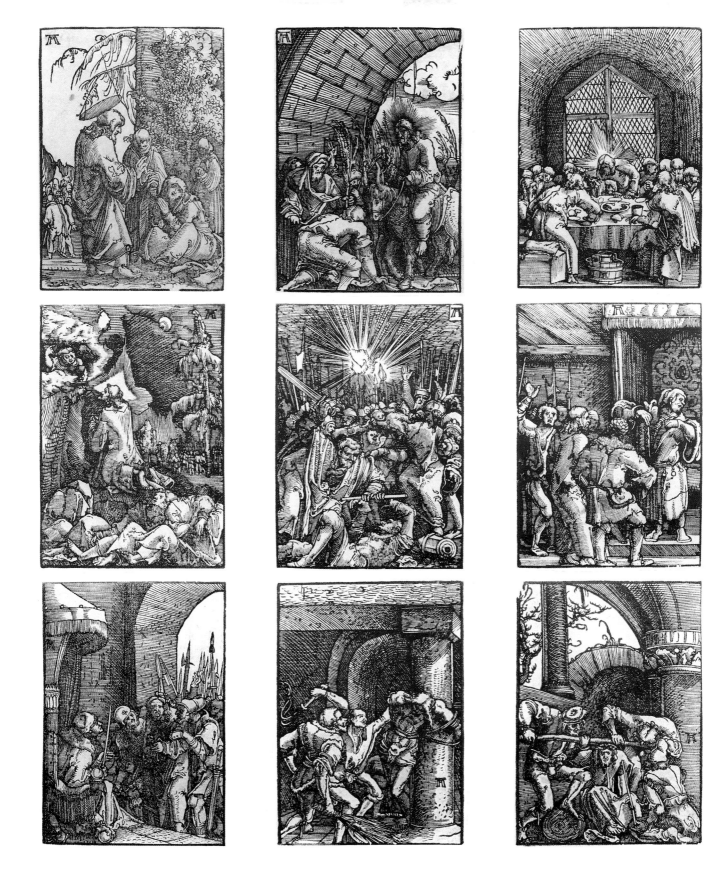

61 to 102 - The Sequence "Fall and Redemption of the Human Race" - Cat. 39 to 80

Mary on a Crescent (187), The Fall (W 26), Expulsion from Paradise (W 27), Joachim's Sacrifice (W 28), The Annunciation of Joachim (W 29), Meeting between Joachim and Anna (W 30), Mary's visit to the Temple (W 31), The Annunciation to Mary (33), Search for a Home (33), Birth of Christ (34), Adoration of the Magi (35), The Circumcision of Christ (36), The Presentation of Christ in the Temple (37), Flight to Egypt (38), Jesus among the Scribes (39), The Transfiguration of Christ (188), Christ's Farewell to Mary (189), Entrance into Jerusalem (192), The Last Supper (191), Christ at the Mount of Olives, The Capture of Christ (193) Christ before Caiphas (194), Christ before Herod (195), Flagellation of Christ (197), The crowning of Thorns (198), Exhibition of Christ, The Ritual Washing of Pilate's Hands, The Bearing of the Cross, Christ is Nailed to the Cross, Erection of the Cross, Crucifixion, Descent from the Cross, The Lamentation of Christ, The Interment of Christ, Christ in Limbo, Resurrection of Christ, Christ Appears to Magdalene, The Ascension of Christ, The Death of Mary, Judgement Day.

Woodcuts.
With monogram, c. 1513.
72×48 mm. B. 1-40, H. 1-40, Wz. 25-64.
Berlin, Kupferstichkabinett, SMPK (Wz. 26-39) and Museen der Stadt Regensburg.

Altogether, this sequence of woodcuts encompasses forty sheets and is generally known under the title *Fall and Redemption of the Human Race*. It depicts scenes from the Old and the New Testaments, from the Fall of Adam and Eve to the Last Judgement, in which, after to the Passion of Christ, the scenes from the life of Mary make up a large part of the sequence.
The large, uncut printed sheets in Erlangen and Cleveland preserved prove that the virgin Mary with Child, standing on a crescent and crowned with angels, forms the beginning of this cycle. It is most likely that Altdorfer knew the woodcut sequence of the small Passion of Christ made by Dürer a few years earlier. Yet one can not speak of an imitation. In their vivid and popular way of narrative as well as in their simple and impressive pictorial form, Altdorfer's woodcuts are completely original and independent. He has handled the small pictorial format in such a masterly manner, that when viewed for a longer period of time the pictures have a distinctly monumental effect. Altdorfer achieved this effect in particular by means of an arrangement of perspectives, in the compositions so that depth appears considerably larger than width. This is most prominent in such examples as *The Meeting Between Joachim and Anna* and in *Mary Visits the Temple*. R.B.

Winzinger, 1963, p. 65 ff. — Cat. *The Danube School*, 1969/70, n° 28/35.

103 - The Holy Family - Cat. 81

Woodcut.
With monogram.
120×95 mm. B. 45, H. 45, Wz. 86.
Paris, Bibliothèque Nationale, Cabinet des Estampes ECN 1502.

Six persons are sitting around a table in a spacious, brightly illuminated hall, which is coated with a coffered barrel vault, has arcature arrangements on the side and an open back wall structured with pillars and pilasters. Mary leads the baby Christ, who has risen from his pillow, to Anna. Joseph on the left and the three husbands of Mother Mary, Joachim, Cleophas and Salomas, the latter of which disappears almost completely in the hard shadows of the side wall, watch the happening with great interest. From the beams of the opened back wall three angels are singing from a book, facing down toward the group of figures. Through the opening, a montain landscape is visible. Winzinger thinks it is possible to date this drawing earlier than the usually suggested date "after 1520", since the completely straight execution of the parallel hachures is not yet present, although it is a major stylistic aspect of Altdorfer's later woodcuts, such as the *Praying Man before Mary*. It is also apparent that Altdorfer was not yet able to depict the constructed room in a completely satisfying manner. M.R.

Winzinger, 1963 n° 86.

104 -The Holy Family at the Fountain - Cat. 82

Woodcut.
With monogram c. 1512/15.
231×175 mm., B. 59, H. 47.
Ratisbonne - Museum der Stadt Regensburg.

In a church space which is depicted in such a manner as to suggest an expanding depth, stands a richly decorated Renaissance fountain. From the upper basin, which is crowned with a crouching male figure, the water flows into three further bulging basins. The lowest basin of the fountain is supported by puttos riding on dolphins. It is so widely outstretched that it seems to fill the entire width of the picture and the holy family which on its flight to Egypt is resting here, can be discerned only upon closer scrutiny of the scene. Mary is wearing a head and shoulder scarf adorned with a fringe and stars in the manner of the byzantine Lucas-Madonna, whose image was highly worshipped in Regensburg at that time. She is holding her child, who is seated on the edge of the fountain. An angel is looking over her shoulder while a second angel is opposite her, playing with a girl. The entire depiction is imbued with a serene and peaceful mood.

Due to its magnificent spatial depth, this woodcut reminds one of the sequence *Fall and Redeption of the Human Race* and the *Annunciation* (cf. cat. 35). In the woodcut in question, Altdorfer has allocated a dominant role to the stone fountain, which one would more likely expect to find in a public square or in the interior court of a Renaissance building than in a church. This motif was treated by the artist in several works, for example in a panel with the same theme, executed in 1510 and in a woodcut made in 1511, which depicts the *Dream of Paris* (cf. cat. 31). His brother Erhard also uses a Renaissance fountain in a drawing of a company of people sitting at a table, in 1506. These scenes were clearly inspired by Italian models executed by artists from the group around Andrea Mantegna, namely by an engraving by Zoan Andrea and another by the so-called Tarocchimaster. R.B.

Winzinger, 1963, n° 38. — Cat. *Kunst der Donauschule*, 1965, n° 103. — Cat. *The Danube School*, 1969/70, n° 46.

105 - Praying Man before Mary - Cat. 83

105 - Praying Man before Mary - Cat. 83

Woodcut with monogram c. 1519.
168×122 mm. B. 49, H. 51, Wz. 87.
Brunswick, Herzog Anton Ulrich-Museum.

Mary has a book and Christ, who in turn is holding a nail from the Cross in his hand, on her lap. She is sitting on a high pedestal, crowned with a baldachin, in a niche the limit of which is marked by a pillar. In front of her, an angel is playing lute. In the deep alignement of the barrel-vaulted room, the attached court with ruined facades, a pagan figure with a trident, and a fire basin, and the landscape appearing at the far end, a man with a Rosary in his hand is kneeling, deep in prayer, before Mary.

Winzinger believes this woodcut to have been done by Altdorfer after a conjectured journey to Italy around 1517/18, due to many details which suggest Italian influences, such as the angel, the nimbi and the lamp hanging down from the ceiling. This woodcut was probably executed in conjunction with the pilgrimage church for the Beautiful Mary and represents, in a didactical manner, a deep inner submersion. It is possible that Altdorfer meant it as a conscious contrast to scenes of ecstatic excess before the picture of the Beautiful Mary (a saint's image which was considered to be endowed with the power to work miracles), as one can find in the woodcut by Michael Ostendorfer.
M.R.

Winzinger, 1963, n° 87. — Cat. The Danube School. 1969/70, n° 47. Cat. *Luther und die Folgen für die Kunst,* 1983/84, n° 14.

106 - The "Beautiful Mary" in the Church - Cat. 84

Woodcut with monogram, c. 1519.
122×95 mm. B. 48, H. 50, Wz. 88.
Berlin, Kupferstichkabinett, SMPK., Inv. n° 145-1891.

Legend has it that in 1519, during the demolition of the synagoge in Regensburg (cf. Cat. 130-131), a stone mason was injured fatally yet was seen alive at the building site that evening. In this period of deep religious unrest, the belief that this incident was to be understood as a miracle performed by the Mother Mary spread rapidly among the population. The chapel, which had been planned to replace the synagoge and meant to house a Byzantine image of the so-called *Beautiful Mary* that had been worshipped already for a long time, was constructed, first in wood, within the next five weeks, since from this time onward a stream of pilgrims poured into the city. This effusive worship of the *Beautiful Mary,* which lasted about four years, interested Albrecht Altdorfer as well as other artists like Michael Ostendorfer and Hans Leinberger.

Aldorfer depicted the *Beautiful Mary* of the Byzantine image (that was thought to be endowed with the power of working miracles), in five woodcuts, at least two copperplate engravings and one drawing. In accordance with the Byzantine image, Mary is wearing a cloth covering her head and her shoulders. Transposed into the late gothic style, however, she has, in accordance with the contemporary artistic taste, a maindely and popular quality. In particular, differs from her severe and exotic model in her intimate affection for the child and her lovely appearance. R.B.

Friedländer, 1923, p. 96. — Winzinger, 1963, n° 88. — Cat. *Kunst der Donauschule,* 1965, n° 107.

106 - The "Beautiful Mary" in the Church - Cat. 84

50Bis - Abraham's Sacrifice - Cat. 28

Woodcut.
With monogram, c. 1520.
123×96 mm. B. 41, H. 42, Wz. 91.
Regensburg, Museen der Stadt Regensburg.

In format and shading technique, this woodcut is closely allied to *Joshua and Caleb* (cat. 27). The main action has been moved far into the foreground. Isaac is kneeling before the already heavily smoking fire of the altar and Abraham, already holding the sword above his shoulder, pauses as a result of the angel's call and turns to see the direction from which the voice is coming. He gazes into the void. Underneath the altar of fire, the ram has gotten caught in the shrubbery. This woodcut, most probably one of the last works done by Altdorfer in this technique, displays a consistent usage fo straight line hachures. Only the wisps of smoke, which guide the view of the observer and thus connect the figures with each other, are not subjected to this system. An interesting analogy with an earlier woodcut can be found in the downward flying angel with drawn-in knees and widely outspread wings. Seen from behind, he already appears around 1513 in the *Annunciation to Joachim,* which is part of the sequence *Fall and Redemption of the Human Race* (cat. 39 to 56) M.R.

Winzinger, 1963, n° 91. — Cat. *The Danube School,* 1969/70, n° 48.

50 - Joshua and Caleb Bring the Fruits of the Promised Land - Cat. 27

Woodcut.
With monogram, c. 1520.
122×95 mm. B. 42, H. 42, Wz. 92.
Regensburg, Museum der Stadt Regensburg.

The Book of Numbers in the Old Testament recounts how, through Moses, the Lord sent out scouts into the land of Canaan, which he had designated for the Israelites. Among them were Caleb from the tribe of Judah and Joshua from the tribe of Ephraim. During their journey they came to the valley of grapes where they cut off a vine, which the two of them had to carry together on a pole. After forty days they returned to Kadesh, where the others were, with their rich gifts (Numbers 13.1-25).
Altdorfer depicts the return of the scouts to the city, which lies next to a wide river and a mountain range. The men enter by a dark city gate and proudly present the fruits, which are elegantly arranged in bowls. Two of them carry a large wreath of fruit on a pole. These two main figures in the procession were inspired by two carriers in Mantegna's painting "Triumpf of Caesar", which had been circulated as an engraving at the time of Altdorfer's own work. The rigorous parallel hachures, used by Altdorfer in this late woodcut, also derive from the Italian shading techniques. M.R.

Winzinger, 1963, n° 92. — Cat. *The Danube School,* 1969/70, n° 49.

107 - The Altar of the "Beautiful Mary" - Cat. 85

Woodcut.
With monogram, c. 1520.
310×240 mm., B. 50, H. 53, Wz. 90.
Berlin, Kupferstichkabinett, SMPK. Inv. n° 498-4.

The *Beautiful Mary* of Regensburg is depicted in the center of an architectural frame in the style of the Renaissance. In 1519 she had suddenly become a desirable center for pilgrimage. At first a wooden structure was errected to house her, while the final stone church was still being designed.
Altdorfer, who as a member of the Outer Council of Regensburg was familiar with these events, treated the *Beautiful Mary* in several of his works. Thus he created, for example, an unfortunately missing woodcut depicting one of the numerous miracles, which were supposed to have occurred. This woodcut was printed on parchment and distributed among the pilgrims. It is generally assumed that the woodcut in question was meant as a sketch for the altar in the stone church. The severe architectural construction, which almost overwhelms the dainty statuettes in the niches, reveals the artists examination of Italian Renaissance forms. R.B.

Friedländer, 1923, p. 95. — Winzinger, 1963, p. 27 ff and n° 90. — Cat. *Kunst der Donauschule,* 1965, n° 109. — Cat. *The Danube School,* 1969/70, n° 45.

107 - The Altar fo the "Beautiful Mary" - Cat. 85

109 Venus and Amor - Cat. 86.
Copper engraving.
With monogram and dated 1508.
102×65 mm. H.43, Wz. 107.
Paris, Bibliothèque Nationale, Cabinet des Estampes.
ECN 1465.

This print from the Bibliothèque Nationale is unique. There is a sketch for this engraving in Berlin (cat. 26 fig. 108) with the figures the other way round. The engraving departs from the sketch in some details. Venus' feather cap is given in greater detail, showing the individual feathers. The areas of light and shade are more strongly contrasted - a result of considerable use of cross-hatching in the shadow areas.

When the sketch was transferred onto the printing plate Venus' left hand, which is preparing to strike Amor on the ear, was turned round. The palm is now turned upwards instead of downwards as before. This distortion might explain why the plate was later cut off below Venus' hip, Whether Altdorfer himself was responsible for this alteration, as Tietze supposes, has not been confirmed. M.R.

Tietze, 1923, p.44. - Winzinger, 1963, n° 107.

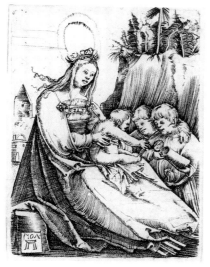

110 - Mary with two Boys - Cat. 87

111 - St. Catherine - Cat. 88

112 - Standing Venus with two
Putti - Cat. 89

113 - Knight - Cat. 90.

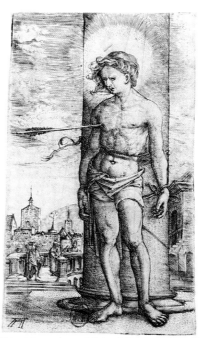

114 - Martyrdom of Saint-Sebastian - Cat. 91

116 - The small Crucifixion - Cat. 92

117 - The Blessing Christ - Cat. 93

118 - The small Standard-Bearer - Cat. 94

119 - Saint George - Cat. 95.

120 - Mary on the half moon - Cat. 96

121 - The Judgment of Paris — Cat. 97

122 - Mary with her Child and St. Anna
at the Cradle - Cat. 98

123 - Allegorical Figure - Cat. 99

125 - Mary with the Blessing Child - Cat. 101
Copperplate engraving.
With monogram, c. 1515.
165×118 mm. B. 17, H. 19, Wz. 122.
Regensburg, Museen der Stadt Regensburg.

This largest of Altdorfer's copperplate engravings seems to be equally indebted to a German and an Italian model. In Dürer's *Mary with a Pear,* (B. 41) made in 1511, Mary sits in a similar fashion with the bless-

are touching the ground, have been conceived in a similar manner by Dürer. In Altdorfer's engraving, however, the figures are in greater contact with the expressive sky. Rather than Dürer's image of Mary without a nimbus, Altdorfer depicts a group with Italian disc-like nimbi, suggesting a link between this engraving and one by Giovanni Antonio de Brescia, *The Holy Family with John the Baptist.* As in the Altdorfer engraving, the child in Brescia's work stands on Mary's thigh. For the primarily parallel running hachures in Altdorfer's engraving it is also more likely that they were modelled on Italian cop-

ing Christ on her lap on a slightly sloping hill with trees. The treatment of the clothes and the coat ends which, separated from the body

perplate engraving techniques than on German techniques. M.R. Winzinger, 1963, n° 122. — Cat. *The Danube School,* 1969/70, n° 54.

124 - Saint Christopher - Cat. 100

125 - Mary with the Blessing Child - Cat. 101

126 - St Hieronymus at the Wall - Cat. 102

Copperplate engraving.
With monogram, c. 1512/15.
122×105 mm. B. 22, H. 24, Wz. 121.
Regensburg, Museen der Stadt Regensburg.

With a book and a crucifix in one hand, a stone in the other and followed by his old lion, the long-legged, lean and bowed Hieronymus paces along an impassable path next to a wall. The wall stretches in a curve almost as far as the left edge of the picture and allows only one other view, namely onto a church with a Romanesque portal.
The figure of St. Hieronymus in this iconographical connection is very unusual, but his depiction can be traced back to Upper-Italian types. The clothes, fitting the body closely like a wet cloth, the slender proportions of the saint, all these characteristic traits, which also appeared during this period in Altdorfer's panel paintings, suggest the Upper-

Italian influence.
Similar spatial arrangements, in the form of a wall ending in an arched doorway, can be found in Dürer's woodcut *Christ in Limbo* (B. 14), of 1510, which is part of his big Passion of Christ. In the church portal, Winzinger detects similarities with the cloister portal of the St. Emmeram's church in Regensburg, which is characterized by doorcasing made of triangular, zigzag and rhombic bands. M.R.

Oettinger, 1959, p. 77. — Winzinger, 1963, n° 121. Cat. *The Danube School*, 1969/70, n° 41.

126 - St. Hieronymus at the wall - Cat. 102

112 - Standing Venus with Two Putti - Cat. 89

Copperplate engraving.
With monogram, c. 1512/15 (?)
59×35 mm. B. 32, H. 39, Wz. 114.
Regensburg, Museen der Stadt Regensburg.

Venus, with a flaming heart in the right hand and a long, slender horn of plenty in the left, stands before a garland and a gnarled tree stump. The one putto in front of her, with Altdorfer's monogram tablet, is reaching for a branch; the other holding a staff, is kneeling on the ground
This engraving goes back to a niello by Peregrino da Cesena, as does the *Couple Led in Triumph*. Altdorfer, however changes the niello which had originally stimulated him. A nude female figure slightly leaning on a bank of earth becomes, in Altdorfer's engraving, a standing Venus. He also reduces the number of winged putti found in Peregrino's niello. The dating of the engraving is disputable. While art historians formerly believed it was created in the twenties, Winzinger dates this engraving somewhere around 1512/15, because he recognizes in the well-proportioned standing motive a nearness to *Sebastian at the Martyr's Pillar*. There are, however, no sure indications as to an exact dating. M.R.

Winzinger, 1963, n° 114.

113 - **Knight** - Cat. 90

Copper engraving.
With monogram, ca. 1512/15.
87×48 mm. B.50, H.62. Wz. 117.
Paris, Bibliothèque Nationale, Cabinet des Estampes. ECN 1476

A knight in 16th century armour, his helmet adorned with ostrich feathers, stands behind an altar. Two steps separate the altar area from an enormous tree. The knight, wearing a long fringed cloth elegantly thrown over his back, is presenting a jug and a loaf of bread. This strangely dressed acolyte is likely to be Melchisedek, King of Salem, who as a priest blessed Abraham of the most high God with bread and wine (Genesis 14,18/19). In medieval typological cycles Melchisedek with his offerings was associated with Holy Communion.
The stance of the figure of the knight corresponds to that of the "Italian Sebastian" (Wz.116; cat.91) and is likely to date from exactly the same period as this engraving. M.R.

Baldass, 1941, p. 184. - Winzinger, 1963, n° 117.

114 - **Martyrdom of Saint-Sebastian** - Cat. 91.

Copper engraving.
With monogram, ca. 1512.
87×46 mm. B:23, H. 26, Wz.116.
Paris, Bibliothèque Nationale, Cabinet des Estampes.
ECN 1453

Altdorfer made two engravings of the St. Sbastian theme, one shortly after the other. The print dated 1511 shows the martyr with outstretched arms and tied to a tree. The arms follow the gentle movement of the branches, the body stands squarely in front of the tree and the figure is not balanced in spite of definite use of supporting leg and non-supporting leg. The landscape is characterised by trees bending in the wind and a wildly pointed mountain crest in the background.
This Sebastian is quite different, with his arms at his side and bound to a pillar. He now stands against a background of architecture. On the right there is part of a house, and on the left a bow-shaped bridge which leads to a town. The silhouette of the mountains in the background is now completely calm.
The saint stands with a distinctly balanced posture. i.e. with supporting leg and non-supporting leg over which the hip sinks and the shoulder rises. It is reminiscent of Italian representations of the theme, such as Andrea Mantegna's painting of Sebastian which is in the Louvre, cf. also the knight (cat. 90 fig. 113). M.R.

Dettinger, 1959, p. 43-45,47 - Winzinger, 1963, n° 116.

110 - Mary with Two Boys - Cat. 87

Copperplate engraving.
Monogram and dated 1507. 70×50 mm. B. 12., H. 16, Wz. 102.
Regensburg, Museen der Stadt Regensburg.

In this broadly laid-out motif of a sitting figure, Mary takes up the front level of the picture. The background is enriched on the left by a city, on the right by an overgrown slope. The strikingly small Baby Christ is stretching his arms out for a bumper which two boys are holding out to him. In this early copperplate engraving Altdorfer still has noticeable difficulties with illustrating volume under garments. To this is added the harsh illumination which represses the plastic qualities of the engraving. It causes Mary's body to dissolve into extensive zones of light and shadow. M.R.

Winzinger 1963, n° 102. — Cat. *The Danube School,* 1969/70, n° 17.

111 - St. Catherine - Cat. 88

Copperplate engraving.
With monogram and dated 1506.
60×39 mm. H. 29, Wz. 98.
Berlin, Kupferstichkabinett, SMPK, Inv. n° 265-1898.

The small-format copperplate engraving shows a young woman dressed in elegant clothes. Sitting between a tree and a wheel in front of a landscape, she holds a sword on her knees.
Her head, adorned with a precious headdress is leaning pensively to one side. The sword and the wheel are symbols of St. Catherine who either as a solitary figure, as is the case in this engraving, or together with St. Barbara and St. Margaret, had been a popular theme since the 12th century. The beautiful and intelligent daughter of the king of Cyprus was condemned to death for her Christian faith, to which she converted a great number of people, including the Empress in Alexandria. By order of Emperor Maxentium she was tortured on a wheel and then decapitated with a sword.
This small copperplate engraving is one of the earliest works of Albrecht Altdorfer. In 1505 he was granted citizenship of the city of Regensburg on the Danube and became a resident there. From 1506 he also inscribed his drawings and copperplate engravings (the woodcuts do not begin until later) with dates. R.B.

Winzinger, 1963, n° 98.

117 - The Blessing Christ - Cat. 93

Copperplate engraving.
With monogram, c. 1512.
73×43 mm. B. 10, H. 11, Wz. 118.
Regensburg, Museen der Stadt Regensburg.

Christ blessing the world, is standing on a rainbow, dressed in a flowing gown with wide sleeves. In his left hand he is holding a globe with a cross as a sign of his sovereignty and of divine omnipotence.
This engraving might possibly have been executed as an imitation of nothern Italian pictures of the *Imperator mundi.* M.R.

Winzinger, 1963, n° 118.

120 - Mary on the half moon - Cat. 96.

Copper engraving.
With monogram, ca. 1520/30.
56×36 mm. B.11, H.12. Wz.119
Paris, Bibliothèque Nationale, Cabinet des Estampes.
ECN 1443

Two iconographical types flow into one another in the representations of Mary on the crescent of the moon. The image of the Madonna with child is connected to that of the apocalyptic woman from the Revelation of St. John the Divine (chap. 12,1): "And there appeared a great sign in heaven; a woman clothed with the sun, and the moon under her feet, and upon her head a crown of twelve stars"... (chap. 12,5):

"And she brought forth a son... and her child was caught up unto God and to his throne".
Winzinger considers it likely that Altdorfer used a sculpture as a model for this print. The dating of the engraving varies between "ca. 1515" in Winzinger and "ca. 1520/30" in the catalogue of the 1938 Aldorfer exhibition.M.R.

Cat. Albrecht Altdorfer und sein Kreis, 1938, n°188. Winzinger, 1963, n° 119.

127 - Serenity During the Flight - Cat. 103

Copperplate engraving.
With monogram, c. 1515/19.
95×48 mm. B. 5, H. 5, Wz. 129.
Regensburg, Museen der Stadt Regensburg.

This slender, alongated engraving depicts, in the foreground, the large, slightly stooping Joseph with a walking stick, and Mary resting on a lawncovered slope. Although the group of figures has been moved far into the foreground of the engraving, the holy persons nevertheless appear to be in intimate contact with the expansive landscape.
A tall tree looms above the standing figure of Joseph; a castle, distinguished by its massive tower, rises behind Mary and combines

with the massif which is equally related to the sitting figures. Serenity is not only the iconographic theme, it is also taken up in the landscape and thus heightened in its meaning.
The dating of the engraving is oriented on the posture of the child. The foreshortening uses the head as its focal point. This motif had already appeared in Altdorfer's work at an earlier date, in the woodcut depicting two horsemen, which is part of the series of woodcuts of camp followers. Later on, the motif inspired by the copperplate engraving in question, also appears on Altdorfer's panel paintings and in the woodcut by Ostendorfer, depicting the Church of the *Beautiful Mary.* (Cat. 106) M.R.

Winzinger, 1963, n° 129. — Cat. *The Danube School,* 1969/70, n° 50.

127 - Serenity during the Flight - Cat. 103

128 - Crucifixion - Cat. 104

Copperplate engraving.
With monogram, c. 1515/17.
144×98 mm. B. 8, H. 9, Wz. 134.
Berlin, Kupferstichkabinett, SMPK.

The so-called large Crucifixion belongs to the most mature achievements of Albrecht Altdorfer in the realm of copperplate engraving. If one looks at his copperplate engravings in the order of their appearance from 1506 to the time this print was done, some 20 years later, one finds here the outcome of his endeavor to reproduce

these appear in the renditions of Mary and John (right) and Mary Magdalen (left).

The pictorial composition of this copperplate engraving, which is of unusually large format for Altdorfer, is based on a rendition of the Crucifixion done several years earlier, as part of a series called "The Fall and the Redemption of the Human Race". In contrast to the first print, the figures here are no longer placed on one level at the front edge of the picture but rather placed in a landscape exhibiting great depth. The figures, lost in pain, the illuminated body of the crucified Christ above their heads, poised against the black nocturnal sky, and the landscape disappearing into the distance unite themselves into a

the human figure. Altdorfer's study of Italian Renaissance artists, above all Andrea Mantegna, can be seen in the well-balanced body-proportions and in the relationship between garments and body as

harmonious picture, which, in contrast to Altdorfer's earlier works, radiates a subdued peace. R.B.

Winzinger, 1963, n° 134. — Cat. The Danube School, 1969/70, n° 55.

128 - Crucifixion - Cat. 104

123 - Allegorical Figure - Cat. 99

Copperplate engraving.
With monogram, c. 1515/18.
94×48 mm. B. 58, H. 77, Wz. 123.
Regensburg, Museen der Stadt Regensburg.

A winged figure with long flowing hair and a wreath of laurels is holding a burning torch facing downwards in the right hand and a staff with ribbons and the little plaque with Altdorfer's monogram in the left hand. It is standing on a star which is irradiating a landscape with trees and a city.
The interpretation of this figure is as yet undecided. Art historians have suggested Lascivia, a picture of a star or Fortuna on a star. The idea for the image can be traced back to Dürer's copperplate engraving *The Big Fortune* (B. 77). In Dürer's rendition there is also a wedge-shaped band of clouds dividing the pictorial field into two zones, in the upper of which stands an allegorical figure. M.R.

Tietze, 1923, p. 177 — Boldass, 1941, p. 148 — Winzinger, 1963, n° 123 — Cat. *The Danube School*, 1969/70, n° 52.

124 - Saint Christopher - Cat. 100

Copper engraving.
With monogram, ca. 1515/20.
60×58 mm. B.19, H.20, Wz 124.
Paris, Bibliothèque Nationale, Cabinet des Estampes.
ECN 1449.

In strong contrast to the 1513 wood-cut of St. Christopher (cat. 38) in which the exhausted saint, bent double, is placed right in the foreground beside a monumental tree, this copper engraving, which dates from a few years later, has a more developed perspective.
The rays of the rising sun, far in the background above a church-tower, form a dome-like vault over the whole scene. As Koepplin fittingly observes (Koepplin, 1967, p.83) it replies "like a worldly nimbus to the Christ child's halo". As a religious symbol it indicates Christ's coming to Christopher who is seeking the true Lord but is as yet unaware of his presence.
The formal layout is likely to have been influenced by Dürer's 1514 copper engraving "Melancholia I" B.74. In that work the bright rays of a comet are similarly represented by narrow sheaves of lines. Wolf Huber was also a decisive influence in the development of the "Danube School sun". M.R.

Winzinger, 1963, n° 124. - Koepplin, 1967, p. 82-92. - Cat. The Danube School, 1969/70, n° 51.

118 - The Small Standard-Bearer - Cat. 94

Copperplate engraving.
With monogram, c. 1516/18.
60×37 mm. B. 52, H. 66, Wz. 126.
Regensburg, Museen der Stadt Regensburg.

As once before, some ten years prior to this date, Altdorfer also executed this standard-bearer standing on a hill as a couterpart to an engraving depicting a mercenary. The standard-bearer, self-confidently placing his right hand on his hip, has been placed far into the foreground of the picture, in front of a hilly river landscape with a settlement close to the water and a citadel on the mountain.
Art historians originally considered this engraving to be dependent on Hans Sebald Beham's *Standard-Bearer,* made in 1519. Stylistically, however, Altdorfer's engraving can be seen to be connected with the woodcuts depicting camp followers, which were probably done before 1519, so that, conversely, a dependency of Beham on Altdorfer is more probable. M.R.

Winzinger, 1963, n° 126.

119 - Saint George - Cat. 95.

Copper engraving.
With monogram, ca. 1515/18. 60×40 mm. B.20, H.22, Wz 130.
Paris, Bibliothèque Nationale, Cabinet des Estampes. ECN 1450.

Altdorfer uses the small dimensions of this engraving to achieve a dynamic representation of this episode. The slender tall format is made to appear even more narrow by the tree on the right-hand edge of the picture, by the adjacent field of boulders and the rock formation. There remains only a narrow field of vision granting us a view of a town in front of mountains which form the background.
Right in the foreground we see the encounter of the considerably shortened dragon and St. George galloping at full speed towards it.
M.R.

Winzinger, 1963, n° 130.

129 - Saint Jerome reading - Cat. 105.

Copper engraving.
With monogram, ca. 1515/20.
104×61 mm. B.21, H.23, Wz.135
Paris, Bibliothèque Nationale, Cabinet des Estampes.

The saint stands in front of an altar with a crucifix on it as well as a litle table leaning against the wall of the cave which has on it the initials serving as Altdorfer's monogram. He is reading out of a folio.
In spite of the completely different surroundings the conception of the theme is reminiscent of that in Dürer's "St. Jerome in his cell" B.60,

dating from the year 1514. The image of the penitent in the wilderness, usually kneeling in front of a cross, has become that of an academic studying, which Dürer had already sketched in 1512 his wood-cut of St. Jerome in the cave.
In this copper engraving Altdorfer is at pains to get a feeling for differentiated tones, as the rather restless relief of the ceiling of the cell shows - it is achieved by overlapping hatching. He reproduced the effect of smooth stone for the altar with the same technique as Dürer used in his masterly engravings of 1514. M.R.

Winzinger, 1963, n° 135. - Cat. The Danube School, 1969/70, n° 42.

129 - Saint Jerome reading - Cat. 105.

130 - The "Beautiful Mary"
on the Throne - Cat. 106

131 - Solomon's Idol Worship -
Cat. 107

132 - Beautiful Mary in Landscape - Cat. 108

133 - Christ drives away
the Money-Changers from
the Temple - Cat. 109

134 - Mary looks for the Twelve
Years Old Christ in the Temple -
Cat. 110

135 - Samson carrying the gates of Gaza - Cat. 111

136 - The centaur - Cat. 112.

137 - Hercules carrying the pillars of Gades - Cat. 113

138 - Hercules overcomes the lion of Nemaus - Cat. 114.

139 - Pomegranate with Foliage - Cat. 115

140 - Samson and Delila - Cat. 116

141 - The Revenge of the Magician Virgil - Cat. 117

142 — Violin-Player - Cat. 118

143 - Horatius Cocles - Cat. 119

144 - Judith with the head of the
Holofern - Cat. 120

145 - Dido - Cat. 121

146 - Venus after the Bath - Cat. 122

147 - The fight for the nymph - Cat. 123

148 - Crouching Venus - Cat. 124

149 - Hercules and the Muse - Cat. 125

150 - Neptune on a sea-snake - Cat. 126

151 - Arion and Nerëid - Cat. 127

152 - Pair of lovers led in triumph by sea-gods - Cat. 128

153 - Portrait of Martin Luther - Cat. 129

Within the image, the inscription reads:

PORTICVS SINAGOGAE
IVDAICAE RATISPONEN
FRACTA. 21. DIE FEB.
ANN · 15 19.

154 - Entrance Hall of the Synagoge in Regensburg - Cat. 130

ANNO·DMI·D·XIX·
IVDAICA·RATIS·A
SYNAGOGA·IVSTO
DE·HVDICIO·FVNDT
EST·EVERSA

155 - Interior of the Synagoge of Regensburg - Cat. 131

Nine landscapes etched in iron by Altdorfer are known. Winzinger believes their date of origin to lie between 1515 and 1520, since on the one hand they presuppose a certain degree of skill in the handling of the technique and on the other they were already being copied by other artists in 1522. The pictorial composition and the execution of the drawn line of this scene show such a clear congeniality with the landscapes by Wolf Huber that an intimate connection between the two artists can be assumed. Altdorfer's etchings, which depict landscapes prosaically, formed the beginning of a new art genre, which soon found approval and attracted a broad following. R.B.

156 - Landscape with a Big Tree - Cat. 132

Etching.
With monogram, c. 1517/20.
235×177 mm. B. 67, H. 85, Wz. 182.
Berlin, Kupferstichkabinett, SMPK. Inv. n° 131-1929.

In this work, as in the largest part of his landscape etching, Altdorfer treats the diversified landscape of the alpine foothills. From the patch of ground in the foreground, the view opens onto rocky slopes covered with trees and onto the grounds of a castle. The tall tree towering closely in front of the eye of the observer, with its gnarled boughs disheveled by the wind, forms a dynamic contrast to the manifold details of the rest of the landscape. R.B.

Winzinger, 1963, n° 182 and p. 116 f. — Cat. *The Danube School*, 1969/70, n° 60.

157 - Landscape with a Dark Wall of Rock - Cat. 133
c. 1517/19. With monogram.
115×155 mm. B. 69, H. 87, Wz. 176.
Plymouth, City Museum and Art Gallery

157 - Landscape with a Dark Wall of Rock - Cat. 133

158 - Landscape with a Double Pine Tree - Cat. 134
c. 1517/20.
110×160 mm. B. 70, H. 88, Wz. 179.
Plymouth, City Museum and Art Gallery.

158 - Landscape with a Double Pine Tree - Cat. 134

159 - Landscape with a Large Castle - Cat. 135
c. 1517/19. With monogram.
108×169 mm. B. 68, H. 86, Wz. 175.
Plymouth, City Museum and Art Gallery.

159 - Landscape with a Large Castle - Cat. 135

160 - Landscape with Two Pine Trees - Cat. 136
c. 1517/20.
110×155 mm. B. 74, H. 91, Wz. 178.
Plymouth, City Museum and Art Gallery.

160 - Landscape with two Pine Trees - Cat. 136

161 - The City at the Sea - Cat. 137
c. 1520.
115×155 mm. B. 72, H. 89, Wz. 180.
Plymouth, City Museum and Art Gallery.

161 - The City at the Sea - Cat. 137

162 - Landscape with a Water Mill - Cat. 138
c. 1520.
174×230 mm. H. 92, Wz. 183.
Plymouth, City Museum and Art Gallery.

162 - Landscape with a Water Mill - Cat. 138

163 - Landscape with a Pine Tree and a Willow - Cat. 139
c. 1517/20. With monogram
115×155 mm. B. 73, H. 90, Wz. 177.
Plymouth, City Museum and Art Gallery.

163 - Lanscape with a Pine Tree and a Willow - Cat. 139

THE ETCHINGS OF THE SPLENDIDLY DECORATED VESSELS

In all, twenty-three etchings in iron by Altdorfer, depicting splendidly decorated vessels are known. With these, like Dürer before him, he made a major contribution to the German goldsmith art of the Renaissance. The goblets, cups the appliances for pouring, the purely ornamental vessels, are all conceived in self-contained, measured classical proportions, which harmoniously combine the Italian Renaissance model with forms of the Gothic goldsmith art. Embassed goblets and cups had been common all over Germany since the second half of the fifteenth century. In the sixteenth century, German goldsmithery reached a high point Nuremberg and Augsburg. Altdorfer's pictorial studies were made at the beginning of this apex. The precious vessels served as presents, as impressive pieces of household equipment for the self-conscious newly-emerging middle class. They also found their place in the Guild or the Council treasury of the city.

R.B.

Winzinger, 1963, p. 118 ff. — H. Kohlhaussen, *Altdorferisches in der Nürnberger Goldschmiedekunst, zeitschrift des Vereins f. Kunstwissenschaft*, Vol. XIX, 1965, p. 185 ff. — J.F. Hayward, *Virtuoso Goldsmiths and the Triumph of Manerism 1540-1620*, London 1976, p. 95 ff.

164 - Goblet with a Lid and Lilies of the Valley - Cat. 140
Etching.
With monogram, c. 1520/25.
207×116 mm. B. 94, H. 117, Wz. 201.
Museen der Stadt Regensburg.

165 - Goblet with a Lid and with a Winged Ball - Cat. 141
Etching.
With monogram, c. 1520/25.
86×112 mm. B. 92, H. 115, Wz. 184.
Museen der Stadt Regensburg.

166 - Goblet with a Lid and Pomegranets - Cat. 142
Etching.
With monogram, c. 1520/25.
180×98 mm. B. 81, H. 104, Wz. 195.
Museen der Stadt Rengensburg.

167 - Goblet with a Lid in a Niche - Cat. 143
Etching.
With monogram, c. 1520/25.
176×124 mm. B. 80, H. 103, Wz. 193.
Museen der Stadt Regensburg.

168 - Double-Goblet with Flat Leaves - Cat. 144
Etching.
With monogram, c. 1520/25.
221×106 mm. B. 85, H. 108, Wz. 198.
Museen der Stadt Regensburg.

169 - Double-Goblet with Angel's Heads - Cat. 145

Etching.
With monogram, c. 1520/25
225 × 108 mm. B. 88, H. 111, Wz. 188.
Museen der Stadt Regensburg.

170 - Goblet with a Lid and Shells - Cat. 146

Etching
With monogram, c. 1520/25.
180 × 98 mm. B. 81, H. 104, Wz. 205.
Museen der Stadt Regensburg.

171 - Double-Goblet - Cat. 147

Etching.
With monogram, c. 1520/25.
260 × 157 mm. B. 90, H. 113, Wz. 187.
Berlin, Kupferstichkabinett, SMPK. Inv. n° 85-1889.

The double-goblet consists of two vessels, of which the upper one is
inverted and sits on the lower vessel like a lid. The shape of the foot,
the threefold jointed shaft and the arrangement of the bosses and acanthus leaves of the lower goblet are repeated, proportionally reduced,
in the second goblet, which only has a flat basin-like edge. R.B.

Winzinger, 1963, n° 187 and p. 120 ff.

172 - Pitcher with a Dragon - Cat. 148

Etching.
With monogram, c. 1520/25.
227 × 109 mm. B. 89, H. 112, Wz. 202.
Berlin, Kupferstichkabinett, SMPK. Inv. n° 258-4

The pitcher with a surbased, hemispherical rounded end is carried by
an elongated shaft, decorated with overlapping acanthus, which is standing on a round foot. The high, slender neck, corresponding to the
waisted shaft, rises with a powerful sweeping upwards motion. On this
neck sits a lid, crowned with foliage. A dragon with a gaping mouth
serves as the spout; a swung, s-shaped shoot, formed from acanthus
foliage, serves as the handle. The sides are fitted with raised and engraved bosses, which are reduced to dense bundles and lined with dainty
profiles. A frieze overlaps the rounded edge and in it is contained
Altdorfer's monogram. With its well-balanced, harmonious proportions and formal elements in the classical style, this pitcher represents
a particularly characteristic example of the German Renaissance style.

Winzinger, 1963, n° 202.

173 - Goblet with a Lid and Grotesquery - Cat. 149

Etching.
With monogram, c. 1520/25.
167 × 111 mm. B. 78, H. 101, Wz. 191.
Museen der Stadt Regensburg.

174 - Three Vessels - Cat. 150

Etching.
With monogram, c. 1520/25.
260 × 142 mm. B. 96, H. 119, Wz. 186.
Museen der Stadt Rengensburg.

164 - Goblet with a Lid and Lilies of the Valley - Cat. 140

165 - Goblet with a Lid and a Winged Ball - Cat. 141

166 - Goblet with a Lid and Pomo-granets - Cat. 142

167 - Goblet with a Lid in a Nice - Cat. 143

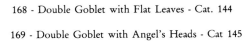

168 - Double Goblet with Flat Leaves - Cat. 144

169 - Double Goblet with Angel's Heads - Cat 145

170 - Goblet with a Lid and Shells - Cat. 146

171 - Double Goblet - Cat. 147

89.

258-4

W. 105.

183 to 186 - Triumphal procession of Emperor Maximilian I - Cat. 158
to 161

175 to 182 - Standard-Bearers and Musicians from the Triumphal Procession of Emperor Maximilian I - Cat. 151 to 157

Austria, Old-Austria, Styria.
Carinthia, Carniola, Swabia.
Alsace, Habsburg, Tyrol.
Gorizia, Pfirdt, Kyburg,.
Nellenburg Hohenburg, Secking-Urach.
Freiburg, Bregenz, Saulgau.
Tibein, Oberwaldsee, Unterwaldsee.
Five trumpet-players on horseback.
Two rows of pipers on horseback.
Limburg, Luxemburg, Geldern.

Woddcuts.
c. 1517
Each about 370 mm. Wide. Wz. 209, 211, 214, 217, 225, 230,233.
Brunswick, Herzog Anton Ulrich-Museum.
Wz 212, 231.
Regensburg, Museen der Stadt Regensburg.

In a freize-like succession of rows, the standard-bearers of the Austrian and Brugundian patrimonial lands, separated from each other by the musicians, lead the triumphal wagon of Maximilian I. In his instructions for the execution of these woodcuts, the Emperor decided how each standard-bearer was to be dressed. The colors of the Austrian patimonial lands were all to be carried on horseback in their respective standards, the bearers were to be dressed with shield, helmet and jewels. Standard-bearers of those lands in which a war had been waged, were to be depicted in armour, whose presentation the executing artist was to vary. Lands in which the Emperor had not fought any battles were to be represented by riders in the most splendid garments of each respective region. All the depicted figures had to wear a laurel wreath. These instructions were followed by an enumeration of all the coats of arms which were to be depicted.
In contrast to the Austrian patimonial lands, Maximilan I allowed no riders wearing armour for the Burgundians. Rather, the standard-bearers were to be dressed in the most maginificent garments and were to wear precious chains. M.R.

Winzinger, 1963, n° 209-240. ⌐ Cat. *The Danube School*, 1969/70, n° 38.

183 to 186 - Triumphal procession of Emperor Maximilan I Cat. 158 to 161.

Baggage carts, Two knights, Cortège and church, End of cortège and sutler's carts.
Wood-cuts.
Ca. 1517/18.
Each 390×390 mm., some cut. Wz. 77,78,80,81.
Paris, Bibliothèque Nationale, Cabinet des Estampes.

The Triumphal Procession of Emperor Maximilian I comprises 138 wodd-cuts. It ends with six wood-cuts of the baggage train by Albrecht Altdorfer, four of which are shown here.
In accord with the scheme of the court historiographer Johannes Stabius the process began with the preparation of drafts in Jörg Kölderer's workshop in Innsbruck. On the basis of these prototypes the Emperor Maximilian I dictated to his secretary instructions for the production of a cycle of miniatures. These instructions were also necessary for the wood-cuts. In the manuscript which has been preserved (Vienna, Nationalbibliothek, Ms. 2835) it states about the cortège: "After that shall come the crowd (of all sorts of servants, labourers and the like) on horseback and on foot all mixed up together/ as befits the crowd/ and all of them shall have laurel crowns on". (Winzinger, 1963, p.75.). Behind a leader the varied retinue to follow the procession on horseback or on foot. They too had to wear laurel crowns.
It was difficult to identify Altdorfer as the designer of the wood-cuts

owing to the fact that the printing blocks were prepared in a workshop. They were cut by different workers in Jost de Negker's workshop in Augsburg. After the initial cutting Jost de Negker went over the blocks again in order to bring some unity to the whole Triumphal Procession.
The lower rank of the crowd allowed Altdorfer to break through the strict frieze composition of the reste of the procession, such as, for example, the standard-bearers. In loose formation the simple people fit in well with the landscape which is never shown in the previous prints of the Triumphal Procession. M.R.

Winzinger, 1963, n° 76 - 81. cat. Kunst der Donauschule, 1965, n° 112. cat. The danube School, 1969/70, n° 36/37. - Winzinger, 1973, 19-27. - cat. Kunst der Reformationszeit, 1983. C2, C2.25, C2.26, C2.27.

The Friezes

The fragments of Altdorfer's friezes from the bishops' residence in Regensburg were discovered in 1887 following a fire. Photographs taken at that time and the draft in Florence for one wall of the room, which unfortunately has not been well-preserved, give an impression of the overall appearance of the frieze.
The oil tempera paintings on dry plaster decorated the so-called "Kaiserbad" of the bishops' residence. The Florentine draft shows the wall with the entrance door. Painted stairs led from both right and left over this portal to a painted balcony. Scenes of men and women adorned the triangles formed by the doorframe and the ascending staircase. On the stairs and in the domed rooms at the sides of the staircase onlookers could be seen watching the bathing which was not at all fitting for life in a religious residence.
This can also be seen in the four fragments exhibited (22 are still in existence), which come from a side-wall. They show a wench bathing who appears to be giving a young man, sitting in a bath, wine or beer from a jug. Eating and drinking was, in fact, an essential part of bathing, one of the most common pastimes.
Altdorfer's friezes in the baths of the bishops' residence are better evidence than any written description of the completely worldly way of life of his patrons. Count Palatine Johann III was elected bishop in 1507 when he was nineteen years old. However, because of his worldliness and his political interests, he was never seriously concerned about being ordained bishop and simply acted as administrator of the bishopric until his death in 1538. Contemporaries have compared his lifestyle with that of the Roman, Lucullus. F.A.

186 Bis - Four Fragments of a Mural - Cat. 162

Oil tempera on dry plaster.
c. 1532.
From the Emperor's bath in the Bishopric in Regensburg.
1070×710 mm in a modern frame. Wz. 86.
Rengensburg, Museen der Stadt Regensburg.

These wall-paintings were discovered in the Emperor's bath 1887 during a fire, and were at that time, judging from old photographs, in comparatively good condition. After the demolition of the building only 22 fragments remained, which, with the exception of one in Budapest, are now all housed in the Stadtmuseum of Regensburg. An idea of what the painted main wall looked like has also been handed down in the form of a very exact square sketch for the mural (Wz. 112, Florence, The Uffizi).
From this sketch, it appears that the wall painting represented an illusionistic two-story interior design, depicting a large bath, in which bathers and observers frolic about. The preserved fragments belong to a side wall. They show a maiden bringing a tin pitcher, placed in front of a window with masterly drawn bull's eye panes and they show the head of a young boy. The face of the woman, with its pointed, vividly contrasting chin, its strong slightly nose and its protruding forehead is typical of Altdorfer. B.B.

Winzinger, 1975, n° 86, p. 48, 120 ff.

Remarks on the Danube school[1]

The initial definition ought to be as non-committal as possible[2]: what we mean by the Danube school is an aspect of German painting in the first thirty years of the 16th century, the two chief representatives of which are Albrecht Altdorfer, who became a burgher of Regensburg in 1505 and died there in 1538, and Wolf Huber, who was living and working in Passau by 1515 at the latest and who died there in 1553.

To painting should be added engraving and above all drawing. This seems to go without saying. At the time, many German painters also did engravings and those who belonged to or who have been included in the Danube School were rather less interested in the technique than others, excepting Altdorfer whose output in this field was as compendious as it was fine. And what painter did not draw? But Wolf Huber, Altdorfer and other artists close to them produced an abundance of drawings which were not studies but completed works intended for sale and whose stylistic and iconographic originality was often greater than their paintings (while this was not exceptional in Germany at the time, the fact nonetheless deserves to be emphasised). Wolf Huber in particular, does not owe his reputation to his paintings but to his many pen-and-ink landscapes, a genre which he cultivated throughout his life.

The notion of a Danuble School has long been extended to include certain aspects of the sculpture of the period, beginning with the work of Leinberger who worked in Landshut, to the south or Regensburg. This extension is easily understandible and ought not necessarily meet with any objection. It was fairly common for statues and even more so for bas-reliefs to be executed after a model supplied by a painter. Bas-reliefs were often designed and composed in the manner of a painting with the same play of perspective, the same display of architecture and vegetation around the human figure, as in contemporary painting, whereas sculpture styles at the time were defined principally by the fold or drapery of the garments. This, however, also played a considerable role in the definition of painting styles, particularly in the Danube style, and in this connection, a number of sculptures executed by Leinberger around 1515 bear a striking resemblance to drawings by Altdorfer from the same period. However, uncertainty in the matter of dates, which are occasionally not easy to establish with exactitude, make it difficult to discern the direction in which the influence worked, if, indeed there were any influence at work. Our image of the sculpture of southern Germany at the beginning of the 16th century is too incomplete for it to be possible to distinguish clearly between what may have been the result of internal development and what may have been contributed by inspiration from without.

An attempt has also been made to bring architecture into

the Danube School. To be more precise, this is a thesis (in the fullest sense of the term) which was put forward at the large-scale exhibition held in 1965 in the Abbey of Saint Florian and in Linz Museum[3]. A section was devoted to

187 - Saint Catherine Being Converted to Christianity - Master HZ
Oil on larchwood - 750 × 471 mm - Museum of Bucarest.

the presentation of photographs of buildings, mostly of religious buildings, from the latter half of the 15th and the beginning of the 16th centuries in Bohemia and in the Austrian provinces. The problems raised by this inclusion were of a different order, for although it is possible to draw formal parallels between painting and sculpture, these latter may not be compared with architecture. It is necessary at this juncture to appeal to the notion of the mood of the times, the famous *Zeitgeist*, or to a common *Kunstwollen*, to use the term coined by Riegel. In the event, the idea of a Danubian style of architecture was justified by a interpretative idea of the Danube School both as the final phase of Gothic art and as the expression of a certain feeling for space, which had long been current where painting was concerned but which, as we shall shortly see, is in reality a purely ideological construct. However, irrespective of the feeling for space in Altdorfer's paintings or in Wolf Huber's drawings, the desire to see it also in the vaults of the Church of Saint Barbara in Kutna Hora belongs to the realm of special pleading or of pure illusion. It is significant that the large number of more or less imaginary architectural constructions with which these two artists enriched their compositions — when they were not the actual subject matter — bear no relation to the exhibits on display at Linz, which were supposed to be representative of the architecture of the Danube School.

This tendency of the exhibition to transform the Danube style into a period style pertaining to all af the arts, so typical of the Austrian tradition of art history, went along with a desire to enlarge its area of activity as far as possible. The Danube School ended up covering all of Central Europe and Switzerland, from Transylvania and Friuli to Bohemia, not to mention more distant (but incontrovertible) ramifications in northern Germany where Erhard Altdorfer, presumed to be Albrecht's brother, had gone to work, and in Leipzig where Lemberger, a painter who may have been related to the sculptor Leinberger of Landshut, lived and worked. This is not the place for a discussion of the excesses to which these claims have led. Resemblances have long been noted, for instance, between the art of the Danube and of the Swiss artists, Urs Graf and Niklaus Manuel Deutsh, but these do not sustain the notion of direct contact since the sole artistic bond between the two regions are the works, or a part of the works of the Zurich artist, Hans Leu the Younger, who, it seems, worked for a time in Nuremberg, which leads one to wonder whether the influence of Franconia has not been underestimated in the history of the Danube School.

Whatever the importance of this or that region, the 1965 exhibition seemed to be putting forward a distinctly geographical definition. The year before, however, in his great work on *The Painting of the Danube School*, Alfred Stange had taken exception to this definition. He refused to extend the appelation to the totality of painted works done in the Danube valley and of the Alpine foreland at the beginning of the 16th century, limiting it to works from which a certain feeling or spirit emanated. While the main protagonists are the same in the exhibition catalogue as in Alfred Stange's book, this is not true of the secondary artists, some of whom, although included in the exhibition, have been categorically excluded from the Danube Shool by Stange whose verdicts do not always appear to be well-grounded. Mere scholarly disputation this, but which reveals, by virtue of the different ideas expressed, the fragility of the notion of a Danube School, or at all events, the problematic nature of the question. It is clear, nonetheless, from both publications that the entity went considerably further than its two main representatives, Altdorfer and Wolf Huber, and the limited circle of their pupils or of the artists whom they directly influenced. Yet all attempts to define a Danube style have been based upon their works and it was from their works, or rather from Altdorfer's work that, historically, the notion of the Danube School first took shape.

* * *

Of all the artists who belonged to this persuasion or who have been included in it, Altdorfer is the only one never to have fallen into oblivion because his prints, especially his copperplate engravings, bearing his monogram, continued to be collected by art lovers. In 1641, an inhabitant of Regensburg donated a small collection of his works to the city, proof of an enduring local reputation. But even without this testimony, he was mentionned by several writers in the course of the 17th century-Quadt von Kinckelbach in his *Teutscher Nation Herlichkeit (Illustration of the German Nation)* in 1609, by the publisher Merian in 1641 in a list of great German painters and, naturally, by Sandrart in his *Teutsche Akademic*[4]. Sandrart claimed that Altdorfer was born in the village of Altdorf in Switzerland but this view was rejected a century later in 1778 in the *Dictionary of Artists of Whom we Possess Engravings* by Heinecken who had obtained biographical details from a Senator of the city of Regensburg.

The curtness of these references were counterbalanced in 1804 by the glowing comments of Friedrich Schlegel on the *Battle of Alexander* which he had seen and admired the previous year in Paris where it had been transported by the French Army from Munich. Schlegel saw it as a sort of precocious romantic manifesto and held it up as an example to contemporary painters. Altdorfer the romantic, an idea which would be taken up again in the 20th century. In the meantime, art history, which was then in the making, took him at first to be one of Dürer's pupils, even if he were on occasion more original than his supposed master. This contention is based on no know fact and was first made, it seems, by Shöber in a book on Dürer published in 1769.[5] In order to magnify the importance of his artist, the author did not hesitate to make him the master of practically all the German artists of the period, excepting Cranach and Holbein, but including Grünewald and... Scorel.

Although completely groundless, the affiliation was accepted, at least for Altdorfer. It seemed to be supported by certain similarities; after all, had not several of his works been attributed to Dürer, such as the series of woodcuts illustrating the *Fall and Redemption of Human Kind* which Fiorillo showed to have been by him? The same Fiorillo also probably contributed to giving credence to the legend of a master-pupil relationship between the two artists when he lent the weight of his authority to this view, in the great history of the painters of Germany and the Netherlands which he published between 1815 and 1820[6]. As his successors were content to reproduce the opinion rather than to verify it, it remained more or less accepted until the end of the century. It was even to be found in the writings of French critics like Hippolyte Fortoul who, of Altdorfer's work, seems to have seen only the *Battle of Alexander* and who found it "curious to observe here traces of the opinion which, in the absence of ancient statuary, German artists had formed of the physiognimy and clothing of the Ancients"[7] - an observation which, at the time, did not err on the side of originality, since it did no more than apply to Altdorfer the regret which had been formulated for generations since the time of Vasari about Dürer himself. Twenty years later, Dr. Lachaise, after referring to Shäuffelein and Grünewald as pupils of Dürer in his *A Reasoned and Practical Guide for the Lover of Paintings*, added that the best-known of these were Beham and "Senator Altdorfer" who was said to have remained with his master for many years and who "was more noteworthy for his detail rather than for his composition which lacks taste, or his perspective which is generally ill-understood"[8].

German writers did not all pass such a negative and esthetically prejudiced judgement on Altdorfer's oeuvre but the notion that he had been trained in Dürer's atelier still interfered with the image that they had formed of his art, although doubts began to be expressed towards the end of the century as to the nature and extent of Altdorfer's debt to Dürer. As modern painting styles have evolved, so also have the attitudes of art historians to the art of painting as long ago as the 16th century. An idea had begun to gain acceptance according to which Dürer had been a pure draughtsman, a great master of line and black and white, that he had not been a true painter, that is to say a colorist[9]. The colorist of German painting was considered to be Grünewald, whose renown dates from this period. In this view of history, it seems possible that Altdorfer had belonged to the same artistic family as Grünewald, whom Janitscheck, in 1890, claims was, if not actually his master, at all events his model[10]. This comparison was too superficial to be accepted for long by art historians but it did amount to a breach in the opinion which had held sway for over a century.

The decisive step was to be taken a year later by Max J. Friedlaender in his doctoral thesis on the Master of Regensburg[11]. Basing his research on knowledge of the oeuvre which has not essentially changed in the intervening century, he demonstrated that Altdorfer's early work, up to 1510, could not have been produced by a pupil of Dürer. His analysis of the two artists' styles led him to carry the distinction between them into outright opposition. Moreover, he did not feel that Altdorfer's painting had anything in common with panel painting at the end of the 15th century. He finally suggested that his antecedents might be sought in miniature painting, where it had been possible for landscape composition to develop in far greater freedom, and he mentioned the name of Berthold Furtmeyr, a miniaturist who had been active in Regensburg in the last quarter of the 15th century, on account of the importance attached to space and nature in his compositions, the style of which was otherwise very traditional.

Space and nature: these two notions have ever since been at the center of definitions of Altdorfer's art and of the style of the Danube. But the crucial role played by Max J. Friedlaender's book did not lie in the importance which he himself gave to the notions; it lay in the fact that, by releasing the Master of Regensburg from dependance upon Dürer, within the confines of which his originality had hitherto been constricted, by affirming his stylistic autonomy, he ushered in a major change in the prevailing view of the art of southern Germany at the beginning of the 16th century and helped to create the conditions for the intervention of the Danube School on to which, for several decades, certain features of German ideology would be projected. It may be worthwhile, in this connection, to note that the relationship between Altdorfer and Dürer, which was manifestly not that of master and pupil, but which Friedlander had tended to underestimate, probably in reaction against an opinion as solidly established as it was unfounded in fact, continues to be a bone of contention between certain specialists, a kind of dividing line between divergent opinions of the Danube School.

In a review of Friedlaender's book in 1892, Theodor von Frimmel remarked that Altdorfer was not an isolated case and that from Regensburg to Linz, early 16th century painting was characterised by common features which distinguished it from contemporary painting in the rest of Germany. This, he said, made it possible to speak of a Danubian style, to the origins of which Hermann Voss devoted a study fifteen years later[12].

In the meantime, the second great figure of what was not yet called a school, Wolf Huber, finally emerged from the shadows. His name was still known to 17th century collectors and was to be found in the catalogue drawn up by Paul Behaim of Nuremberg in 1618 and, half a century later, he was mentioned as one of the artists whose work figured in the Künast collection in Strasburg[13]. But Sandrart did not speak of him and he seems to have fallen into total oblivion by the following century. In 1858, Nagler rediscovered the meaning of the monogram on his few engravings and in 1891, W. Schmidt found a resemblance between it and the monogram on a great many pen-and-ink drawings. Two doctoral theses were devoted to him in 1907, one in Basel by Riggenbach, and the other in Heidelberg by Hermann Voss who included his findings in a book on the origins of the Danube School which was published that same year[14]. Both writers regarded him as a pupil of Altdorfer, an opinion which was already being challenged at the time and which has since been abandoned, although the very close relations between the two artists have never been subjected to close or conclusive investigation. It is true, however, that in books about the Danube School, Wolf Huber long remained in the shadow of the Master of Regensburg. This may be explained in several ways. Firstly, he was thought to have been a few years younger than Altdorfer, since 1510 was the earliest that a work of his could be attested, the celebrated *View of the Mondsee* (a lake in the Salzburgerland). A pen-and-ink landscape dated 1505 is so different in style from the rest of his work that it was looked upon as a mere piece of juvenalia and even as a work of doubtful attribution. In his monumental study of Huber, published in 1979, Franz Winzinger dated the artist's first work as far back as 1502; earlier, therefore, than Altdorfer's first work, but this section of the catalogue leaves unresolved, and even gives rise to, a great many problems of attribution and dating[15].

The other, and main reason for his relative obscurity lay in the fact that his painted work is neither as extensive nor as diverse as Altdorfer's. Lastly, unlike what happened in the case of Altdorfer, ideas about Huber's output were far from definite when Voss and Rigenbach were writing up their findings, and have continued to alter substantially right up to the recent past.

Advances in research have, however, been of greater benefit to lesser artists, mostly anonymous or known only by monogram, whose works have been progressively identified, published and then assembled according to hand, with all of the uncertainty that such a procedure implies. The way in which our knowledge has been enriched may be seen from a comparison of the book by Hermann Voss, the catalogue of the *Altdorfer and his Circle* exhibition in Munich, organised on the occasion of quatracentenary of the artist's death, and the catalogue of the exhibition on the Danube School in Linz in 1965[16]. For Voss, the Danube School could be reduced practically to two artists, Altdorfer and Wolf Huber; in 1938, it seemed to be synonymous with the entourage of Altdorfer, in which Wolf Huber was included; in 1965, Altdorfer was no more than the most important of a large number of other, mostly anonymous artists.

The evolution was not merely quantative. It coincided with a changed view of the phenomenon itself. The idea of a regional school, of a period style or of a combination of the two progressively came to replace the notion of the influence of a powerfully original painter on his entourage. However, as has long been the case — as is still the case — with attitudes to the esthetics of impressionism, defined by what is imagined to be contained in the canvases of Monet and none other, definitions and interpretations of the Danube style have been based mainly upon the attitude of their authors to the art of Albrecht Altdorfer. The history of art is already too full of other examples of such inconsequential methodology.

Ever since Max F. Friedlaender, it has been above all the role of nature and space, but especially of nature, that has engaged the attention of the specialists. Friedlaender himself belonged to a generation that had been formed at the time of the triumph of Impressionism, at the end of a century during which the study of nature, in other words of landscape, had been to the forefront, or so it seemed, of painterly preoccupations. While he himself spoke only in passing of 19th century art, it is easy to see from his writings that his taste had been shaped to a certain extent by the period in which he grew up. His interest in Altdorfer's work thus becomes clear, as does the counter proof of his negative verdict on the marvellous Budapest *Calvary*, with its archaistic gold background and the compact crowd that crams the horizon[17].

With few exceptions, nature occupies a prominent place in Altdorfer's drawings (including a series of landscape etchings) and also in his painting; he it was who painted two canvases which were long looked upon as the first landscapes in the history of Western painting - the Munich *View of the Danube* and the London *Landscape with Bridge*. These pure landscapes (were it not for the presence in the

Munich canvas of a tiny figure, unnoticed until recently) appeared to be the culmination of a logical progression, foreshadowed in the art of painting as early as the 15th century, but which had accelerated in Germany after 1500, especially in the Danube region. Landscape was considered to have begun as a mere backdrop erected behind the figures who depicted an episode from the Lives of the Saints and who occupied the foreground. In German-speaking regions throughout the 15th century, the only artist to have gone further than this was Konrad Witz, particularly in his *Miracle of the Fishes* in the Musée de Genève, with its view of Lake Geneva. Then other features of landscape began to move forward: from being a backdrop, they became the wings and the way they were arranged created an illusion of depth. The figures were no longer located in the foreground but blended into the space behind. At the same time, they forfeited their relative importance in the composition, were progressively consigned to the role of accessory, and then melted into the natural setting, before finally disappearing altogether.

This is the general outline, tempered by observation of particular works, upon which most studies of Altdorfer's style during the first half of the 20th century have been based. It is, in fact, a double outline, since it relates to two distinct phenomena, the conquest of space by the depiction of depth, in which Altdorfer (and also Wolf Huber) would seem to be greatly indebted to the masterful perspectives drawn by Michael Pacher in the panels of his *Altarpiece of Saint Wolfgang* and also by an interest in the pageantry of nature, more especially in trees and the vegetation in woods, which would lead to the composition of pure landscapes. Despite the connections which may have existed between these two evolutions, one of Altdorfer's works, dated 1510, is a good illustration of the fact that they were relatively independent. Saint George and the dragon is entirely covered by a vast curtain of foliage, and the distances are indicated by no more than a tiny patch of sky which may even have been painted in later.

But what was long looked upon as the specific character of Altdorfer's art and even more so of the Danube School, was less a liking for landscape than a certain vision of nature and of the relation of man to nature. Neither Altdorfer nor Wolf Huber, not to mention the anonymous artists in their entourage, have left any *studies* of trees, or plants or rocks or clouds... They always depict a whole setting, even when a particular motif, such as a tree trunk, is given a prominent place in the foreground. It would be easy to interject that the drawings and engravings which have come down to us, are complete compositions, with the artist's monogram more often than not, frequently dated and doubtless intended for sale and that

188 - Hunting the Boar - Rueland Freuauf the Younger
(Altarpiece of the Legend of Saint Leopold) - Monastery of Klosterneuburg.

there is no reason to suppose that they were not preceded by preparatory studies which have long since disappeared (a few architectural studies by Altdorfer have survived). This, however, would mean entering an area of investigation which has long been neglected by art historians, who seem more inclined to describe and examine the significance of formal developments than to consider the tangible requirements and material conditions of artistic creation.

Not only did the artists of the Danube School not distinguish between the constituent elements of the landscape that they drew or engraved or, on occasion, painted, by means of differentiated treatment, in fact, they endowed their scenes with unity by using a graphic style which was less concerned with conveying appearances than with expressing the forces at work in nature. Even the human figures appear to have been submitted to the same treatment, so that man, instead of standing in opposition to the world around him, appears to melt into it like a simple element into the cosmos.

We should remind the reader that theses remarks are not intended as a definition of an artistic style but as a résumé of the manner in which that style has been perceived over a lengthy period. For this is an area in which ways of seeing may long outlast the circumstances which first gave rise to them. In the event, this view of the Danube School was originally voiced by a generation of art historians, among others by Otto Benesh and Alfred Stange, who were finishing their studies immediately after the First World War. Despite the substantial differences of opinion between them on specific matters, they shared a common body of ideas, at least where their writings on the Danube School were concerned. These were related to the views expressed by Oskar Hagen in his *Deutsches Sehen* (the first edition of which was published in 1919) which belong to the renewal of romanticism that marked German thought for over half a century.

The very term *romantic,* appears again and again in relation to the Danube School, as do comparisons between Altdorfer and certain 19th century German painters, in particular Ludwig Richter. In order to characterise the earliest manifestations of the Danube style, Ludwig Baldas wrote that it was necessary to borrow the terms romanticism and *Sturm und Drang*[18] from literary history. There was a particular reason for this necessity: romanticism was more or less clearly conceived of, or felt to be, the natural form of expression of the German soul, particular manifestations of which happened to give rise to the coining of the term around 1800 but which were no more than a late avatar of a constant presence. German painting had never been as brilliant as at the end of the 16th century: it must, therefore, have been romantic. Fur-

thermore, it offered the two sides of romanticism to view, the grandiose and the impassioned in Grünewald ("for Grünewald is romantic through and through, as are Rembrandt and Wagner", wrote Franz Bock as early as 1907 in the review *Walhalla*), idyllic in the landscapes and biblical or legendary scenes of the Danube School. It is easy to imagine the sort of critical commentary aroused by Altdorfer's small-scale canvasses, his *Nativities* plunged in darkness yet lit up by a magic brilliance, and the figures of his globular period, which might have come straight out of an illustrated book for children. Is not the high foliage under which his Saint George (the 1510 canvas) slays the dragon the forest dear to the heart of the romantics? And does his drawing of a savage of 1508 not belong to the same universe as Moritz von Schwind's Rübezahl?

In 1939, a novel by Watzlik, *The Master of Regensburg,* extended this vision into caricature, a completely involuntary kind of caricature, which in no way interfered with the book's success, as 6 000 copies had been sold two years later and it has frequently been re-edited. Among other protagonists, Uberto Vistosi, a Venetian antique dealer, a typically unscrupulous *welsch,* full of scorn for Germany, exclaimed when Altdorfer presented him with his *Saint George,* "But this is *maniera gotica!* It is barbarous!", to which the poor painter made the charmingly ingenuous reply: "I am a child of the forest. That is why I paint the forest"[19].

Although romantic, Altdorfer's inspiration also had its roots in the popular consciousness. One recalls the infatuation of the romantics, from the end of the 18th century onwards, for folk poetry, folk songs and folk legend, to which they tried to give a new lease of life. But they were children of the Enlightenment and could not escape their destiny. Neither their faith nor their inspiration could any longer be endowed with that purity and ingenuity that they attributed to medieval faith and which they felt to have surged forth from the very soul of the common people. But Altdorfer was considered to have lived in those happy times. As early as 1907, in his book on the origins of the Danube style, Hermann Voss had compared the work of Altdorfer and Wolf Huber with old folk songs as they were conceived of at the beginning of the 19th century by the poet Uhland; without attempting to explain the apparently common source of inspiration, he found in both the same love of vegetation, of foliage and of forests.

The book was reviewed in such implacably critical terms by Robert Stiassny that the author felt obliged to reply - thereby giving rise to one of those vigorous polemical exchanges which were such a common occurence between art historians at the time but which have regrettably fallen out of fashion in those circles[20]. Apart from the fact that it was probably exacerbated by personal animosity, the dispute had an unmistakeable ideological dimension above and beyond the quarrel over attributions and who discovered what first. Stiassny based his interpretation of the Danube School on a general theory of civilisation which, he held, always moves in the same direction, from the mountains to the plains. Thus, the cradle of the Danube style should be sought in the Alps, from Bavaria to Styria, and not in the region of Regensburg. Thirty years later it would be located in Lower Austria; but this is not the main point, although Stiassny's thesis may have been useful as an explanation of the link which was believed to have existed between the Danube School and certain Swiss artists. What is important is Stiassny's "ethnographical" vision of movements in art. The affinity between art works of the "Danube style" as he understood it, that is to say the Alpine Renaissance with its tendency towards baroque excess and a penchant for representation of nature, and the painting of the Danube basin, with its markedly rustic flavor, was to be explained by a common source in the age-old people of Bavaria, *der gemeinsame altbajuwarische Volkskern*"[21].

There was nothing new or original about the intellectual substrate upon which Stiassny's view was based. Clothed in the pseudo-scientific garments of ethnography, it was a continuation of the romantic idea of the *people,* the quasimystical idea of a collective entity that transcended social categories because it contained all of them, although its essential features were to be found preserved in their purest form in the peasantry. Anybody even slightly acquainted with romantic thought and its ramifications down to the middle of the 20th century will realise what a complex knot of ideas and feelings is embodied in the terms *Volkstum* (the essence, or collective characteristics, of a people) and its adjective, *volkstümlich.* These were to crop up for over fifty years in almost all of the writings devoted to the Danube School. "It was a form of popular art (*'volkstümlich'*), this Danube School" wrote Fritz Dworschak in 1963, adding, two years later, that: "The popular or folk character of this style is due also and above all to its highly romantic feeling"[22]. The illusion was so complete that Wolf Huber's art was actually described as being rustic (a term that is obviously never clearly defined by those that use it), whereas his early drawings display an exceptional power of abstraction and refinement.

This definition of the Danube School attached it to the Late Middle Ages and contrasted it with the Renaissance, unless it be an autonomous and separate Northern, as distinct from transmontane Renaissance. The Middle Ages was the period when the soul of the people had expressed itself with greatest purity; it was also the period of Gothic, which was felt to be an essentially Germanic art form, the term being taken to mean, *pace* Wilhelm Worringer, not the system of construction invented in the Ile-de-France in the middle of the 12th century, but the incarnation of a specific spiritual attitude in an artistic style. Taken in this sense, Gothic had reached its high point just before Italianate forms invaded the Germanic regions. The Danube style, like Grünewald's art, belonged to this final, and most brilliant flowering.

German painting of the 15th century is regarded as the age of provincial schools. There was Swabian painting, Bavarian painting, Franconian painting... all with their own individual characteristic styles. Of the varied possible explanations of such diversity, one at least seemed self-

evident: it reflected the diversity of character of the peoples who lived in the various provinces, in other words, of the different Germanic ethnic groups, the legendary tribes *(Stämme)* which made up the body of the German people. This view situated the Danube School as the last of the provincial schools which had prospered in the 15th century, as a late manifestation of Gothic painting. The *Stamm* which had given birth to it was the Bavarian group, whose area of expansion stretched as far as the Ostmark, or Eastern Mark, the present Lower Austria. These were the terms in which, in the wake of Robert Stiassny and many others, Franz Winzinger described the phenomenon in 1965 as "the grand contribution of the

189 - Saint Bernard Praying for a Good Harvest - Jörg Breu the Elder Austria, Monastery of Zwettl.

Austro-Bavarian ethnic group to German painting at the time of Dürer"[23]. The only dissenting voice in this chorus was that of Götz Fehr for whom the roots of the Danube style stretched back into a Celtic idea of form[24]. This hypothesis at least had the merit of laying itself open to verification, in so far as we possess a series of works from which it is possible to imagine what "Celtic idea of form" those ancient Celts may have had, whereas we do not have the same good fortune where the original Bavarian *Stamm* is concerned! For this reason, we shall limit our remarks to the prudent comment made by Oskar Hagen: "This is not the place for an exhaustive investigation into the origin of the eternal and collective forms with which each individual *Stamm* expressed itself"[25].

Whatever this mysterious Austro-Bavarian character may have been - and, incidentally, no writer has sought to define it - the theory did have certain definite consequences. Thus, for instance, the sources of the Danube style were alleged to have been found in the region itself. Alfred Stange, who mentions a great number of painters who were working and living in Bavaria towards the end of the 15th century, provides the latest and most accomplished example of this method; but there is so little in common between the art of these painters and the art of Altdorfer that one looks in vain for the common characteristic enabling one to identify the expression of a single ethnic group[26]. An attempt to explain the formation of the style by the presence in Regensburg of the atelier of the already mentioned Berthold Furtmeyr, a miniaturist, may appear to be better-founded. But although the opinion has been repeated by several writers, it has not obtained general acceptance, any more than has the recent attempt to establish a link between the art of Wolf Huber and that of a painter named Hans Huber who was born, lived and worked in Feldkirch.[27]

As early as 1928, however, Otto Benesch, curator of the Albertina in Vienna, was stressing the importance of Austria, and more especially of Lower Austria in the origin and development of the Danube style. He emphasised the role played by three painters who had worked there at the beginning of the century, Rueland Freuauf the Younger, from Passau, Jörg Breu the Elder, from Augsburg, and Lucas Cranach the Elder[28]. He also insisted on Altdorfer's debt to Marx Reichlich, a pupil of Michael Pacher, who worked in Salzburg. But other historians have not unanimously acceded to this view, which remains disputed, when not actually glossed over in silence, whereas Freuauf, Breu and Cranach were rapidly recognised as the "shepherds" of the Danube School, to use the title conferred upon them at that time. This view

has remained current down to the present day, in spite of the reservations which it should have inspired and occasionally did.

Around 1500, Freuauf painted a number of altarpieces for the Klosterneuburg Monastery near Vienna. On the panels of one of them, he depicted the legend of Saint Leopold, the individual episodes of which he located in wood-covered landscapes whose idyllic serenity have been looked upon as foreshadowing the landscapes of the Danube School. The same importance has been attached to a landscape painted by Breu on one of the panels of an altarpiece intended for the Abbey of Zwettl. The artist collaborated in the painting of this work during a stay in Melk, on the banks of the Danube, between 1500 and 1502. Cranach's presence has been attested in Vienna in 1502 and until recently, historians have tended to locate his stay there between 1500 and 1504. His work during this period, the earliest to have survived, is characterised by an expressive power which was quickly to disappear when he went to live in Wittenberg, and also by the importance of the natural setting. As early as 1908, Voss and Stiassny, for once in agreement, saw in them the beginnings of the Danube style. At first sight, the link with Altdorfer's earliest work seems clear: was not a celebrated drawing of 1504 attributed to both in turn? Whatever the outcome of the fresh examination to which this question ought to be subjected, Altdorfer had no need to go to Vienna to familiarise himself with the art of Lucas Cranach who had probably already left Austria when he executed his most striking works of this period - the great *Crucifixion*, known as the *Crucifixion of Schleissheim*, dated 1503, the *Rest During the Flight into Egypt*, of 1504 and the drawing of *Saint Martin*, also dated 1504.

Baldass had already estimated the slightness of Breu's and Freuauf's contributions to the formation of the Danube School and it is to be regretted that his prudent example has not been followed[29]. Freuauf's style belongs to a tradition derived from Flemish painting which he inherited from his father. At the beginning of the 16th century, an artist like Altdorfer could only have judged such art as being extremely old-fashioned. Breu's art, with its almost brutal violence in the Passion scenes, bears little relation to the Danube style, except perhaps in that the violence led to comparisons with that of Cranach during the same period. But the notion that the Austrian sojourn of the two painters was a sort of prelude to the Danube School was sustained by a parallel with the history of romantic literature, which had been preceded by the *Sturm und Drang* movement. Similarly, the Austrian period of Cranach and Breu was looked upon as a form of *Sturm und Drang*, after which the romanticism of the Danube School was free to blossom forth[30].

Breu, a native of Augsburg, was Swabian and Cranach was Franconian. Of the three, only Freuauf represented the Bavarian *Stamm*. For those who regarded the Danube School as a manifestation of the genius of the *Stamm*, this should have posed considerable difficulties. Although these do not seem to have concerned Benesch, they could or should have impaired his thesis at a time when land and blood, the infamous *Blut und Boden*, were widely used as an explanation of history. But its success was assured because circumstance was of more consequence than principle. The idea that the origins of the Danube School were to be sought in Lower Austria, at the eastern frontier of the *Ostmark*, that Cranach, Breu and Freuauf had come into the region to produce work which, according to Buchner in his Preface to the catalogue of the exhibition entitled *Albrecht Altdorfer and his Circle* in 1938 should be included as the freshest and most powerful of old German painting, this idea was extremely attractive at the time. Its power may be assessed from the final remarks of the same Preface: "In conclusion, let us draw attention to the profound symbolic significance of the exhibition. It demonstrates the inner coherence and the cultural unity of the old Bavarian Ostmark from the Lech to the Leitha, down whose center flows the Inn, on whose banks is situated Brunau. The setting up of a united Reich has given this unity its ultimate ratification"[31].

Four years later, Karl Oettinger put forward an analogous view in his book on *Old German Painters of the Ostmark*[32]. If this area of German art had been neglected for so long, unlike the schools of Nuremberg and Cologne, this was because of the power of the baroque style in Austria and of the feeble impact of romanticism there. But the fall of the Austro-Hungarian monarchy after the war had forced the Germanic region of the Ostmark, in other words the Austrian provinces, to rediscover their affinities with the first Reich, that is to say to turn towards Germany, thus enabling a new generation of historical research to glorify those forgotten treasures, It was true, he confessed, that the artists who left the most lasting impression had come from outside, from Bohemia and Bavaria, from Swabia and Thuringia. But did the fact that the borders between artistic provinces were not absolute not prove "the authentic organic unity of all our people above and beyond individual Stämme"?[33]. And was not this precisely the official doctrine of the new régime?

The arguments developed by Oettinger to sustain the Austrian origin of the Danube School were used to opposite purposes after 1945. He claimed that the Ostmark had possessed the power of attracting foreigners, of overcoming them with its charms, of beguiling them into singing its praises: "it is not in Swabia nor in Thuringia that

Breu and Cranach got their inspiration: the fountainhead of the art of the Danube that they created and of which Altdorfer is the pinnacle, sprang from the traditions and forces that lie here, in this very earth"[34]. More or less the same idea was taken up twenty years later by Fritz Dworschak, except that he pitched his argument in a totally different register: the obscure attraction of the earth referred to by Oettinger gave way to the charms of the countryside and of the vineyards, to the mild climate and the hospitality of the inhabitants of Lower Austria, all of which sufficed to explain the influx of painters and the

felicity of their inspiration[35]. It mattered little that Cranach and Breu, both nearly 30, were already fully trained artists by the time they arrived and that no solid argument has ever been put forward proving that Altdorfer and Wolf Huber had come to the region before they were in full possession of their styles. The Danube School was an Austrian affair and the 1965 exhibition was going to provide the proof.

From this point of view, it constituted a rejoinder, as it

190 - Saint Wolfgang and Saint Blaise - Master of the Bishops of Budapest
Budapest, Fine Arts Museum.

were, to the 1938 exhibition, which by endeavoring to show that one single art form had held sway from the Lech to the Leitha, recalled that the *Ostmark* belonged to the Holy Roman Empire, just as the *Anschluss* had joined Austria to the Third Reich. The 1965 exhibition, on the contrary, by virtue of the importance attached to peripheral provinces such as Moravia, Carinthia, Friuli or even to regions outside the Empire altogether, like Slovakia, Hungary and distant Transylvania, appears to have been an ideal attempt to give a new lease of life to the Hapsburg Empire. The Danube School thus came to be coterminous with the entire artistic output of the early 16th century, from the Tyrol to the Carpathian mountains; an extraordinary collection of works were thus gathered together under an aegis which, needless to say, was devoid of the slightest stylistic unity.

That unity had to be sought in the collective spiritual force that had inspired the works, in the *Volkstümlichkeit* upon which nearly all the contributions to the catalogue or to the debates organised for the occasion, insisted. But national preoccupations and cultural antagonisms cropped up here also. Franz Lipp spoke of the religiosity of the people as one of the *motors* of the art of the Danube[36]. There is no need to go into the detail of his remarks, based essentially on confusion between the kind of commissions contracted by the artists and the spiritual meaning of their style; but he vigorously denounced the theory outlined by Alfred Stange in his book on the Danube School published the previous year and which had presented their art as the pictorial expression of the *devotio moderna*, a doctrine and form of religious life that appeared in Flanders towards the end of the 14th century. According to Lipp, the *devotio moderna* met with a total lack of understanding among ordinary people; it prefigured the Reformation, the success of which deeply impaired popular religiosity, which was not restored, in an allied form, until the Baroque period. Thus it was that the artistic unity of Bavaria and Austria asserted by the author and explained by recourse to the community of the *Stamm*, turned out to be, first and foremost, the cultural community of the Catholic areas of the South in contrast to the Germany of the Reformation, to what the Catholic regions called, simply, Prussia.

The attack on Stange's view was all the more revealing in that the latter had not set *devotio moderna* against popular religiosity, far from it. Quite the contrary, convinced as he was of the rightness of the notion of *Volkstümlichkeit*, he insisted on the popular character of the Danube style and denied any link with humanistic thought. But his conception of *devotio moderna* is substantially different from that of Franz Lipp, who drew attention to the emphasis placed on Faith as distinct from good works, which foreshadowed Lutheran doctrine and contrasted with popular religiosity, whereas for Stange,

devotio moderna was a form of mysticism, of direct communication with the godhead. In fact, of course, neither writer mentioned any research on the movement nor even quoted the writings of its founders; they seem rather to have conjured up an idea simply to suit their own purposes. Lipp's approach was clear. And the *Geistesgeschichte* was not really the realm of Stange, that great man of learning; for while he may have been the first person to refer to the *devotio moderna* in connection with the Danube School, he did not support his opinion with the slightest argument of solidity or conviction. As well, his book returned to other older theses in a purely cumulative way, with no concern for the incoherence thus caused.

The first of these had been put forward by Benesch in 1938 in his monograph on Altdorfer's painted work, subsequently taken up again and systematised in his essay on the discovery of landscape in painting[37]. The art of the Danube, he alleged, was based on the same panvitalist conception of the universe as was expressed in the writings of Paracelsus. But since Paracelsus, born in 1493, could not have influenced the development of the style, it had to be a question of resemblance or parallel, which still required analysis - other than by appeal to the circumambient ethos. In 1938, Benesch compared an Altdorfer canvas, *The Two Saints John*, or, to be more exact, his description thereof, with a description by Paracelsus of the natural elements and their metamorphosis. Such comparison is as inconclusive and arbitrary as quotations from mystical writers to account for the use of light in Grünewald's paintings! He later placed particular emphasis on the notion of the man-microcosm universe-macrocosm correspondance to which the artists of the Danube School were supposed to have given shape when they blended their characters into the landscape by treating them pictorially in the same manner as the vegetation. It seems pointless to scrutinize the oeuvres of Altdorfer and of Wolf Huber for evidence in support of this view; suffice it to say that this was how Benesch and after him Stange (who took up the same line of argument) perceived the matter, but they did so in order to erect a view of the Danube School on that foundation. Let us say simply that the art of Altdorfer and Wolf Huber lent itself more obviously than any other to such interpretation, but that the interpretation becomes more intelligible when one recalls the role played by Paracelsus in the intellectual life of his day... and in 20th century German thought, or in a segment of it at all events, for which he was the commendable hero of irrationality.

The other thesis taken up by Stange did not immediately concern Altdorfer. It concerned Michael Pacher, that great painter of the Southern Tyrol who was active in the second half of the 15th century and went to live in Salzburg late in life. One remembers the influence which his Altarpiece in Saint Wolfgang is supposed to have exerted on the art of Altdorfer and Wolf Huber; it is claimed that the sense of space and perspective in their work was made possible by a study of his composition (this may appear a somewhat prudent presentation of the facts, but it is not yet proven that a study of Mantegna's engravings had not been at least as beneficial from this point of view). It was this sense of space, already present in Pacher's compositions, that led his biographer, E. Hempel, to draw a comparison between his art and the philosophy of that great thinker, Nicolas de Cues[38]. Where Pacher was concerned, the comparison was enhanced by an external — and therefore utterly meaningless — consideration; Nicolas de Cues had been Bishop of Brixen (Bressanone) when Pacher had his atelier in the neighbouring town of Bruneck (Brunico). As scientist, as philospher and as theologian, he meditated on the notions of the One and the Infinite: this was enough to establish a link between his thought and the art form of the Danube, in which the twofold idea of organic unity and infinite space had been expressed, despite the fact that the Bishop's discourse was articulated in terms so abstract that any analogy with a particular style of painting can only appear arbitrary. The truth of the matter is that the twofold feeling that was to emanate from the work of the Danube School was not to be found in de Cues' writings but in German romanticism, or in the general understanding of German romanticism in the 20th century. It was to be found in the section on space in Oskar Hagen's book, *Deutsches Sehen*, in which it was contrasted with the rational vision of the Latin races who where said to draw distinctions, to measure dimensons and to set limits.

But even if one were to look upon it as the last of the regional schools, the Danube School was too novel and had too many obvious links with the rest of German art at the beginning of the 16th century (even though Winzinger tried, a little late in the day, to minimise Altdorfer's debt to Albrecht Dürer) to be excluded from what is called the Renaissance. Although emphasising its *Volkstümlichkeit* and without flinching at the apparent contradiction, F. Dworschak defined the school as recently as 1965 as "the art of German humanism in the Danube region"[39]. But this had been a *German* Renaissance, a *German* humanism. Paracelsus' panvitalism had been German, Nicolas de Cues' philosophy had been German, or was interpreted thus[40]; the *devotio moderna,* as defined by Stange, that is, a form of direct communication with the divinity present throughout the universe, was a Nordic phenomenon. Ever since Jacob Burckhardt, it had been thought that the Renaissance was the time when the human individual acquired an awareness of himself as an individual; but his mistake, wrote Winzinger in 1952, was to restrict the origin of the historical phenomenon ex-

clusively to the Italian world picture[41]. A different form of individualism, characterised by a greater sense of irrational subjectivity, had developed in the North. Speaking of Nicolas de Cues, Winzinger encapsulated the very essence of the art of the Danube in the following phrase: — "Man stands alone in the face of the Infinite" ("der Mensch steht vor dem Unendlichen einsam"). There is one work, a celebrated work, in German art which

perfectly illustrates this interpretation of the Danube School, so perfectly, indeed, that one wonders whether it may not have more or less inspired the remark: but the work is not by Altdorfer, nor by any of his contemporaries: it is the *Monk by the Sea*, completed by Friedrich in 1810!

Other German works of art have been used to sustain commentary of the same order, from the statues of Naumburg, to the paintings of Friedrich and the churches of

191 - The Burghers of Regensburg Imploring Saint Wolfgang - Monogramist WS Nuremberg, Germanisches Nationalmuseum.

Balthasar Neumann, whose interiors, with their complex mobility, also seemed to communicate that same feeling of the incommensurable and the infinite. Few, however, were canvassed quite as much as those which made up what is called the Danube School, so much so that it may be wondered whether the very notion of the Danube School may not owe, if not its initial appearance, then its continued presence in the history of art to its reflective power, to its capacity to satisfy a need for identification.

The appeal it exerted did, however, have one positive result, that of leading to a quest for works and documents, of encouraging learned investigation and the publication of catalogues, and in particular of giving rise to that monumental contribution to the glory of Altdorfer and Wolf Huber by the lately lamented Franz Winzinger who worked on the 1938 exhibition and who subsequently devoted his energies to a study of the two artists. Apart from the great figures, Dürer, Grünewald, Cranach, Baldung, no other area of German painting has been so attentively explored. But the new generations of German art historians who grew up during or after the Second World War, have turned away from the period, perhaps because they had the impression that everything had already been said, that there was nothing left to be discovered, but more probably on account of the interpretations that it had inspired. It is true that there has been no lack of learned contributions to this or that point of detail, but the time did not seem ripe for a fundamental reassessment, despite a few isloated protests at the use of the adjective *volkstümlich* to describe the art of Altdorfer or of the Danube School[42].

Over the past fifteen years or so, however, there would seem to be evidence of a renewal, as if at last it were becoming possible to take a fresh look at this art, as if at last the mists of what Ferguson called, in his fine book on interpretations of the Renaissance, a romantico-nationalistic ideology[43], had been blown away. At the same time, the United States have been making contributions to the question, evidence of an interest in German art which extends to other periods[44]. But the outlines of a new overall vision are nowhere visible in the studies of G. Goldberg and C. Meckseper on the *Battle of Alexander,* nor in Charles Talbot's thesis on *Altarpiece of Saint Florian,* nor in Joseph Harnest's thesis on perspective in German painting at the time of the Renaissance, nor in the research of Achim Hubel. And this is only to be expected[45].

For the only possible overall vision would be one in which individual elements adhered and the Danube School never was that coherent entity so long asserted by art history. Even if one were to take it in its largest and vaguest sense, the term *school* implies a certain stylistic unity due to a community of tradition or of education. Its use may be justified in the 15th century for what are called regional schools, the existence of which can be explained, not be the *Stämme*, as has been alleged, but in part at least by the concentration of artistic production in a number of large centers and important ateliers. Activity was also favored by a substantial increase in commissions for altarpieces. In is extremely enlightening introduction to his article on the painting and sculpture of Lübeck, Max Hasse laid emphasis on the consequences of the economic difficulties within the profession around 1500, at least in a number of German cities for which documents are available: the corporations resumed malthusian regulations to control numbers and artists were scattered in an internal diaspora, forced to look for work or to live in towns of lesser importance[46].

Added to the dispersal of artistic activity was the growing importance of engraving in the training of artists, who did not merely borrow motifs or compositions but might also retain a certain graphic style, a way of rendering garments, a conception of the human shape... Altdorfer certainly owes more to the engravings of Dürer, Mantegna and Jacopo da'Barbari than to the unknown master to whom he was apprenticed. Finally, a break, perhaps deliberate, with the art of the preceding period seems to have occured in southern Germany at the beginning of the 16th century; the style of Grünewald (despite a slight debt to Holbein the Elder), of Cranach in 1502 or of Wolf Huber in his first landscape drawings, such as *View of Mondsee*, are so new that it is impossible to relate them to any atelier tradition discernable in the last twenty years of the 15th century.

After this period of fracture, of radical innovation, which it would be easy but inadeqaute to explain by the genius of a few exceptional individuals, traditional modes returned. Certain artists attached to Dürer's atelier or in his orbit, such as Hans Suess, Schäuffelein, later on Pencz and the Beham brothers, were deeply influenced by his style and their own bore the Master's imprint thereafter. Art history does not, however, speak of a school where they are concerned, whereas the work of Wolf Huber's and Altdorfer's entourages was no more stylistically coherent. Wolf Huber's landscape drawings were copied and imitated but he is not known to have had many pupils, except perhaps for a painter who was subsequently active in the Rhineland. Altdorfer's style, on the other hand, underwent so many changes and he was productive over such a long period of time that there is practically no correlation between what an artist might have learned in his atelier towards 1510, when the Master of Pulkau seems to have had close contacts with him, and what might have been observed at the end of his life, when Hans Muelich was his collaborator.

The Danube School did not, therefore, exist. What existed was a fairly dense network of complex and varied stylistic relationships which in no way entitle one to draw boundaries, since certain painters who are usually included in the "school" differ more from each other than from artists who have never been admitted to its ranks. What is the common feature, for instance, that might allow one to speak of affinity between the Master of the Legend of Saint Philip and the Master of the Song of Songs, or between the Master of Innerochsenbach and the artist who painted the Altarpiece of Gutenstetten? What stylistic definition may be proposed to include them all, as it includes Altdorfer and Wolf Huber, particularly if, like Alfred Stange, the monogrammist HG of 1514 and the Master of the Bishops of Budapest are excluded, but the artist of *Saint John at Patmos* in Munich and Master WS of the Cross of Malta are included? In fact, one is dealing here with a juxtaposition of works of art that is both incoherent and arbitrary.

If then, there was neither Danube School nor Danube style, it may seem somewhat pointless to examine their significance, whether it be in the *devotio moderna* or elsewhere. Even an output as clearly circumscribed, as clearly defined by subject and function as the pen-an-ink landscapes of Wolf Huber or the small-scale devotional canvasses by Altdorfer poses a series of problems which it is at present, and may well always remain, impossible to resolve. We possess no historical documents relating to the personality, tastes or clientèle of the two artists. As far as we know, no writer of the time spoke of either. It should be added, however, that the judgements pronounced by several writers, among the most famous, on the art of Cranach and Dürer are, in the main, so platitudinous, and the information they provide on their characters and lives so anecdotal that too much ought not to be expected from such sources. At the most, the silence that surrounds Altdorfer and Wolf Huber may be evidence of lesser reputation or lesser esteem but it would be mistaken to conclude from this that they had no contact with humanist circles.

Humanism flourished at the Cathedral Court of Passau[47] and even more so in the venerable but declining city of Regensburg. It seems improbable that no personal contact existed between the artists who worked there and Altdorfer and Wolf Huber. More important than neighbourly relations, however, was the destination of their work. Altdorfer's drawings as, indeed, his copperplate engravings, presuppose the existence of a public interested in fine works of art. The purchase and collection of pen-and-ink drawings, of landscape etchings and of chiaruscuro drawings whose biblical or romancic subject matter frequently served as mere pretexts for the display of a natural or architectural setting, of what the Italian Bishop, Paolo Giovio called in 1527, the *parerga*, seems to have been a novel occurence in the Germany of the time

and probably coincided with a profound change in the way works of art were perceived[48].

The inventory of Altdorfer's estate after his death revealed that he had possessed a collection of antique coins and his interest in ancient art is clear from the study he made of engravings and niellos from Northern Italy. Considerations of a theoretical nature are far from absent from his work, be they in the realm of perspective or of the architectural forms of the past. No image could be more false than that of the naïve painter endowed with a kind of childish spontaneity which art historians were content to create and then to perpetuate for so long, unless it be the image of Wolf Huber as a peasant artist.

The limits of the Italianate or classical character are, nonetheless, too obvious for it to be worthwhile discussing them. Are these limits evidence of profound natural resistance? In his recent book on the German sculptors of the period, Mr Baxandall has put forward a different point of view which, despite its fragility and apparent inconsistency, deserves to be included in the debate[49]. Baxandall quotes two verses written around 1530 by a Nuremberg woodcut engraver named Peter Flötner, in which a distinction was drawn, where Flötner's work was concerned, between an Italian manner (*welsch*) and a German manner. When German humanists turned their attention to antiquity, they did not thereby break with national or popular traditions as they were accused of doing at a certain period[50]; quite the contrary, they felt they had discovered in Tacitus, in the Tacitus of *Germania*, that very tradition and a Germanic identity which had been occluded by the Empire for centuries. The notions of *Stämme* and of *Volkstümlichkeit* appeared at this time. They emerged from historical and ethnographical research inspired by the example of the ancients and encouraged by a feeling of hostility towards Rome and Italy which was then widespread in Germany. The most exalted forms of erudition did not prosper in isolation, far removed from political passion and national resentment, any more than they do in our own day!

Dürer was driven by a spirit of competition with Italian artists, as witness a number of his statements and the inscriptions on several of the works that he himself regarded as paramount. But he went on to their ground to equal or, even better, to surpass them. Might it not be imagined, *a contrario,* that others, by deliberate recourse to a manner deemed to be German, sought to assert that Germanity, which the writings of Konrad Celtis or of his follower, Aventin, may have helped them to grasp? Was not this the style that Cranach had been looking for when he studied, as shown by Charles Sterling, the *Tabula magna* in Tergernsee, a work that had been executed two generations previously?[51] Even if he owes him little or nothing, or at all events less than has been claimed, might Altdorfer not have followed the same course? This would account both for his reaction to the work of Dürer and to the Italians, whom he took as models much as if he wished to set them at a certain distance. It is true that the period during which he might have acquired a specifically German manner is not easy to ascertain, even if examples of deliberate archaisms are far from absent in his work. Baxandall sees an illustration of this in a sculpted altarpiece attributed to the monogrammist HL who was undoubtedy linked in some way or other to the so-called Danube School, although it is not clear precisely how. Baxandall compared it to a famous 13th century sculpture in Bamberg Cathedral on account of the small parallel pleats in the garments which was a style adopted by Altdorfer for a time and which the Master of Pulkau seems to have borrowed from him and to have used throughout his life. But did not Altdorfer and HL borrow the technique directly (like the 13th century sculptor) from ancient ruins or from some more recent Italian work in the antique vein?[52] In which case, what can have been its significance? But is not to ask such a question to attribute an attitude to the art of the past which was prevalent in the 19 th century and which remains so today? Are we not committing the great sin of anachronism which is bound to bedevil any interpretation of past works of art that is not based upon what is occasionally called, not without a certain degree of unconscious irony, formal evidence?

Pierre Vaisse

1. Most of the ideas contained in the following article were contained in the dissertation submitted by the writer after research in the Sorbonne in 1960-61, under the supervision of André Chastel, and in a paper read to a colloquium on *German Humanism*, organised in Tours in 1975. The proceedings of the colloquium were published in 1979 (Munich: Fink Verlag and Paris: J. Vrin Bookstore). Reinhild Janzen's book *Albrecht Altdorfer. Four Centuries of Criticism*, (UMI Research Press) was published the same year in the United States. Its conclusions are similar to those outlined in the present essay. But Mr. Janzen's descriptions of certain aspects of Altdorfer's art (comparisons with the *devotio moderna* and with the writings of Paracelsus, in particular) in a chapter entitled *The Quest to Identify Altdorfer's Intellectual and Spiritual Position*, separate from the chapter in which the ideological misappropriation of the artist's work are denounced (*Altdorfer and Ideologies*), the author omits to demonstrate that these interpretations were all produced by the same ideological nexus from which all of the misappropriations in question proceeded. We should immediately add that this is in no way to prejudge the strictly political opinions of the writers who formulated the interpretations, nor their attitudes to the Third Reich. Moreover. Janzen regards a number of questionable hypotheses as facts duly established by research, as, for instance, the influence of B. Furtmeyr on Altdorfer and above all the date commonly ascribed to his small-scale woodcuts known as the *Mondseer Siegel* - a point of scholarship with immense consequences for opinions of the artist's education and training.

2. French readers will find a different definition in the article by Artur Rosenauer in the *Petit Larousse de la Peinture*, Paris 1979, vol I, p. 432-433. Mr. Rosenauer accepts all of the opinions which in the present essay regards as without foundation.

3. *Die Kunst der Donauschule 1490-1540*, Stift ST. Florian und Schlossmuseum Linz, 1965.

4. Quadt von Kinckelbach, *Teutscher Nation Herlichkeit*, Cologne, 1609, p. 425; Mathäus Merian, in his edition of Thoma Garzoni, *Allgemeiner Schauplatz aller Künste*, Frankfurt/Main, 1641, p. 721 (quoted by W.K. Zülch, *Der historische Grünewald Munich*, 1938, p. 380); Joachim von Sandrart, *Teutsche Akademie*, Muremberg, 1657, p. 231. In Regensburg itself, in 1651, a collector donated to the city a series of drawings and most of Altdorfer's engravings as well as a painting attributed to him (Peter Halm, Eine Altdorfer Sammlung des 17. Jahrhunderts, *Münchner Jahrbuch der bildenden Kunst*, 1960, p. 162-172).

5. Schöber's book was quoted by St. Eucker, *Das Dürerbewusstsein in der deutschen Romantik*, Marburg/Lahn, 1936, p. 18.

6. J.D. Fiorillo, *Geschichte der Zeichnenden Künste in Deutschland und in der vereinigten Niederlanden*, Hannover, vol II, 1817, p. 406-409.

7. Hippolyte Fortoul, *De l'Art en Allemagne*, vol. II, Paris, 1842, p. 189.

8. Dr Lachaise, *Manuel pratique et raisonné de l'amateur de tableaux...*, Paris, 1866, p. 226.

9. On the evolution of opinions on the use of color in Dürer's work, see Fedja Anzelewsky, *Albrecht Dürer. Das malerische Werk*, Berlin, 1971, p. 15ff and Kristina Fiore-Hermann, Das Problem des Datierung bei Dürers Landschaftsaquarellen, *Anzeiger des Germanischen Nationalmuseums* 1971/1972, p. 122ff.

10. H. Janitscheck, *Geschichte der deutschen Malerei*, Berlin, 1890, p. 411.

11. Max Friedländer, *Albrecht Altdorfer. Der Maler von Regensburg*, Leipzig, 1891.

12. Theodor von Frimmel, *Repertorium für Kunstwissenschaft*, 1892, p. 417. For H. Voss's book, see note 14.

13. Paul Behaim, Verzeichnis allerley Kunst... cilligiert und zusammengebracht durch Paulus Behaim juniorem. 1618, p. 73 (this was the document that enabled Nagler to identify the monogram WH in 1838); the catalogue of the Künast collection was quoted by W.K. Zülch, op.cit. (supra, note 4) p. 381.

14. Rudolf Riggenbach, *Der Maler und Zeichner Wolfgang Huber (c. 1490-nach 1542)*, Bale, 1907; Hermann Voss, *Ueber Wolf Huber als Maler und einige Meister des Donaustiles*, Leipzig, 1907 et id., *Ursprung des Donaustils. Ein Stück Entwicklungsgeschichte Deutscher Malerei*, Leipzig, 1907.

15. Franz Winzinger, *Wolf Huber. Das Gesamtwerk*, Munich-Zurich, 1979.

16. *Albrecht Altdorfer und sein Kreis. Gedächtnisausstellung zum 400. Todesjahr Altdorfers*, Munich, 1938; on the Linz exhibition, cf. supra., note 3.

17. A judgement formulated in his book, *Albrecht Altdorfer*, Berlin, 1923, p. 138 (see P. Vaisse, review of Franz Winzinger's *Albrecht Altdorfer. Die Gemälde*, Munich-Zurich 1975, in *Zeitschrift für Kunstgeschichte* 1977, 3/4, p. 320-321)

18. Ludwig von Baldass, *Albrecht Altdorfer*, Vienna, 1941, p. 24: "To describe this art with precision, we are forced to borrow from the terminology of the late 18th century; we speak of romanticism to depict the magical atmosphere of these landscapes and of *Sturm und Drang* to describe the overwhelming force of the altarpieces".

19. Hans Watzlik, *Der Meister von Regensburg. Ein Albrecht Altdorfer-Roman*, 1939; our quotations are taken from the Augsburg edition, Adam-Kraft Verlag, 1955, p. 194.

20. Robert Stiassny, Die Donaumalerei im sechszehnten Jahrhundert, in *Monatshefte für Kunstwissenschaft*, 1908/1, p. 421-435, and Hermann Voss, R. Stiassny zum Thema des Donaustiles. Eine notgedrungene Selbstwehr, ibid., p. 442-447.

21. p. 432. *Bajuwarisch* is an old version of *bayrisch* (Bavarian); it is used today with mildly ironic or ethnographic intent. It crops up frequently in writings on the Danube School.

22. Fritz Dworschak, Die Donauschule - Malerei und Plastik, in *Die Gotik in Niederösterreich*, Vienne, 1963, p. 149, et id., Die Ausstellung, in the Linz cat., 1965 (*supra*, note 3) p. 11.

23. Franz Winzinger, Zur Malerei der Donauschule, in the Linzcat, 1965 (*supra*, note 3), p. 18.

24. Götz Fehr, Architektur, ibid., p. 207.

25. Oskar Hagen, *Deutsches Sehen. Gestaltungsfragen der deutschen Kunst*, 3 rd. ed., Munich, 1933, p. 6.

26. Alfred Stange, *Malerei der Donauschule*, Munich, 1964, p. 41ff.

27. The hypothesis according to which Altdorfer might have been influenced by Furtmeyr was put forward by Friedlaender in 1891, as we have seen, but Friedlaender remarked in a later essay that is was when he had reached maturity that the painter had adopted a style reminiscent of the art of miniature (in *De l'Art et du connaisseur*, French translation, Paris, 1969, p. 240); it was taken up by Alheidis von Rohr in a doctoral dissertation on *Berthold Furtmeyr und die Regensburger Buchmalerei des 15. Jahrhunderts*, *Bonn*, 1967, and frequently reappeared in writings on Altdorfer and the Danube School, but the comparisons upon which it is based are fare from convincing. On Wolf Huber and Hans Huber, see Thomas Brachert, Die Malwerkstatt des Meisters hh (Hans Huber von Feldkirch), in *Montfort*, 1966/2, p. 280-324, in particular, p. 319-320.

28. Otto Benesch, Zur altösterreichischen Tafelmalerei, *Jahrbuch der Kunsthistorischen Sammlungen*, 1928, p. 63-118, rééd. dans Otto Benesch, *Collected Writings*, vol. III, New York, 1972, p. 16-72 (p. 69).

29. Baldass, *op.cit.* (*supra*, note 18), p. 31-32.

30. *Sturm und Drang* (the most representative literary works are *Werther* and the first *Faust*, by Goethe) was generally considered in literary history as the prelude to romanticism. That this may have been the case or that, as claimed by Lukacs, it was the fulfillment of the Enlightenment is not germane.

31 .E. Buchner, in the Munich cat. 1938 (supra, note 16). p. III-IV. It should be recalled that Hitler was born in Brunau.

32. Karl Oettinger, *Altdeutsche Malerei der Ostmark*, Vienna, 1942.

33. ibid., p. 6.

34. ibid., p. 6.

35. F. Dworschak, *op.cit.* 1963 (*supra*, note 22); p. 144.

36. Franz Lipp, Volksart und Volksfrommigkeit als Treibkräfte der Kunst der Danauschule, *Werden und Wandlung. Studien zur Kunst der Donauschule*, Linz, 1967, p. 20-36.

37. Otto Benesch, *Der Maler Albrecht Altdorfer*, Vienna, 1938, and *The Art of the Renaissance in Northern Europe*, London, 1965 (1 ed., 1945), chap. III, The New Attitude towards Nature.

38. Eberhard Hempel, *Das Werk Michael Pachers*, Vienna, 1937.

39. F. Dworschak, Linz cat. 1865 (*supra*, note 3) p. 15.

40. The idea that the thought of Nicolas de Cues was specifically German is questioned by Maurice de Gandillac, *La philosophie de Nicolas de Cuse*, Paris, 1931, p. 31, note 1.

41. Franz Winzinger, *Altdorfer Zeichnungen*, Munich, 1952, p. 29.

42. In particular by Dieter Koepplin, Das Sonnengestirn der Donaumeister, *Werden und Wandlung* (op. cit. supra., note 36), p. 114, and by Eberhard Ruhmer, Albrecht Altdorfer, Munich, 1965, p. 30-33 (but with a far too narrow definition of volkstümlich).

43. W.K. Ferguson, *The Renaissance in historical thought*, trad. fr. *La Renaissance dans la pensée historique*, Paris, 1950.

44. Charles W. Talbot, *The Passion Cycle by Albrecht Altdorfer at St. Florian: A study of program and style*, Phil. Diss. 1968, New Haven, Conn., Yale Univ.; cat. expo. *The Danube School: Prints and Drawings from the Danube School*, Yale University Art Gallery, 1969; Patricia A. Rose, *Wolf Huber Studies: Aspects of Renaissance thought and practice in Danube School Painting*, Phil. Diss. New York, 1973, Columbia University; and R. Janzen's book referred to in note 1.

45 For recent studies on the *Battle of Alexander*, see the essay by Gisela Goldberg in the present catalogue; on Charles Talbot's view, see

previous note; Joseph Harnest Das Problem der konstruirten Perspecktive in der altdeutschen Malerei, Diss. University of Munich, 1971; Achim Habel, Albrecht Altdorfer als Maler.

192 - Saint John in Patmos - Unknown Master
Munich, Bayerisches Nationalmuseum.

Beobachtungen zu Form, Farbe, Licht, Albrecht Altdorfer und seine Zeit, Schriftenreihe der Universität Regensburg, Vol 5, Regensburg, 1981.

46. Max Hasse, Lübecker Maler und Bildschnitzer um 1500, *Niederdeutsche Beiträge zur Kunstgeschichte*, III (1964), p. 285 ("Die Überfüllung im Gewerbe der Maler und Bildschnitzer zu Anfang des 16. Jahrhunderts").

47. Gustav Künstler, Wolf Huber als Hofmaler des Bischofs von Passau Graf Wolfgang von Salm, *Jahrbuch der Kunsthistorischen Sammlungen in Wien*, 1962, p. 73-100.

48. On Paolo Giovo's text (on the painter Dosso Dossi), Creighton Gilbert, On Subject and Not Subject in Italian Renaissance Pictures, *Art Bulletin*, 1952, p. 204, and E.H. Gombrich, Renaissance Artistic Theory and the Development of Landscape Painting, *Gazette des Beaux-Arts*, 1953/1 p. 346.

49. Michael Baxandall The *Limewood Sculptors of Renaissance Germany*, Yale University, 1980, p. 135-142.

50. Paul Joachimsen, Der Humanismus und die Entwicklung des deutschen Geistes, *Vierteljahrsschrift für Literatur und Geistesgeschichte*, 1930, p. 419-480 (in particular, p. 476 against Friedrich Paulsen and the "modern Gothics").

51. Charles Sterling, Grünewald c. 1500-1505, Proceedings of the Round Table discussion *Grünewald and his Work*, University of Strasburg, 1974, p. 132.

52. Luise Böhling, Prinzipielles zum deutschen Parallelenfaltenstil *Zeitschrift für Kunstgeschichte*, 1938, p. 20-40.

194 - The Stigmata of Saint Francis - A. Altdorfer
Oil on Limewood - 236×103 mm - 1507 - Berlin, K., SMPK.

195 - The Repentance of Saint Jerome - A. Altdorfer
Oil on Limewood - 235×204 mm - 1507 - Berlin, K., SMPK.

196 - The Birth of Jesus - A. Altdorfer - 1507
Oil on paper - 418×315 mm
Bremen, Kunsthalle.

197 - Saint George in the Forest - A. Altdorfer - 1510
Oil n Limewood - 282×225 mm - Munich, Alte Pinakothek.

198 - The Family of Satyrs - A. Altdorfer - 1507 - Oil on Limewood - 230×205 mm - Berlin, K., SMPK.

199 - Christ on the Cross with Mary and Saint John - A. Altdorfer - Oil on Limewood - 1020×1165 mm - Kassel, Gemäldegalerie.

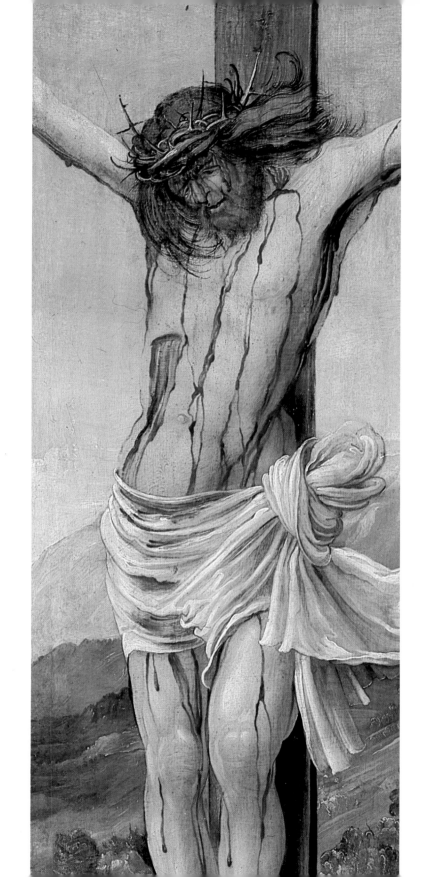

200 - The Two Saint Johns - A. Altdorfer - Oil on pinewood - 1732×2336 mm - Regensburg, Museen der Stadt Regensburg.

201 - The Birth of Christ - A. Altdorfer
Oil on limewood - 360×255 mm - Berlin, K., SMPK.

202 - The Flight into Egypt - A. Altdorfer - 1510
Oil on limewood - 582×392 mm - Berlin, K., SMPK.

203 - The Holy Family and Saint John the Evangelist - A. Altdorfer - 1515
Oil on limewood - 225×205 mm - Vienna, Kunsthistorisches Museum.

FANTASTICISM OF THE EARTH AND OF MAN: ALTDORFER

I

A thousand leaves, a hundred thousand fragments
of the tree
A hundred arcs, three thousand
marble shimmers
The galaxy
of characters tangled in combat
The wind
of the loincloths
of torture
The fluid faces
The flesh
ravages
- destructured features -
The arms out reaching - too late
Without doubt
it is too late for the God
Saviour

II

Two realities
of the World,
from Saint George to Suzanne in the garden
of Calvary - that of the Monastery of St. Florian -
to the bodies thrown out of the water of the Saint
that of Nuremberg

Two realms
of fantastic
or
the same
That of the Earth
That of Man

III

Lives of the forest
of the man dominated
Uproar
or murmer
of Society, human suffrance - so human God that God is gone -
or is us?

Calm
of the woods, invading space, but where the tree Flows downward
and wants
to touch the lichen's ground
claws
of a Vegetation which expresses
- which thinks?
structuring the air
Knotting
The dialogue with he
subjected

IV

The joy
of those who
violate
torture
oppress
judge

gestures
of Man satisfied
repeated
and innumerable - so quotidian -
created to reduce
Who knows Freedom
Who is
Truth

V

But the apostles walk
the garden is
- or not -
throughout
a Ray of light before them
- Or within?

Maurice Guillaud

204 - The Saint Florian Polyptych: Christ on the Mount of Olives - A. Altdorfer - 1518 Oil on pinewood - 1285×940 mm.

205 - The Saint Florian Polyptych: The Arrest of Christ - A. Altdorfer - 1518
Oil on pinewood - 1295×970 mm.

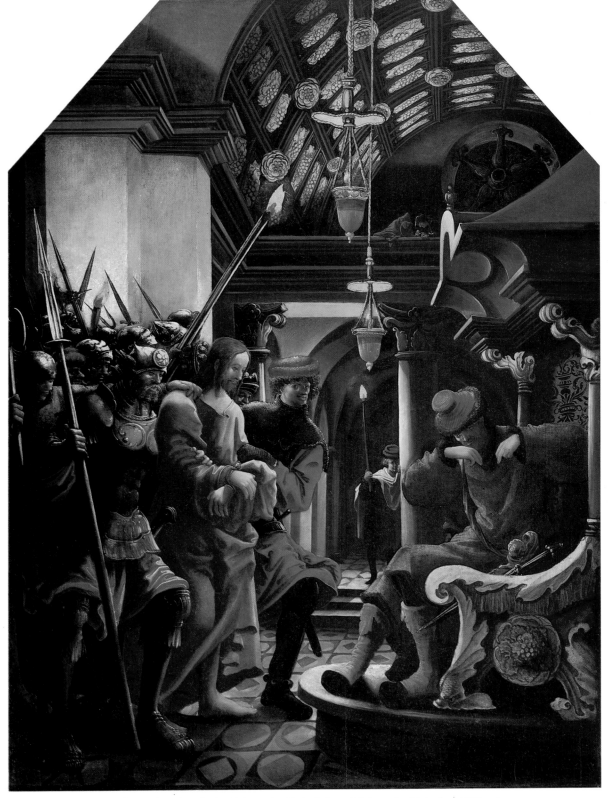

206 - The Saint Florian Polyptych: Christ before Caiphas - A. Altdorfer - 1518
Oil on pinewood - 1295×970 mm.

207 - The Saint Florian Polyptych: Christ Being Scourged - A. Altdorfer - 1518
Oil on wood - 1280×935 mm.

208 - The Saint Florian Polyptych: The Crowning of Thorns - A. Altdorfer 1518
Oil on pinewood - 1120×940 mm.

209 - The Saint Florian Polyptych: Pilate Washes his hands - A. Altdorfer - 1518   (erratum: inversed illustration)
Oil on pinewood - 1140×960 mm.

210 - The Saint Florian Polyptych: Christ Carrying the Cross - A. Altdorfer - 1518
Oil on pinewood - 1140×960 mm.

211 - The Saint Florian Polyptych: The Crucifixion - A. Altdorfer - 1518
Oil on pinewood - 1122×945 mm.

212 - The Saint Florian Polyptych: Saint Sebastian Before the Judge - A. Altdorfer - 1518

Oil on pinewood - 1280×937 mm.

213 - The Saint Florian Polyptych: The Martyrdom of Saint Sebastian - A. Altdorfer - 1518
Oil on pinewood - 1285×943 mm.

214 - Polyptych of St Florian : St Sebastian - A. Altdorfer - 1518
Oil on Pinewood - 1124×940 mm.

215 - The Saint Florian Polyptych: The Corpse of Saint Sebastian is Taken from the Water - A. Altdorfer - 1518
Oil on pinewood - 1125×945 mm.

216 - The Saint Florian Polyptych: Saint Margaret and Saint Barbara
A. Altdorfer - 1518 - Oil on pinewood - 855×335 mm.

217 - The Saint Florian Polyptych: The Entombment of Christ
A. Altdorfer - 1518 - Oil on pinewood - 705×373 mm.
Vienna, Kunsthistorisches Museum.

218 - The Saint Florian Polyptych: The Resurrection
A. Altdorfer - 1518 - Oil on pinewood - 710×378 mm
Vienna, Kunsthistorisches Museum.

219 - The Saint Florian Polyptych: Prior Peter Maurer
A. Altdorfer - 1518 - Oil on pinewood - 852×356 mm.

THE ALTAR OF ST. FLORIAN'S

The 12 panels of the Sebastian Altar in the gallery of St. Florian's Monastery near Linz in Austria and the four small panels in Vienna's Art Museum are what remains of a large winged altar. The wooden sculptures which once formed the centre of the altar (as in Matthias Grünewald's Isenheim Altar) have long been lost.

Originally the four scenes depicting St. Sebastian's Martyrdom formed the exterior of the retable, which was known as the everyday side. Above (from left to right) were the following scenes: the Interrogation of the Saint — the Ordeal; and below: the Saint is Cast Down — the Saint's Body is Saved.

On the predella (Vienna) were the following: on the left, sitting, Saint Margaret and Saint Barbara, and, on the right, kneeling, Peter Maurer, Provost of St. Florian's, who donated the altar.

When the outer wings were opened on Sundays and feast days the following could be seen - above:

Praying on the Mount of Olives - Christ's Arrest - Christ before Caiphas - the Flagellation of Christ.

Bellow: Christ being Crowned with Thorns - Pilate Washing his Hands - Christ carries the Cross - the Curcifixion.

In the predella:

Left: Christ is laid in the Tomb; right: the Resurrection.

(On important Holy Days the inner wings were opened. The inside of the wings was probably carved).

The panels of St. Florian's Altar are Albrecht Altdorfer's most extensive piece of work. The building of the altar was probably commissioned by Provost Peter Maurer (1508-1545 reg.) soon after he took office, at the latest following the consecration of the altar mensa on 29.4.1509. The year 1518 on the panel depicting the ressurection may be the date of completion. The twelve paintings must have required an enormous amount of work if one takes the drafts and preparation involved into consideration.

Winzinger has emphasized to what extent Altdorfer, who was not yet thirty years old, was rather unsure of himself at the time of this first commission, which involved a great many full-sized figures. Their proportions are not homogeneous; often, as is the case in the Ressurection, their size exceeds all probability. Where architecture is concerned, the forms of the Renaissance predominate, and he has not yet mastered the relationships of size and perspective. The outdoor scenes are all the more convincing. It is obvious that Altdorfer was above all concerned with the intense movement, theatrical at times, that animates the various scenes. With this in mind, he paid extreme attention to the unity of composition of the pictures consituting the diferent façades. F.A.

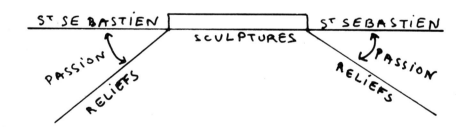

220 - The Saint Florian Polyptych: diagram.

221 - Christ Bidding Farewell to Mary - A. Altdorfer
Oil on pinewood - London, National Gallery.

Three panels of the Florian Legend

A total of seven pictures of the cycle of the Florian Legend painted by Altdorfer for the altar of St. Florian's are still in existence; an eighth has been lost. Traces of paintings found on the backs of certain pictures in this sequence suggest that they must also have been intended for the wings of an altar. We may assume that these paintings were intended for St. FLorian's since they not only portray the legend of the patron, but also show the miraculous fountain fo St Florian's. They could therefore have a direct temporal connection with the large altar, circa 1516/18.

Altdorfer's style has clearly evolved. The figures are now more stocky and uniform in size. He is in complete control of the perspective, as seen in the *Arrest of the Saint*. The scene is arranged on a curved bridge. The planks of the bridge emphasize perspective. (A painting in the Uffizi Palace in Florence features the same bridge, seen from below). *St. Florian before the Governor,* an episode played out in an inner room, the perspective construction of which is emphasized.

222 Panel of the Legend of Saint Florian:
   The Corpse of Saint Florian Being Taken from the Water -
   A. Altdorfer - Oil on pinewood
   815×653 mm - Nuremberg, Germanisches Nationalmuseum.

223 -Panel of the Legend of Saint Florian:
   Saint Florian Before the Praetor - A. Altdorfer -
   Oil on pinewood
   781×661 mm - Nuremberg, Germanisches Nationalmuseum.

In the third painting, the *Saving of the Body of St. Florian,* Altdorfer is obviously in his element. It is dusk and, having rescued the drowned man from the river, two men and tow women are laying the body on a cart.

All the scene of the legend are marked by their peaceful, unemotional character, in striking contrast to the Sebastian Altar of St. FLorian's. The Seitenstetter apostles, dating from 1517, are also typical of Altdorfer's change in style.

The following scenes are included in the cycle:
1. St Florian takes his leave, Florence (81,4×67 cm)
2. Arrest of the Saint, Nuremburg (78,4×65,1)
3. The Saint before the Governor, Nuremburg (78,1×66,1)
4. The Saint is Cast Down, Prague (81,5×67)
5. The Saint is Thrown from the Bridge, Florence (76,4×67,3)
6. The Body of the Saint is Saved, Nuremburg (81,5×65,3)
7. The Miraculous Fountain fo St. Florian's, formerly in a private collection in Berlin (81,5×67,5) F.A.

223 bis - Panels of the Legend of Saint Florian:
   The Arrest of Saint Florian - A. Altdorfer - Oil on pinewood
   784×651 mm - Nuremberg, Germanisches Nationalmuseum.

224 - The Birth of Christ - A. Altdorfer - Oil on limewood
443×360 mm - Vienna, Kunsthistorisches Museum.

225 - Landscape with Bridge - A. Altdorfer
421×351 mm - London, National Gallery.

226 - Mary and the Infant in Glory - A. Altdorfer
Oil on limewood - 660×430 mm
Munich, Alte Pinakothek.

227 - The Apostles' Farewell - A. Altdorfer - Oil on limewood
422×325 mm - Berlin, K., SMPK.

228 - Calvary - A. Altdorfer - Oil on limewood
405×331 mm - Nuremberg, Germanisches Nationalmuseum.

229 - The Crucifixion - A. Altdorfer - 286×209 mm - Berlin, K., SMPK.

230 - Suzanne and the old men - Cat. 162 Bis

231 - Suzanna Bathing - A. Altdorfer
Oil on limewood - 750×613 mm
Munich, Alte Pinakothek.

232 - The Gists of the Three Kings - A. Altdorfer
Oil on limewood - 1085×780 mm - Frankfurt, Städelesches Kunstinstitut.

233 - Allegory - A. Altdorfer
Oil on limewood - 289×410 mm - Berlin, K., SMPK.

234 - Danube Landscape near Regensburg - A. Altdorfer
300×220 mm - Munich, Alte Pinakothek.

235 - Lot and his Daughter - A. Altdorfer - 1537
Oil on limewood - 1075×1890 mm - Vienna, Kunsthistorisches Museum.

Albrecht Altdorfer: the Battle of Alexander the Great against the Great Persian King Darius III at Issus in 333B.C. (The Battle of Alexander)

What is it in the picture of the *Battle of Alexander* that so fascinates the observer? One is drawn to it like a magnet, much more so than towards any other of the paintings in the *Pinakothek,* especially of course in the Exbihition Room. Other paintings with a composition similar to that of the Battle of Alexander are hung there — and yet it stands out very markedly from these.

At a first glance, the panel which was originally somewhat higher — (it has been reduced at the upper edge; the pompous panel was almost twice its present size) — seems to present two areas. In the lower half of the picture, tones of green, brown, red and grey predominate, and in the upper half a radiant luminous blue; zones corresponding to those of the earth and the sky.

If this picture calls to mind the expression "infinite", this may quite rightly be an apt description of the upper half of the painting. It is not, however, simply a question of dividing the picture into two halves. To choose to define the picture in terms of one area denoting the earth and the other denoting the sky although correct, would lack a certain subtlety. At the point where the blue area begins to take over in the middle of the picture, the earth's surface is still represented in the form of islands, rivers, mountains

236 - Tabletop with the Battle of Charles the Great - Unknown Master - Nuremberg - Germanisches Nationalmuseum.

237 - The Battle of Alexander: Mosaic in the House of Fauna in Pompei, 2nd/3rd century.

and plains. These only reflect, as do the countless pieces of shining metal armour in the lower half of the picture, the colour of the sky which spans the entire composition. The eye is drawn into the furthest distance right up to the point where, to the left, the sky becomes indistinguishable from the earth, and where, to the right, the sunlight clearly marks the horizon. The firmament extends to the very fore of the picture. The spatial value of the composition is defined by means of the ingenious shaping of the horizon with its downward-curving lines, towards which the low-lying strata of clouds descend. In the foreground this immense volume of space is delimited by the large pompous panel which seems to swing on its own axis.

The observer looks down on the event from a high viewpoint and at the same time his eye is drawn into the farthest distances. He finds himself lifted out of the picture and is able to feel the violent forces of nature manifest in the turbulent movements of the cloud formations and in the expansive tumult of the battle, as if he were witness to an immense drama.

The source of light is not external to the picture, as is often the case in the paintings of the late Middle Ages, but is clearly visible: the warm golden light of the setting sun lightly skims over the sea, the landscape and warriors. It borders the clouds and mountain ranges, shines into the midst of the dense clusters of clouds and is reflected on the sea's surface in the background of the picture. The observer is literally dazzled.

The motif of the sun, as a light source within the picture itself, is used in a higly developed manner by Albrecht Dürer, Albrecht Altdorfer and Wolf Huber. In *the Battle of Alexander,* one can surely compare the distance which separates the observer from the sun, with the space travelled to reach the limits of the cosmos. In the few moments before the sun disappears below the horizon, the last rays of light cover the earth once more and give a final warm blaze of colour. These colours will soon be extinguished by night: it is already approaching with the star on the left. Day has gone but night has not yet descended, a time of transition for both stars. The observer feels the tension of the brief remaining moments of twilight.

The seething clouds, the red bands flapping violently in the wind, create a feeling of agitation and restlessness. The direct confrontation of the opposing armies is decisive for the course of the conflict in the front and back areas of the battle field, but a new situation has sprung up in the heart of the battle. In front of the brightly illuminated ruins the spears are no longer pointing at each other. They are in an upright position because the infantry and cavalrymen are turning back. Far in front of this "side-scene", the battle's final outcome is being decided, for here a finely dressed knight on his white horse is pursuing a fully equipped chariot drawn by three horses, which is to all appearance not profiting from the advantage it has over the knight in

pursuit.

From the style of the architecture, armour and dress one could easily think that Albrecht Altdorfer was depicting a contemporary event in this picture, dated 1529. The numerous inscriptions, however, indicate that this is a battle from Antiquity between the Macedonian king, Alexander the Great, and the Great Persian King Darius III. For a long time it was uncertain exactly which battle between the Macedonians and Persians was represented. But finally the group of women portrayed near to the Persian King revealed that this was, in fact, the battle which had taken place near the town of Issus, in south-east Asia Minor in 333 B.C. Tradition has it that Alexander, the victor at the battle of Issus, honoured Darius's mother, wife and children, who all belonged to the Great King's retinue. The geographical site also helped to identify that this was beyond any doubt the Battle of Issus. The view is taken from a north-south direction over the eastern part of the Mediteranean Sea as far as the Red Sea and the Nile Delta.

The adversaries of the pursuit scene situated in the centre of the battle are identifiable: Alexander is pursuing Darius. The battle is, therefore, at its final stage, which is also indicated by the constellation of the heavenly bodies. According to a report of battle, it began in the morning and by evening was concluded.

In iconography the simultaneous representation of the sun and moon is often encountered. For example, the portrayal of Christ's crucifixion and also the "Battle of Joshua against the Amorites" (Old Testament, Joshua 10, 12ff; representation in the *Schatzbehalter,* Nuremberg 1491): in these two themes, it seems that what is being expressed is the standing still of time, whereas in *the Battle of Alexander* it is rather the passage of time.

Alexander the Great (356-323 B.C.; ruled 366-323) was the son of King Philip II of Macedon. He is reknowned not only as the greatest general of all times, but also as a paragon of noble and knightly virtue (cf. the Greek story of Alexander's life written c. 220 B.C.) After consolidating his power in Greece, he began in 335 preparations for his great Persian campaign. To the west, the Persian Empire of Darius comprised the lands of Lydia, Phrygia, Cappadocia, Sicily, Palestine, Egypt and Libya, and consequently constituted a continual threat to Greece. In the spring of 334 the march of the Macedonian army began. The Persian army seemingly had a great advantage over the Macedonians as far as number was concerned, and this led them to underestimate the approaching danger. Alexander gained his first victory in north-west Asia Minor near the River Granicus. The coastal towns of Asia Minor, including Ephesus and Miletus, fell not long afterwards. Alexander set up his winter quarters in the Phrygian capital of Gordieum (The Episode of The Gorian Knot) and in the following spring he advanced down to the south coast of Asia Minor. As Darius drew nearer with the army which he had raised

238 - The Battle of Alexander - A. Altdorfer - 1529
Oil on limewood - 1582×1205 mm - Munich, Alte Pinakothek.

in Mesopotamia, Alexander set out from the town of Tarsus. It was in the two-kilometer wide valley of Issus that he awaited his enemy, which he succeeded in overrunning due to his advantageous position. Darius was put to flight and Alexander assured the family of Darius, which remained behind, of his magnanimity.

The successive stages in Alexander's Persian campaign:

332 The conquest of Tyrus and Gaza. The liberation of Egypt (in Memphis Pharaoh is crowned). The founding of Alexandria.

331 Victory over the Persians at Gaugamela and Arbela. The taking of Babylon and Susa. The conquest of Persepolis. Alexander thereafter becomes ruler over the whole of the Persian Empire.

330 The subjugation of the eastern Persian Empire: Darius is murdered at Hecatompylos by the Satrap of Bactriana.

327 Beginning of the Indian Campaign. He marries Roxana, daughter of Oxyartes, Duke of Bactriana.

326 The crossing of the Indus; victory over the Indian King, Poros. He begins his retreat from the river Hyphasis.

324 In Susa, Alexander marries the eldest daughter of Darius, and Parysatis, daughter of Artaxerxes III.

323 The court transfers from Ecbatana to Babylon; preparations for an African expedition. Death of this exceptionally successful general.

Let us return now to the painting:

The extremely precise detail of this large-scale composition is astonishing. The examples are numerous: the physiognomy of Darius as he looks back in despair; his chariot driver lying at his feet, pierced by an arrow; the fire-spitting dragon on Alexander's helmet; the women clinging desperately to one another in search of consolation, the ruins, left of centre, with dead cattle and chariot wheels lying close by; the encampment in front of the city.

It is certainly not easy to discern the enemy armies within the violent eddies of the battle. But the protagonists are immediately distinguishable. The tassel hanging from the pompous panel indicates the central axis of the picture and the "position" of Alexander.

The number of dead are indicated on the flags held by the soldiers: 300 of Alexander's 32.000 strong infantry have fallen, 150 of this 4.000 knights are dead.

Darius has lost 12.000 of his 300.000 infantrymen and 10.000 of his 100.000 knights. Further numbers are shown on the large pompous panel: 100.000 of the Persian infantry have fallen, 10.000 Persian knights, 1.000 Persians have fled. The losses of Alexander's army are not mentioned. The latin text, probably written towards the end of the 16th century, has replaced an original German text. Most flags and penants bear pictures of apparently fantastical weapons and emblems. For Alexander we find a griffin and a female figure with garlands in her hands; for Darius, a naked, winged, male figure kneeling in a boat with a torch (?) in his upheld right hand, and a sovereign figure bearing a flaming sword. Both camps have differently coloured diagonally-striped flags. Alexander and Darius are identified by their

actual names: ALEXANDER MAGNUS can be read on two discs of his horse's saddlery; DARIUS is written on a disc on his chariot.

The artist seems not to have been acquainted with the *classical source texts* (Quintus Curtius Rufus, *Historia Alexandri Magni*. III, 21-31 (written during the reign of Emperor Claudius 41-54); Flavius Arrianus, *Anabasis*. II, 8-II (written in the 2nd Century A.D.). It must be assumed that he came to know the description of the battle through the court historian Aventinus *(Das erst puech der Baierischen chroniken... 1526. I, chapter 153, chapter 158).*

Technical details, Signature, Dating and Inscriptions:
Lindenwood, 158.4 × 120.3 cm. The surface of the picture has been cut off on all sides. The signature, ALBRECHT ALTDORFER ZV REGENSBURG FECIT is found on the lower frame of the pompous panel, to the right of the tree trunk in the lower left-hand corner, the picture bears a second signature in the form of an intertwined monogram AA; it is dated 1529.

The present latin text reads:
ALEXANDER M DARIVM VLT SVPERAT
CAESIS IN ACIE PERSAR PEDIT C M EQVIT
VLRO X M INTERFECTIS MATRE QVOQVE
CONIVGE LBERIS DARII REG CVM M HAVD
AMPLIVS EQVITIB FVGA DILAPSI CAPTIS
(Alexander The Great defeated the last Darius, after 100.000 Persian infantrymen had fallen and over 10.000 cavalrymen had been slain. Whilst Darius was able to flee with no more

than 1.000 of his cavalry, his mother, wife and children were taken captive.

The reduced pompous panel that is visible today, must have originally been about 10 cm. higher. The original 23-line inscription was formerly in German. Fragments of the text, which on the lower border of the picture are visible to the naked eye but which on the upper border can only be made out with technical aid, are reminscent of similar wordings found in the historical writings of Aventinus. The inscriptions on the flags read as follows: . ALEXANDE / . HET . AN . FVES / VOLCK . 32000 / . DAR . AVS IST / . ERSCHLAGE . / NIT . MER .. / 300 (upper right); . ALEXAND / HET WENIC / VOLCK RAISI / 4000 / DAR AVS / ERSCHLAG / ORDEN / 150 (center right); . DARIVS . / HET RAISIGS . ZE / IG 100 000 DAR / AVS IST DOT / ERSCHL . / AGEN . 10 000 (on the left near to the group of women followers); . DARIVS . / . HET . MANCHERLAI . / VOLCK . ZV . FVES . / 300 000 / DA . AVS . ERSCHLAGEN / 12000 (on the right above Alexander); DAR / IVS . BRVEDE / OXATHR / ES. (on one of the center penants). On various penants and flags reference is made to Alexander: ALEXANDER; ALEXAND; ALE. Alexander and Darius, as we have said above, are named in the pompous panel. The sequence of letters on one of the penants situated to the right thus far remains unexplained: KHMIN A. Inventory number of the Bayerische Staatsgemäldesammlungen: 688.

The Battle of Alexander in Paris

Around 1800, during the wars, the picture was brought to Paris. The story often found in literature, that Napoleon hung the *Battle of Alexander* (which, however, was returned to Munich in 1815) in his bathroom at St. Cloud, is difficult to prove. It is more likely that the painting, if it was ever at St. Cloud, was simply stored there. In 1803 Friedrich Schlege (1772-1829) a philospher of art and culture and a literary historian and critic who was living in Paris at the time, mentions the picture as being in the restoration rooms of the Louvre.

Schlegel saw *the Battle of Alexander* through the eyes of an early romantic. He described the painting in 1803 in his Paris-edited revue *Europa*. "How can I describe the amazement which overcame me when I beheld this wondrous work. I was like one who, until that moment, had known only the light charming poetry of Italy and had taken this to be the only true poetry, someone who suddenly, quite unexpectedly, saw unfolding before his eyes the characters of Shakespeare's enchanted world. This, however, is to describe only the plenitude, the richness and the depth of Altdorfer's painting, of his poetry, and not the knightly spirit which reigns therein, so much so that one could indeed speak of it as a painting of chivalry. It portrays Alexander the Great's victory over Darius, yet in no way is it an imitation of the classical manner. He renders it rather in the poetic style of the middle Ages, as the greatest adventure of ancient chivalry. The costume is totally German and chivalric; men and steeds clad in armour and iron, the gilt or embroidered heraldic uniforms, the spikes on the steeds' foreheads, the glittering lances and stirrups, the multitude of weapons — together create a magnificence and richness beyond description. Nowhere do we find blood and horror, nor dismembered limbs and deformations. Only in the immediate foreground, on close inspection, can one discern below the hordes of cavalry charging headlong at one another, under the hooves of their steeds, several rows of corpses intertwined as in a woven cloth; as if to form the supporting tapestry for this universe of war and weapons, of glistening iron and even brighter glory and knighthood. The action is a world in itself, a small world contained in a few square feet; the hordes of soldiers rushing against each other from all sides are innumerable and infinite, and the view into the distant background also conveys this feeling of infinity. This is the sea of the world; historically inexact, perhaps, but which nevertheless embodies a true and very important allegory. Here we have the sea of the world, the lofty mountain ranges, the distant warships and the clusters of ships; and then to the left the sinking moon, to the right the rising sun; a symbol as clear as it is great, of the story protrayed... It should be noted once and for all that the meticulousness of detail in this painting, though it appears to have suffered not a little, is nonetheless such as one nerver finds in the attention given to precision in the otherwise fine paintings the old Italian School, and which is, in fact, only to be found in the high style of the old German School. What diversity, what expression, not only in the individual characters of the combatants, but also in the groups themselves; here a group of back archers surges down the mountainside with the anger of a swollen river, wave after wave pressing forward; on the other side, high up the rock a scattered band of fugitives are turning back in a narrow pass. All one can see of them are their helmets reflecting in the sun; and yet everything is so distinct even at this distance. The decisive and focal point of the composition as a whole stands out from the centre by its brilliance. Alexander and Darius are both in gleaming golden poanoplies; Alexander on Bucephalus, his lance outstretched and well ahead of his men, is giving pursuit to the fleeing Darius, whose chariot-driver has already fallen across the white steeds and who is looking back at his victor with the grief of a defeated king. If one stands far enough back from the picture so that the rest becomes indistinguishable, then this group stands out distinctly and moves the heart to an inner compassion. Through its language of colours, this small Iliad was able to teach the artist, who was reflecting on and

struggling to find great new themes, who souht perhaps to abandon the sacred domain of Catholic allergory and create a truly romantic painting, the essence and real meaning of chivalry. If other pictures of such great worth are to be found in Munich, then German artists should make a pilgrimage there as they would to Rome or Paris."[1]

Albrecht Altdorfer's *Battle of Alexander* is one of a *cycle of pictures* painted between 1528 and 1540. The commission was given by Wilhelm IV, Duke of Bavaria and his wife Jacobaea, née Margravine of Baden, to various south-German artists: *from Nuremberg* Barthel Beham (1502-1540), *from Augsburg* Jörg Breu the Elder (1474/76-1537) and Hans Burgkmair (1473-1531), from *Regensburg* Albrecht Altdorfer (c. 1480-1538), *from Ingolstadt* Melchior Feselen (c. 1495-1538), *from Munich* Abraham Schöpfer (active c. 1533) and Ludwig Refinger (c. 1510/15-1549).

The project must have started at the latest in 1527. It is astonishing that the greatest of the German painters was not included (he was active in southern Germany). Dürer died in 1528.

The cycle of at least 16 paintings portrayed the heroic deeds of men and women from the distant past, namely from Greek, Roman, Jewish and early Christian history.

Leaving aside the various conclusions of the attempts made so far to explain the cycle of pictures, it may first of all be said that the sequence of paintings should be considered in relation to the portrayal of heros frequently found at that time in the presentation rooms, which the patrons of the arts used, to profess their attatchment to the noble models and desirable ideals such as courage, valour, justice, honour, etc.

The paintings are divides into upright and oblong formats: the former portray famous heros and the latter, scenes from the lives of famous heroines. The upright formats are characterized by an aerial perspective covering a broad expanse of land with the horizon placed high in the picture, whilst in the oblong formats we find close foreground zones with a tapering perspective in the middle and background areas. It is naturally tempting to assume that the earliest dated compositions of the oblong and upright series served as models for the later paintings of the cylce. Two of the earlier pictures are also, in our opinion, the

most outstanding from an artistic point of view: Hans Burgkmair's *Story of Esther* (1528) and Albrecht Altdorfer's *Battle of Alexander* (1529). It is only a supposition that the Bavarian court historian, Aventinus (1477-1534) was called in for consultation on the scholarly aspects of the project.

It remains unknown even to the present day for which room(s) of his Munich Residence (fig. 239), including the garden buildings, Duke Wilhelm IV of Bavaria originally intended these paintings. On the basis of a description of Munich in 1565 (Samuel Quickelberg), in which mention is made of paintings executed by way of a competition for Duke Wilhelm IV's larger gardens, scholars are of the opinion that the cycle of historical paintings decorated the "summer house" in the old gardens of the Residence. Thus far this theory has been neither conclusively proven nor refuted, since there is no extant description of the building, detailed enough to give an exact idea of the aspect and dimensions of the interior. On the occasion of Emperor Charles V's ceremonial entry into Munich, the Emperor's Italian escorts described in their letters the Residency gardens and the buildings found therein. In addition to the round building which is thought to have been the summer house, they refer to a palace-like structure in the grounds which may have contained the audience chamber: it is worth considering whether or not it was for this location that the paintings were executed. A cycle of historical paintings, very similar to that commissioned by Wilhelm IV of Bavaria, is definitely known to have existed in the Munich Residence in the early 17th century, in the Emperor's Room (Kaisersaal) built in 1611. These pictures must have been painted not long before the first known mention is made of them (1613); the artist is Andrea Vicentino (born c. 1540/42 probably in Vicenza; died in 1617 in Venice). As far as the basic thematic idea is concerned there is a great correspondence between the two cycles. It may be assumed that Vicentino Cycle replaced the older one, as we know that this latter was already by 1598 no longer in its original

place of destination. The oldest authenticated inventory, dated 1598, of the Munich museum art collection mentions the pictures as belonging to the ducal museum.

The cycle of historical paintings is the oldest authenticated group of the Bayerische Staatsgemäldesammlungen — the centre-piece, as it were, of the *Alte Pinakothek*. Today, however, the complete cycle is no longer to be found at Munich. During the Thirty Years War several of the paintings were taken back to Stockholm by the Swedes and three of the upright formats are now to be found in the Stockholm National Museum. From the inventory entries we know that two further paintings belonging to the cycle are now lost.

Certain paintings in the cycle bear the arms of Wilhelm IV, either alone or along with his wife's, as a sign of the ducal commission. Others have no heraldic markings, and among these we find *The Battle of Alexander*.

The series of pictures comprised, as far as we know, the following, sixteen paintings:

Upright Format Panels (1-8):

1) ALBRECHT ALTDORFER: Alexander the Great defeats the Persian king, Darius, at the Battle of Issus (333 B.C.) *(The Battle of Alexander)*. Signed and dated 1529.

Lindenwood, 158,4×120,3 cm. the surface of the picture has been cut off on all sides. Bayerische Staatsgemäldesammlungen. Inv. No. 688 (Munich, *Alte Pinakothek)*.

2) JÖRG BREU THE ELDER: Publius Cornelius Scipio defeats Hannibal at the Battle of Zama (202 B.C.). Signed. Painted aroud 1530.

The personage of Publius Cornelius Scipio: Publius Cornelius Scipio Africanus (235-183 B.C.) already figured in Antiquity among the heros due to his oustanding exploits and personality. He was a Roman army leader and son of the general, Publius Cornelius Scipio (212), who was defeated by Hannibal at Ticinus, although he had won several victories over the Carthaginians. He participated in the Battles of Ticinus and Cannae. As Proconsul he received the supreme command of Spain in 211 and suceeded in keeping the Carthaginians out of the country until 206. Despite opposition from the Senate, he crossed from Sicily into Africa and there gained a decisive victory over Hannibal at Zama in 202.

Pinewood, 162×120,8 cm. The surface of the picture has been cut off at the top and on both sides, only the bottom edge remains intact.

Bayerische Staatsgemäldesammlungen. Inv. No. 8 (Munich, *Alte Pinakothek)*.

3) HANS BURGKMAIR: Hannibal defeats the Romans at the Battle of Cannae (202 B.C.) Signed and dated 1529.

The personage of Hannibal: Hannibal (247/46-183 B.C.), widely recognised in Antiquity as a genius of generalship, was a Carthaginian army leader. He was still only a child when, under the orders of his father, Hamilcar Barcas, he swore his undying hatred for Rome. His entire life bore the imprint of the arduous battles waged between Rome and Carthage. At the age of nine he left with his father for the theatre of war in Spain where in 221 he assumed supreme military command. It was essentially by his doing that Carthage consolidated its power in Spain. In 219 (the capture and destruction of Saguntum), he disregarded the treaty concluded several years beforehand between Carthage and Rome by which Carthage was forbidden to engage in hostilities against cities allied to Rome. In 218 Hannibal crossed over the River Ebro with large forces, which was also forbidden by the terms of the treaty. As Hannibal's surrender, provided for in the treaty, was not forthcoming, Rome declared war (the Seconde Punic War). With the intention of waging war not in Spain but in Italy itself, Hannibal immediately interrupted his actions in northern Spain and that same year crossed the Pyrenees with a large army (infantry, cavalry and elephants), through Gaul, over the Alps into northern Italy. In Gaul, Publius Cornelius Scipio was unable to check his advance and the loss of life was considerable. Leaving Bologna he crossed the Apennines and the marshlands of the Arno in 217. Following the battles at Lake Trasimenus he invaded north Apulia with the intention of freeing Italy from Roman rule. At the time, Hannibal's adversary was the Roman dictator, Quintus Fabius Maximus Cunctator: by means of cautious delaying tactics and by avoiding full-scale confrontation he was able to thwart Hannibal's plans for a swift conquest in their early stages. For Rome, however, such tactics were not sufficiently spectacular, since they brought no news of victory. When the dictator's term of office expired the two consuls, Lucius Aemilius Paullus and Gaius Terentius Varro, were appointed to the head of the Roman army. The opposing armies met on the River Aufidus (now called the Ofanto), near to the Apulian city of Cannae (now known as Canne). Here the overpowered Roman troops were surrounded and decimated by Hannibal. Despite their heavy defeat, Rome refused to negotiate. The much feared seige of Rome, however, did not take place. Hannibal, who was summoned back, to Carthage in 203, was overcome by the Romans under the leadership of P. Cornelius Scipio at Zama in 202 B.C.. In 183 Hannibal put an end to his life in Libya.

Pinewood, 162×121,5 cm. The surface of the picture has been cut off at the top and on both sides, only the bottom edge remains intact.

Bayerische Staatsgemäldesammlungen. Inv. No. 5328 Munich, *Alte Pinakothek)*.

4) MELCHIOR FESELEN: Julius Caesar beseiges the city of Alesia (52 B.C.) Signed and dated 1533. (fig. 242).

The personage of Caesar: Gaius Julius Caesar (100-44 B.C.), general, statesman, orator and author, descended from the old Roman patrician family of Julia. Since the time of Augustus, Caesar's adoptive son, the title of "Caesar", which formerly had been used only as a nickname by Julia's patrician family, was added to the names of the Roman Emperors (from this derive the titles of "Kaiser" and "Zar"). From the Middle Ages the memory of Caesar has survived in chronicles and fictitious accounts as being the first Roman emperor, a general,

257

world-conqueror and hero. He stands as the symbol of noble virtue and valour. It was as Quaestor that Caesar began his real political career in 68. He became Aedile in 65. In 63 he went on to be elected president of the Priests College (Pontifex Maximus), with the support of Marcus Licinius Crassus and the city's populace. After a year spent as consul (59), Caesar became governor of Dalmatia, Gallia Cisalpina and Gallia Narbonensis. Between 58 and 51 he subjugated the rest of Gaul. Among his adversaires were Ariovist and Vercingetorix, the latter of whom he defeated in 52 during the siege of Alesia. He gives his own account of the Gaulish battles in his book *De Bello Gallico*. After defeating the last of his enemies in Africa in 46 and in Spain in 45, he became emperor and dictator until the end of his life. He was murdered by the two conspirators, Marcus Brutus and Caius Cassius, on the Ides of March in 44 B.C..

Pinewood, 162×121,5 cm. Upper border of the picture has been cut off.

Bayerische Staatsgemäldesammlungen. Inv. No. 686 (Munich, Alte Pinakothek).

5) LUDWIG REFINGER: Horatius Cocles defending the Tiber Bridge (507 B.C.) Dated 1537.

The personage of Horatius Cocles: Horatius Cocles, the One-eyed, is a heroic figure of the Roman history legend, the famous example of Roman *virtus*. In 507 B.C. he had defended single-handed the right-bank Tiber Bridge in Rome against the troops of the Etruscan king, Porsenna. The latter had wanted to lend aid to the expelled Roman King Tarquinius Superbus in his plans to return to Rome. The downfall of Tarquinius Superbus and the expulsion of his family had been brought about by the outrage committed by his son against Lucretia, the wife of his nephew, Tarquinius Collatinus. After their expulsion from Rome the

239 - The Residence of William IV, Duke of Bavaria
Nikolaus Meldeman - 1530
Munich, Alte Pinakothek.

Republic was proclaimed. Horatius Cocles along with Mucius Scaevola and Cloelia are said to have defended the Republic against Porsenna. Livius *(Ab urba condita.* II, 10), amongst others, describes the heroic exploit of Horatius Cocles in his famous legend: this man fought alone on the bridge against several enemies until the bridge could finally be destroyed behind him. The Etruscans thus found that their entry to the city had been cut off. At the last moment Horatius Cocles saved himself by jumping into the Tiber, fully clad in armour. According to Livius' account he reach-

ed the bank alive.

Lindenwood, 161,7×114,7 cm. The top border has been cut off.

Stockholm, National Museum. Inv. No. NM 294.

6) LUDWIG REFINGER: Titus Manlius Torquatus defeats a Gaul in single combat (360 B.C.)

The Personage of Titus Manlius Torquatus: Titus

240 - Wilhelm IV, Duke of Bavaria and Jacaboea von Baeden, Duchess of Bavaria - Munich, Alte Pinakothek.

Manlius Torquatus (4th cent. B.C.) descended from the Roman patrician family of Manlius, who saw its golden age during the first six decades of the 4th century B.C.. Titus Manlius Imperiosus was the most famous bearer of the family name and had earned his surname "Torquatus" on account of the necklace he had won in single combat against a Gaul. Titus Manlius Imperiosus Torquatus was considered as the exemplum of Roman severity and the following events have been handed down to better illustrate this character trait: the courageous plea he made on behalf of his father before the People's Tribune, Pomponius, in 363; his single combat against a Gaul of much greater stature than himself in front of the gates of Rome in 360; his severity, even with regard to his own son, whom he had executed for having fought the enemy without orders, even though he was victorious.

Pinewood, 160,8 × 109 cm. Right, left and upper edges cut off.

Stockholm, National Museum. Inv. No. NM 296.

7) LUDWIG REFINGER: Marcus Curtius sacrifices himself for the Roman people. (362 B.D.) Dated 1540.

The personage of Marcus Curtius: Marcus Curtius is a hero from the Roman history legend. The incident recounted in the legend is said to have happened in 362 B.C.. Livius also gives us his account of it *(Ab urbe condita*. VII, 6) "It is said that in the same year the market place (Forum Romanum), through an immense fissure in its middle, caused either by an earthquake or some other violent cause, sank down into a bottomless pit. And it was impossible to fill up the abyss with the earth brought there for that purpose until, heeding the counsel of the gods, the search was undertaken to find the true strength of the Roman people. For this, prophesied the seers, should be consecrated to this place, if they wished the Roman community to continue. Whereupon it is said that Marcius Curtius, a youth who had distinguished himself at war, reproached the sceptics and asked if the Romans had ever had a greater good than their weapons and courage. When all had fallen silent, he looked towards the temples of the immortal gods, built above the Forum, stretched out his hands to the heavens and then to the yawning abyss and the gods of the underworld, and consecrated himself to death. He mounted his jewelled steed and plunged armed into the abyss. Gifts and fruits of the earth were thrown after him by a multitude of men and women".

Lindenwood, 162,4 × 123,1 cm. The surface of the picture has been cut off on the top and sides, only the lower border

has been preserved intact.

Bayerische Staatsgemäldesammlungen. Inv. No. 687 (Munich, *Alte Pinakothek)*

8) ABRAHAM SCHÖPFER: Mucius Scaevola stretches his hand into the fire as a sign of courage, in front of the Etruscan king Porsenna (507 B.C.). Signed and dated 1533.

The personage of Mucius Scaevola: Gaius Mucuis Scaevola is a hero from the Roman history legend. Gaius Mucius Cordus, who later received the surname Scaevola (the left-handed), is said to have made an attempt on the life of the Etruscan King, Porsenna, in 507 B.C.; Porsenna was at the time at war against Rome. By mistake, however, he killed the king's scribe and later at his trial revealed to Porsenna his real but unfulfilled intention. As proof of his fearless love for his fatherland, which would not let him shrink from trying yet again to kill Porsenna, he thrust his right hand into the altar flames. Porsenna showed great admiration for this heroic act, released the culprit and ended his heroic act, released the culprit and ended his seige of Rome. Livius, among other authors, has given an account of this event *(Ab urbe condita*. II, 12).

Lindenwood, 156,9 × 119,7 cm. The upper border has been cut off.

Stockholm, National Museum, Inv. No. NM 295.

The Oblong-Format Panels (9-14)

9) BARTHEL BEHAM: Empress Helena finds the holy cross and has it put to the proof by Bishop Makarios. (Early 4th century A.D.). Signed and dated 1530 (fig. 241).

The personage of Helena: Helena (c. 257 - c. 330) (Flavia Julia Helena) is a Christian heroine. According to varying traditions, she is said to have been of either low birth or royal stock. She bore a son, Constantine, to the future Caesar Constantius. In 312 she converted to Christianity, and since the end of the 4th century, legend has it that she found the Holy Cross the Holy titulus, the nails and the crosses of the two robbers. She set up numerous churches in the Holy Land, including the Church at Mount Olive in Jerusalem. Her name is also linked with the memorials for the Martyrs of the Thebes Legion in Cologne, Bonn and Xanten, as well as the transferal of the relics of Apostle Matthew and Saint Rock to Trier. She died in Rome or in Nicomedia. She was first buried in Rome but Constantine brought her remains to Constantinople. In the 9th century her remains arrived in Haut-villiers (Reims diocese) and since the French Revolution they are to be found in Paris, at St. Leu, except for the head which lies at Trier.

Pinewood, 101,1 × 149,8 cm. The surface of the picture has been cut off on all sides.

Bayerische Staatsgemäldesammlungen. Inv. No. 684 (Munich, *Alte Pinakothek*).

Bayerische Staatsgemäldesammlungen. Inv. No. 7969 (Munich, *Alte Pinakothek*).

10) JÖRG BREU THE ELDER: Lucretia stabs herself to death after having been dishonoured (508 B.C.). Signed and dated 1528.

The personage of Lucretia: Lucretia is a Roman heroine, whose legend has in fact a real historical basis. The story is said to have occurred at Collatia near Rome in 508 B.C. and is recounted by several authors including Livius (*Ab urbe condita* I, 57-59). — Lucretia was the wife of Lucius Tarquinus Collatinus, who in about 508 B.C. took part in the seige of Ardea undertaken by his uncle, the last Roman king Tarquinius Superbus. During a banquet attended by the royal princes and their cousin, Lucius Tarquinus Collatinus, a dispute arose concerning the virtuousness of their wives. Lucius Tarquinius Collatinus set his wife, Lucretia, above all other women and suggested that his claim be put to the test by rendering her an unexpected visit there and then. The company hastened to Rome and on to Collatia; the outcome of the wager fell in Lucretia's favour. The beauty and acclaimed virtue of this woman aroused Sextus Tarquinius and he sought to possess her by force. Unknown to Lucretia's husband, he returned to Collatia several days later. He abused the hospitality accorded to him and at night he forced his way into her chamber and threatened to kill her if she did not surrender to him. She staunchly refused his demand, whereupon he tried to achieve his ends by threatening to ruin her reputation: should she still refuse to give herself, he would kill not only her but also her slave, whom he would then place unclothed in the conjugal bed. He would spread the news that he had caught her by surprise in shameful adultery and slain them for this reason."... this threat overcame her virtue" (Livius). — Lucretia immediately demanded that her father and husband avenge her. Everyone consoled the desperate woman. They recognized her blamelessness since she had been forced. "I free myself of my sin", said Lucretia "but I cannot escape the punishment. Never shall an unchaste woman keep her life by Lucretia's example." She then plunged a dagger into her heart. Vengeance was sworn over her dead body and the overthrow of the royal house was called for.

Pinewood, 103,5 × 148,5 cm. The surface of the picture has been cut off on the upper and lower edges, the right and left sides remain intact.

11) HANS BURGKMAIR: Queen Esther intercedes before her husband, King Ahasuerus, for the deliverance of the Jews in their kingdom (c. 500 B.C.). Signed and dated 1528.

The Personage of Esther: Esther is a heroine of the Old Testament (Book of Esther, chap. 1-10, 3). Esther became the wife of the great Persian King Xerxes I, a descendant of the House of Achaemenides, and who is known as Ahasuerus in the Old Testament, after he had divorced Vasthi. Ahasuerus/Xerxes I (c. 519-465; reigned from 486) is, among other things, known for his campaign against Greece which ended in defeat at Salamis ("The Persian Wars"). According to the Old Testament, Esther was made queen by King Ahasuerus without her having revealed her Jewish origins. Haman, one of the King's closest attendants, had ordered that all the Jews in Ahasuerus's Kingdom be put to death. He had reacted with indignation as the Jew Mardochai had refused to kneel to him in respect. Mardochai, the Queen's foster father, had in the past foiled an attempt on the King's life, which had been plotted by Bagathan and Thares. He asked Esther to intercede before the King in order to spare the Jews living in the kingdom. Esther presented herself to the King unannounced, which was strictly forbidden, and much to her surprise was received. She expressed the desire that the King dine at her house the following day with Haman. At the meal she did not voice her real request but only repeated the invitation for the next day. Just before the following meal Haman, at his wife's demand, had a scaffold built for Mardochai as the latter had refused to show him due respect. Meanwhile the King had remembered that Mardochai has once saved his life and was informing himself on how Mardochai had been repaid. As this matter had been neglected, he ordered that the latter should now receive his due reward. He called Haman to him to discuss the affair. Haman was asked in what way the King could favour a man with his good will. Haman presuming that the honoured man was himself, recommended to the King that "the man to be honoured should be given royal clothes accustomedly worn by the King, a steed mounted by the King and a royal crown should be placed on his head, and such clothes and such a horse should be presented by the hands of a prince and the man should ride through the city on horseback... The King said to Haman: Go quickly and take the clothes and horse as you have said and give them to Mardochai the Jew, who is sitting before the King's door; and do not fail to accomplish all that you have recommended..." Deeply offended, Haman executed the King's command and hurried to the meal. Once again, the King asked Esther what she desired. She then revealed why she had craved the grace of the King's hearing: that her persecuted people be spared. Ahasuerus immediately passed the death sentence on Haman, to be carried out on the very scaffold that Haman had built for Mardochai. Mardochai was then appointed as Haman's successor.

Pinewood, 103 × 156,3 cm. Tfhe upper and lower borders of picture have been cut off, only the right and left sides remain intact.

Bayrische Staatsgemäldesammlungen. Inv. No. 689 (Munich, *Alte Pinakothek).*

12) MELCHIOR FESELEN: Cloelia and the other Roman women held as hostages were freed because of their courage (508 B.C.). Signed and dated 1529.

The personage of Cloelia: Cloelia is a heroine from the Roman history legend at the time when Rome was under seige by the Etruscan King Porsenna in 508 B.C.. Following the description of Mucius Scaevola's heroic exploit, Livius recounts (Ab urbe condita. II, 13): "After his deed had been so honoured, the women also were moved in their desire to serve the state. Among the hostages that Rome had been forced to surrender as a pledge for the safe departure of the Etruscan soldiers who had been laying seige to the Gianicolo was the young Cloelia. When the Etruscan army neared the Tiber, she duped the guards and swam across the river at the head of the maidens, under the enemy's arrows. Safe and sound they were taken to Rome back to their families. At first the King was enraged on hearing the news and sent ambassadors to Rome, demanding that the hostage Cloelia be returned. He was not concerned with the rest of the girls. Soon, however, he came to admire his act even more than the deeds of Cocles and Mucius. He categorically stated: should the hostage not be delivered he would regard the peace as being broken. But should she return, he would send her back unharmed to her family. Both sides kept their promise. The Romans delivered Cloelia as a gage of peace. The Etruscan king assured not only her safe conduct

241 - The Story of the Empress Helen - Barthel Beham - 1530
Oil on wood - 1011×1498 mm - Munich, Alte Pinakothek.

but also paid tribute to her courage. He praised the girl highly and gave her some of the hostages as a gift. Peace was thus reestablished. Such bravery was new in a girl, and as a token of their esteem the Romans rewarded her with an equestrian statue..." In addition to Livius, other classical writers also speak of this heroic deed.

Lindenwood, 103,3 × 167,6 cm. The surface of the picture has been cut off at the top and on both sides, only the lower edge remains intact.

Bayerische Staatsgemäldesammlungen. Inv. No. 13 (Munich, *Alte Pinakothek).*

13) HANS SCHÖPFER: Virginia is stabbed to preserve her honour (c. 450 B.C.). Signed and dated 1535.

The Personage of Virginia: Virginia is a heroine of the Roman history legend, who is said to have lived towards the middle of the 5th century B.C. Apart from Livius (*Ab urbe condita.* III, 44 ff) other classical authors have also recounted the story of Virginia, who descended from a rich plebian family. — Because of her beauty and youth she had aroused the attention of Appius Claudius Crassus Inregillensis Sabinus, Decemvir between 451 and 449 and opponent of the plebians. As he was not able to win Virginia by legal means, he tried to take her by force. He took advantage of the absence of her father, Lucius Verginius, who was on military service at the time, and declared that Virginia had been born a slave and that Virginius's paternity had been falsely attributed to her. Following this, Marcus Claudius, a client of the Decemvir, claimed her as his slave. When Virginia was on her way to school he accosted her and ordered her to follow him. The people rose up in revolt at this procedure and immediately exacted a trial which was in progress when Lucius Verginius was summoned the next day. Appius Claudius was president and decided in his client's favour. Virginius asked to speak with his daughter and took advantage of the interview to kill her, for he wanted to preserve her honour and save her from the pursuits of Appius Claudius. Her death lead the army to revolt and Appius Claudius and the other people's tribunes were withdrawn from their functions.

Pinewood, 94,7 × 167,8 cm. The upper and lower borders of the picture have been cut off.

Bayerische Staatsgemäldesammlungen. Inv. No. 13099 (Munich, *Alte Pinakothek).*

14) HANS SCHÖPFER: Susanna repells the lustful old men and remains innocent. Dated 1537.

The Personage of Susanna: Susanna, whose story is found in the apocryphal appendix to the Old Testament Book of Daniel (chap. XIII, I ff), was the beautiful and pious wife of the rich Babylonian Jew Joachim. As he was well esteemed, the Jews met together daily at his house and amongst these, two old men who served as judges. At midday when the crowd had departed, Susanna would visit her husband's park. Each day the two old men would see her leave and were consumed with love for her. Although at first they did not confide their desire to each other, they met by chance in the park, lying in wait at the same place and so confessed the reason for their unusual behavour. They decided from then on to leave together as soon as Susanna left unaccompanied for the park. One very hot day the opportunity presented itself. Susanna had just ordered her two servants to fetch oils and ointments as she wished to take her bath in the park. The servants had scarcely left, when the tow old men came out of their hiding place, threw themselves on Susanna and attempted to rape her. But she told them "I know, if I do this, I am vowed to die, and if I do not do this, there is no escape from your hands; but it is better not to do this and fall into your hands than to sin in the eyes of the Lord". At this the old men gathered the people around them and accused Susanna in a slanderous fashion of having committed adultery under their eyes. Only by the intervention of the youth Daniel was the injustice revealed. The two old men were found guilty and finally lapidated.

Lindenwood, 100,8 × 149,9 cm. The upper and lower borders of the picture have been cut off.

Bayerische Staatsgemäldesammlungen. Inv. No. 7775 (Munich, *Alte Pinakothek).*

The Missing Pictures (15 and 16):

According to an inventory of 1598 it would appear that two pictures (today missing), representing:

15) the Queen of Saba and

16) Judith and Holofernes,

must also be considered as having belonged to the cycle.

The Patrons

Duke Wilhelm IV of Bavaria (Bavaria-Munich), nicknamed "the teadfast", was born in Munich on 13th November 1493 and died there on 7th March 1550 (fig. 240).

He was the fourth child and eldest son of Duke Albrecht IV of Bavaria and his wife Kunigunde of Austria, daughter of Emperor Friedrich III and sister of Emperor Maximilian I. Among the seven children there were two brothers: Ludwig (b. 1495) and Ernst (b. 1500). According to the law of primogeneture introduced by his father, Wilhelm took over the government which was directed by a Regency Council until 1511, when he reached his eighteenth year and majority. From 1516, after protest from his younger brother Ludwig who had strong political support, he shared his rule with the latter until Ludwig's death in 1545 and from then on he ruled alone.

"Albrecht IV's law of primogeneture and thereby the internal cohesion of the state were put to severe test during the years prior to 1516. During the political strife of these years the unity of the state was to be reestablished and refortified. Wilhelm IV's relationship with his younger brother Ludwig and with the provincial diets evolved amidst eventful struggle and let to a state of affairs which was to prove a sound and durable basis for the following decade. The political and religious crises which Bavaria came up against from 1519 did not succeed in shaking this foundation during the reign of Wilhelm IV. The many-sided and risky nature of Bavarian politics at the time of the Reformation presupposed the stability and continuity of the internal structure which had been achieved with great effort during the troubles of the eight years following the death of Albrecht IV..."[2]

One of the most important counsellors of Wilhelm IV was Leonhard von Eck, an opponent of the Reformation, as was the Professor Johann Eck from Ingolstädt.

After his father's death — Wilhelm was only fifteen years old at the time — he no longer followed any regular education. His great passion was jousting: between 1510 and 1518 he fought in thirty one jousts. His political ambition was pronounced: He lived with the idea that the Wittelsbachs, the Carolingians and the Agilofingians were of one and the same lineage. This meant that he considered his family to be much more distinguished and ancient than the Hapsburgs. At the end of the twenties it was hoped that the royal election would fall in favour of the Wittelsbachs. (We shall not here go in the armed conflicts in which Wilhelm IV participated).

At the beginning of his rule Wilhelm IV had the reputation of living a life of debauchery. Despite his somewhat clumsy manner in dealing with others at this time, his intelligence was later to come to light. He is even said to have been the most eloquent speaker among the German princes.

In 1522 he married Jacobaea Maria of Baden, the eldest daughter of Margrave Philip of Baden and his wife Elizabeth, daughter of Philip I, Elector of the Palatinate. She was born on 22nd June 1507 and died on 16th November 1580 in Munich. The marriage bore four children:
— Theodo, b. 1526; betrothed to Anna, the daughter of the emperor, Ferdinand I, in 1533; died in 1534.
— Albrecht V, b. 1528; betrothed in 1535 to Maria, daughter of Ferdinand I. (however, she married Duke Wilhelm of Cleves eleven years later); married Anna, daughter of Emperor Ferdinand I in 1546 (who previously was betrothed to: 1) 1533 Theodor of Bavaria, 1534; 2) 1534 Charles of Orléans, son of King François I of France); died 1579.

— Wilhelm, b. 1529, died 1530.
— Mechtilde, b. 1532; betrothed in 1551 to Duke Philipp Magnus of Brunswick, who died two years later; betrothed in 1556 to Margrave Philibert of Baden, whom she married in 1557.

Wilhelm IV also had a natural son (Johann Georg Dux von Hegnenberg who in 1525 took part in the Battle of Pavia; died 1596).

Wilhelm IV was an ardent enemy of the Reformation. He called the Jesuits into Bavaria but during his rule the Societas Jesus was unable to implant itself. The Peasant War did not have much importance in Wilhelm IV's territory.

242 - The Siege of Alesia - Melchior Feselen
Oil on wood - 1620×1212 mm - Munich, Alte Pinakothek.

243 - Saint Mary Magdalen at Christ's Tomb - A. Altdorfer
Oil on limewood - 650×429 mm - Munich, Alte Pinakothek.

Wilhelm IV and Court Art

"Until the end of the 16th century the residence of the Munich dukes had been the Old Palace. Wilhelm IV was the first to move into the "Neuveste" which now gained importance as the seat of the fortified principality and which was developed accordingly. It should not be forgotten in this context that the Italian Renaissance was introducing new forms of Christian art which found a favorable reception at Munich.

"In the person of Wilhelm IV came a ruler who, apart from the fact that he was to rule over the entire Duchy of Bavaria, had received an excellent humanist education for the times: with him the Renaissance made its entry into Munich. The princes Wilhelm, Ludwig and Ernst were educated at Burghausen, Munich and Landshut by the tutor Aventius who had acquired his learning in the first universities of the time and who was to become the leading historian of Bavaria.

"The influence of Wilhelm's humanist education may be felt in his first artistic undertaking, the creation of the rosegarden and his summer house on the east side of the Neuveste. The garden was screened off from its surroundings by a circular wall and was linked by a bridge to the Neuveste. It was laid out with hedges, pergolas, mazes and water basins, with a polygonal, two-storeyed summer house in the centre. On the ground floor of the house, in a columned room with painted vaulting, there was a bronze fountain with numerous statues. Unfortunately, the name of the designer responsible for this first important layout of the Wittelsbach gardens, which must have cost four thousand ducats, is unknown. This is all the more regrettable as the arrangement was admired by all the visitors, including Emperor Charles V."

"Samuel Quickelberg again wrote in 1565...: "I should not like to fail to inform the best art lovers of the special liking that Wilhelm IV of Bavaria, the extremely discerning father of Duke Albrecht, showed for fine paintings. For he had the best German artists paint certain pictures, that is to say the most wonderful creations of their art, in a well reputed art contest for his larger Munich gardens, giving to each one of the artists the dimensions of the pictures... And his love of great arts has been transmitted to his sons and grandsons."

"The paintings referred to by Quickelberg concern a series of twice eight pictures, examples of masculine and feminine virtue in the humanist style and manner, based on the deeds of women and men from the Old Testament and Antiquity. It is still unknown to this day if these paintings were, in fact, intended for the first floor of the summer house or for another room in the Neuveste. The design of Wilhelm IV's summer house has already been attributed to

Albrecht Altdorfer who, as is well known, was the city architect at Regensburg. The ultimate decisions concerning building at the Munich Court seems, however, to have lain in the hands of the court architect, Leonhard Halder, who descended from an old local family of stonemasons. He had been working at the Munich court since 1518. In 1538, he was appointed architect to the Duke for the rest of his life... Under Halder's direction was constructed on the east side of the Neuveste the round-roomed building, the so-called *Rundstubenbau* a two-storeyed wing in the style of a *palazzo*, built onto the south bastion of the Neuveste. This provided the living space needed for the court to be transferred from the Old Palace. Halder's most important work inside the Neuveste was perhaps St. George's Chapel, which needed enlarging because of the court's increasing size. The chapel, consecrated in 1540, now extended beyond the limits of the old outer courtyard and had a straight eastern wall and galleries on three sides. It was, in fact, to judge by the miniatures of Hans Mielich (1516-1573), still basically a chapel in the medieval style... This is all the more remarkable as in other respects Wilhelm IV was manifestly interested in the Renaissance. One should not overlook the fact that up to the middle of the 16th century, "architecture" — not only at Munich — was to a great extent the concern of master craftsmen who had come from the traditional craft of stonemasons. Or was it intentionally that the palace chapel of the Duke, who since 1522 had become the champion of the Counter Reformation, was built in the conventional style? The chapels of protestant castles built at about the same time took their inspiration much more from contemporary Italian architecture and its theories. Our image of the court art of Wilhelm IV is defined to a large extent and in line with the German Renaissance as a whole, in terms of painting and small objets d'art. In the sculpture of the twenties preference was also given to small formats, especially mannered statuettes and reliefs. One of the leading artists in this domain was Friedrich Hagenauer who in 1525 arrived from the Middle Rhine at Munich, where he stayed for two years. From about 1522/25 to 1535/40 the sculptor Loy Hering executed for Wilhelm's Court a series of six square bas-reliefs out of Jura limestone, one of which represented the bust of Duchess Jakobäa of Baden and the five others with feminine figures bearing coats of arms in decorated borders... Besides his work for Wilhelm's history gallery, Barthel Beham worked above all as a painter. From 1530-1535 he executed for Wilhem IV a series of ducal portraits, continuing in a certain manner the series of portraits by Wertinger..."[3]

The MOTTOS of the ducal pair read:
Wilhlem IV: I have him in my heart
Jacobaea: My heart is entirely yours.
These wordings appear, for example, on the back of the diptych of the portraits of Wilhelm and Jacobea, painted by

Hans Wertinger (1465/70-1533) — (Alte Pinakothek) — and a wooden dowelled chest (Munich, Bayerisches Nationalmuseum) with richly engraved ivory inlays of Italian ornamental art, executed in 1530/40.

Jacobaea's wedding chest has also been conserved. The work which dated from c. 1522 was executed by master craftsmen from northern Italy or south Tyrol. The marquetry is in different kinds of wood: maple, walnut, oak, spruce and plum. On the sides there are representations in perspective of open cupboards and musical instruments, games and utensils (Munich, Bayerisches Nationalmuseum).

Several illuminated manuscripts also testify to the artistic activities at the Court of Wilhelm IV and Jacobaea: the marriage prayerbook (Pommersfelden), the garment book and the tournament book (Munich, Bayerische Staatsbibliothek), the choirbook (Wolfenbüttel; this is the oldest of at least 25 authenticated choirbooks of Wilhelm IV).

The inventory of Jacobaea's estate drawn up in 1580/81 enumerates, along with a great number of everyday objects, many artistic items, unidentifiable with any conserved object.

A momento of the death of Duke Wilhelm IV of Bavaria (Munich, Bayerisches Nationalmuseum) shows a portrait of the dead man and mentions in a short accompanying text the last words exchanged by the couple, which lead to believe that Wilhelm's death was a sudden one: "... my honoured wife / said: Sire, ye fall / yet die as a de / vout Christian, his Princeship / replied, yes / that was his honour's: last word."

"The mention of the Duke's last words at the very moment of his sudden death is all the more important and all the better done, as the dying man's wish for a Christian end stood in a lieu of the last sacraments."[4]

Aventinus, the presumed author of the Historical Cycle

"Johannes Turmair was born on 4th July 1477 at Abensberg in Bavaria; it was from the original latin placename, Aventinum (fig. 245) that he took his name Aventinus. After studying at Ingolstadt, Vienna, Cracow and Paris universities, he returned to Ingolstadt in 1507, became the private tutor to the princes Ludwig and Ernst of Bavaria in 1509 and accompanied the latter on an educational voyage to Italy in 1515. In 1517 Wilhelm IV, Ludwig X ans their brother Ernst commissioned him to write the history of Bavaria. He himself describes how he crossed the Bavarian provinces on horseback, bearing letters of recommendation from the Court, in order to gather and study useful historical source material for his work.

"Unlike the compilations of the Middle Ages, Aventinus began "a work of thorough research and active deepening of the general history in which we are all still implicated today" (Ranke) and through this he earned the nickname of a "Father of Modern Historiography". He translated his

Annales Bojorum from 1522 onwards into an original and forceful German, much like the language used by Luther. An extract of this Bavarian Chronicle appeared in Nuremberg in the same year. By 1533 the work, which began with an account of bibical events, was completed. For Aventinus classical history is linked to the history of Bavaria since the people originating in the region of the lower Danube were considered to be Bavarians *(Bojer)*. Owing to his relations with the protestants, Aventinus was imprisoned in 1528 but with the help of the Bavarian chancellor Leonhard von Eck he was soon released. From then on he lived in Abensberg and Regensburg, where he died on 9th January 1534.

"*The Annales Bojorum* and their German translation appeared for the first time in their full edition in 1553."[5]

A few remarks on the life and work of Albrecht Altdorfer

By 1529, the year in which he created *the Battle of Alexander,* Albrecht Altdorfer had already painted numerous important works commissioned both by the church and the laity, for example:
— the great altarpiece for the Augustinian Monastery at St. Florian (near Linz in Austria) for which the final date of execution is mentioned on the predella as being 1518 (St. Florian and Vienna);
— the wings of a small altar (painted in the 1520's) with scenes from the legend of St. Florian, either for the above-mentioned monastery or for St. John's Church at St. Florian (FLorence, Nuremberg, Prague and formerly Berlin);
— single panels of large format: the three pictures of the *Crucifixion* (Cassel) the two figures of John (Regensburg) painted around 1510, and the representation of the *Nativity of the Virgin* painted ten years later for an ecclesiastical building (Munich, Alte Pinakothek);
— small format pictures: in 1510 *St. George in the deciduous forest* and in the 1520's *Danube landscape* with Wörth Castle, near Regensburg (fig. 234) the oldest conserved landscape in oils (both paintings in Munich, Alte Pinakothek).

If the construction of the church's interior in the painting of the *Nativity of the Virgin* already shows the masterly use of space, then the picture of *Susanna bathing* painted three years before *the Battle of Alexander* (Munich, *Alte Pinakothek)* represents the coming to terms with the landscape's volume as a perfectly solved artistic assignment.

Altdorfer's vision of the cosmos in the *Battle of Alexander* appears as a logical development of the ideas already present in his previous works, both regarding the volume and landscape and also the figures interwoven therein. In Altdorfer's work the motif of *contre-jour,* mentioned above, which at the same time dazzles and yet attracts the spectator, is often found. Here we shall only mention the painting of *Saint Magdalene at Christ's Tomb* (Munich, *Alte Pinakothek)* (fig. 243) dated about 1525: the eye is directed from the tomb's obscurity towards the brightly lit landscape. The sun itself is shining over the horizon.

Altdorfer's vision of the infinite in landscape and sky is overwhelming and does not seem to depend on any precursor. But the correlation with Leonardo da Vinci (1452-1519) in the representation of landscapes which extend into the cosmic is remarkable (cf. Leonardo's brillant study (Windsor) for the painting of Anna-Selbdritt (Paris), c. 1510.

When he participated in the realisation of the History Cycle for Duke Wilhelm IV of Bavaria, Altdorfer already had a great deal of experience in "teamwork": he belonged, like Dürer, to the group of artists engaged by Emperor Maximilian I to illustrate his prayerbook in 1515 and to execute the monument for his posterity (wood carvings of the Triumphal Arch in 1515 and the triumphal porocession in 1526).

There also exist several battle scenes in German painting from before 1529. Certainly a contemporary event, the Battle of Pavia in 1525, greatly contributed to making this theme a topical subject (1529: painting by Rupert Heller (active c. 1530) (Stockhlom); c. 1530: drawing by Wolf Huber (c. 1485-1553) (Munich).

As mentioned above, the artist did not portray classical subjects in a historically exact manner, but rather as a contemporary event. Friedrich Schlegel (cf. above) was the first to recognize this fact.

It is tempting to compare Altdorfer's *Battle of Alexander* to the most famous *classical representation of the Battle of Issus* (fig. 237). Philogenes of Eretria (active c. 300 B.C.) is known to have painted a picture of the battle between Alexander and Darius for King Cassandros (306/297). The mosaic of a battle of Alexander (Naples, National Museum), dated 2nd/2nd century, for the Satyr House in Pompeii is probably a copy of the painting by Philogenes of Eretria. As in a relief, the characters of the wide-angled scene are represented as large foreground figures. The centre and background constitute the second "plane" in much smaller proportion. The army is suggested by countless lance bearers. The decisive detail of the battle is seen close up: here the situation is being decided dramatically in Alexander's favour. Coming from the left into the heart of the battle, he is forcing the war chariot in which Darius is standing into rapid flight. In this picture also, Darius is looking backwards at his conqueror recognizing the hopelessness of his destiny. A single tree serve to suggest the landscape in this painting.

244 - Miniature from the Book of Obligations of the City of Regensburg - Hans Muelich 410×275 mm - Regensburg, Stadtarchiv.

The enormous importance of the landscape in Altdorfer's painting becomes all too clear in this comparison: he sees the decisive outcome of this world-important battle the representatives of the Occident and the Orient in a cosmic setting.

Chronological Summary of Altdorfer's Life

Painter, draftsman for woodcuts, engraver, printmaker and architect. Born in 1480, probably in Regensburg.

Nothing is known of his artistic background. In 1505 he obtained the citizenship of Regensburg and is listed as coming "from Amberg". In 1512/1513 he was already taking part in the artistic projects of Emperor Maximilian I. He bought a house in Regensburg in 1530. In 1517 we find him member of the Regensburg City Council for External Affairs (fig. 244). "In this capacity he seems to have been closely involved with the events of 1519, connected with the expulsion of the Jews and the setting up of the pilgrimage to the *Schöne Maria*... In 1525 he figures among the nine members of the Council for External Affairs which elected the mayor and the Council for Inner Affairs. One year later he even becomes member of the latter Council, as well as city architect, although this title is not mentioned in the city electoral lists. In view of the Turkish threat, he received in 1529 the commission of fortifying the city walls. In 1527/28 he took part in the trial of the Anabaptists. Altdorfer was elected mayor in 1528, to serve office from the Quarter of St. Emmerami until the Birthday of Christ, against which he raised pressing arguments, in particular the fact that he had undertaken to finish an important work for Duke Wilhelm... In the following year (1529) the town granted him "release from office", so that he could terminate his "work" for the Duke of Bavaria. This was of course the *Battle of Alexander*[6]. Albrecht Altdorfer died in Regensburg in 1538.

Observations from two 20th century artists will bring this essay on the *Battle of Alexander* to a conclusion:

(Oskar Kokoshka (1886-1980): "... To think that in the *Battle of Alexander* one did not recongnize sooner the earliest baroque picture!... The Earth is spinning round in this picture, which was created before Galilei taught us of this planet's motion. I should describe the *Battle of Alexander* as a work of absolute art. It grips one, as if a curtain had been ripped away in front of an abyss rather than in front of a penny peepshow. It is the other side of reality laid bare, in no way transcendental, but one which man, who has not really learnt to observe, does not see... The course of time... has here become part of the picture... Yet oddly enough, one thing has escaped the onlookers of this picture. They are ready to acclaim its romantic nature, and yet are inclined to regard the human element rather as a child's game with lead soldiers. It rings as a paradox to say that what has escaped the experts is the monumental miniature in the centre of the picture! It is not easy, even after intensive study, to try and find the tiny gem, no bigger than a pinhead, of Darius' face amidst the ten thousand strong multitude. It is even more difficult to catch the look of defeat in the turned away face of the king of kings, who is fleeing in his war-chariot... I shall not submit... "I shall not submit! I cannot perish!" So speaks the look of a man, the eye of Darius, a grain of colour in the middle of Altdorfer's cosmic picture. However infinitesimally small the face, the entire figure, or indeed the ten thousand — strong army and the Greek army might appear to us — the experience that stands out for us against the monotonous history of mankind, what remains, is the deeply grieved look of a man who is consciously turning his face away from the glory of the setting sun. He recognizes that he is defeated!... In the fleeting passage of time, the look of this defeated man drew me to a halt and awakened me." (1956).[7]

Otto Dix (1891-1969): "For me, one of the world's great wonders in painting is the Battle of Alexander by Altdorfer" (1958).[8]

GISELA GOLDBERG

245 - The Tombstone of Jean Aventinus in St Emmeram - Regensburg.

For the current state of affairs in research see: G. Goldberg, *Die Alexander-schlacht und die Historienbilder des bayerischen Herzogs Wilhelm IV. und seiner Gemahlin Jacobaea für die Münchner Residenz.* (Bayerische Staatsgemäldessammlungen. *Künstler und Werke.* 5.) Munich 1983.

1. Quoted from: K. MARTIN, *Die Alexanderschlacht von Albrecht Altdorfer,* Munich 1969, p. 12 f.
2. *Handbuch der bayerischen Geschichte,* II. Edited by M. Spindler. Munich 1969, p. 297.
3. H.H. STIERHOF, "Die Wittelsbacher und die bildende Kunst", in H.E. VALENTIN, E. VALENTIN, E. NOLLE, H.H. STIERHOF, *Die Wittelsbacher und ihrer Künstler in acht Jahrhunderten,* Munich 1980, p. 332 ff.
4. H. RIGGAUER, "Ein Sterbeandenken an Herzog Wilhelm IV"in: *Jahrbuch für Münchener Geschichte,* I, 1887, p. 416 ff (in particular p. 421).
5. K. MARTIN (opus cited in 1.), p. 29, note 4.
6. F. WINZINGER, *Albrecht Altdorfer, Die Gemälde,* Munich-Zurich, 1975, p. 10.
7. Quoted from: K. MARTIN (cf. opus cited), p. 14 ff.
8. Letter from Otto Dix of 12th March 1967 in the Archives of the Staatlichen Kunstsammlungen Dresden (quoted in: H. Marx, *"Die Aussicht... ins ganz Unermessliche". Albrecht Altdorfer zum 500. Geburstag.* In: *Dresdener Kunstblätter,* 14, 1980, p. 166.

138 - Hercules overcomes the lion of Nemaus - Cat. 114.

Copper engraving
With monogram, c. 1520/25.
43×36 mm. B.26, H.31, Wz 144.
Paris, Bibliothèque Nationale, Cabinet des Estampes.
ECN 1455.

Both Hercules and Samson had to contend with a lion in the course of their heroic lives; both strangled them with their naked hands. Samson was unarmed, Hercules in the first of his twelve heroic deeds had to fight with the lion of Nemäus whose skin was impervious to all weapons.
Here the ancient hero crowned with laurel is represented with his ineffectual bow and arrows and breaking the lion's jaws as Samson had done.
This engraving probably goes back to an Italian model. M.R.

Tietze, 1923, p. 176. - Winzinger, 1963, n° 144.

146 - Venus After the Bath - Cat. 122

Copperplate engraving.
With monogram, c. 1525/30.
61×41 mm. B. 34, H. 41, Wz. 167.
Regensburg, Museen der Stadt Regensburg.

Both works belong to a series of small-format engravings with which Altdorfer inspired, if he did not actually found, the artistic genre of Little Master Engravings in Germany. For this reason, he was formerly considered one of the "Little Masters", whose most important representatives were the brothers Sebald and Barthel Beham, and Georg Pencz, all three of whom are nearly a generation younger than Altdorfer.
In both scenes, Altorfer follows the style of the engravings by the Italian Marc Antonia Raimondi. R.B.

Winzinger, 1963, n° 166 and 167. — Cat. *Kunst der Donauschule,* 1965, n° 146, n° 147 and 148.

153 - Portrait of Martin Luther - Cat. 129

Copperplate engraving.
With monogram and inscription D.M.L. (Doctor Martin Luther), c. 1525.
60×40 mm. B. 61, H. 80, Wz. 171.
Museen der Stadt Regensburg.

A daintily engraved Renaissance ornament frames the bust of Martin Luther with his doctoral hat. The medallion form and the profile view of the Reformer continues in the traditon of classical portraiture, which gives the depiction an official and impressive quality. Altdorfer engraved this portrait of Luther after an etching by Daniel Hopfer, which in turn was a copy of an etching made in 1521 by Lucas Cranach the Elder (B. 26). One may assume the date of origin for the copperplate engraving by Altdorfer to have been around 1525, since this is the period in which the reformation movement spread in Regensburg. This would also explain why this copperplate engraving was printed in high numbers. R.B.

Winzinger, 1963, n° 171. — Cat. *Kunst der Donauschule,* 1965, n° 149. — Koepplin/Falk, 1974, n° 38.

135 - Samson carrying the gates of Gaza - Cat. 111.
Copper-engraving.
With monogram, ca. 1520/25.
43×36 mm. B.2., H.2, Wz.142
Paris, Bibliothèque Nationale, Cabinet des Estampes.
ECN 1434

The Old Testament (Judges 16,5) reports how Samson, to whom God had given superhuman streingth, escaped from the town of Gaza. The Philistines wanted to kill him to avenge the thousand men he had slain with the jaw-bone of a donkey. However, Samson freed himself from his prison by ripping the doors of the city gate from their hinges and carrying them away to the top of Mount Hebron.
The very low horizon line makes the armed figure of Samson stand out from the town in the background. With powerful strides he climbs up the mountain. A knotted cloth which holds the donkey's jaw-bone also holds the doors together on his back. M.R.

Winzinger, 1963, n° 142.

136 - The centaur - Cat. 112.
Copper engraving.
With monogram, ca. 1515/25.
37×30 mm. B.37, H.38, Wz 154.
Paris, Bibliothèque Nationale, Cabinet des Estampes. ECN 1467.

An old centaur with pointed ears proceeds towards the left bearing a conical vessel, perhaps a coal-apn, on his shoulders and a staff which is thickened at the end. Slung around his left arm a ragged lion skin flaps in the wind.
This engraving goes back to an Italian model which was also worked into a tondo in the Palazzo Medici-Riccardi in Florence and a little plaque which is now in Berlin. All three works can finally be traced back to a Hellenistic-Roman sardonyx cameo which used to be in the possession of Lorenzo di Medici and is now stored in Naples. M.R.

Bode/Knapp/Vöge, Königliche Museen zu Berlin. Beschreibung der Bildwerke der christlichen Epochen, vol.2, Die italienischen Bronzen, 2nd ed., Berlin 1904, n° 526, plate XXXIX. - Tietze, 1923, p. 176. — Winzinger, 1963, n° 154. - Wester/Simon, Die Reliefmedaillons im Hofe des Palazzo Medici zu Florenz, in, Jahrbuch der Berliner Museen, N.F. VII, 1965, p.15-91.

137 - Hercules carrying the pillars of Gades - Cat. 113.
Copper engraving.
With monogram, ca. 1520/25.
43×36 mm. B.27, H.32, Wz 143.
Paris, Bibliothèque Nationale, Cabinet des Estampes.
ECN 1456

Hercules's tenth task involved stealing the herds of the giant Geryones in Iberia. On the way there Hercules planted the tow pillars of Gades. The composition of this engraving is similar to that of "Samson with the gates of Gaza" (cat. 111). As in that work a town lies in the background at the feet of a hero who is standing on the top of a hill. This formal similarity corresponds to the typological interpretation of both heroes as precursors of Christ. M.R.

Winzinger, 1963, n° 143.

139 - Pomegranate with Foliage - Cat. 115
Copperplate engraving.
With monogram, c. 1515.
30×37 mm. P. 108, H. 97, Wz. 151.
Regensburg, Museen der Stadt Regensburg.

The motif of this small, ornamental engraving, the pomegranate bursting open with an overlapping leaf, was used by Altdorfer several times to decorate the round towers in the *Gates of Honor of Emperor Maximilian,* an extensive piece of woodcuttery, which occupied Altdorfer at the latest from 1515 onwards. The cut section of the cut bough, with its rolled-up bark at the lower left-hand corner of the scene, is repeated in another ornamental engraving (Wz 127) and in the margin drawings for the prayer book of Emperor Maximilian. The ornamental engraving depicting vegetables, which probably served as a model for this engraving, has its origin in the gothic crabs that Martin Schongauer in the late 15th century already rendered in such a way as to resemble vegetables. R.B.

Winzinger, 1963, n° 151. — Cat. *Kunst der Donauschule,* 1965, n° 137.

140 - Samson and Delila - Cat. 116.
Copper engraving.
With monogram, ca. 1520/25.
44×36 mm., cut
B.3, H.3, Wz. 145.
Paris, Bibliothèque Nationale, Cabinet des Estampes.
ECN 1435

After Samson had escaped from the city of Gaza he met Dalila in the Sorek valley and fell in love with her (Old Testament, Judges 16,4-22). The Philistines bribed Dalila to discover the secret of his strength. Three times he deceived his beloved, but the fourth time he confided to her that his invincibility lay in his hair. As he was a consecrated man of God from birth, his hair had never been cut. If anyone were to cut his hair he would be weak and defenceless. When Samson had fallen asleep a servant called in by Delila his locks off. The Philistines imprisoned him and tore his eyes out.
Delila's harsh face is made to stand out from the rest of the engraving by means of the wall framing it, the house on the left and the tree on the right. Delila sits on a stone block with the scissors in her hand. Samson has fallen asleep in her lap. The shortened recumbent figure of Samson with his legs clothed is reminiscent of the lying figure of Christ in the representation of the mourning on an unfinished woodblock by Altdorfer dating from 1512 in Munich. M.R.

Winzinger, 1963, N° 145.

151 - Arion and Neréid - Cat. 127
Copper engraving.
With monogram, ca. 1520/25.
60×40 mm. B.39, H.46, Wz 165.
Paris, Bibliothèque Nationale, Cabinet des Estampes.
ECN 1469

This print used to be called "Triton and Nereïds". Triton is usually portrayed as a sea-god with a fish's body. Arion on the other hand was, according to Herodotus, a famous citharist and the inventor of the dithyramb and is said to have been robbed and thrown overboard by the crew of a passenger ship while travelling from Tarent to Corinth. He was allowed to sing once more. Then he jumped into the water. There he was caught by a dolphin and taken in safety to Tainaron. In this print Arion is seen riding on the back of his rescuer the dolphin, with his fiddle and bow. A neréid accompanies him holding up an anchor (the symbol of hope). In the background there is a castle and a third dolphin approaching. The engraving was probably based on an Italian model, probably a niello. M.R.

Tietze, 1923, p.176. - Winzinger, 1963, n° 165.

141 - The Revenge of the Magician Virgil - Cat. 117

Copperplate engraving.
With monogram, c. 1520/30.
75×45 mm. B. 43, H. 50, Wz. 155.
Brunswick, Herzog Anton Ulrich-Museum.

In the Middle Ages, Virgil was considered as a magician. Legend had it that he fell in love with the king's daughter, who pretended to comply with his courtship. He let himself be drawn up to her window in a basket. Halfway up, however, she left him hanging so as to make a public laughing-stock of him. With the help of his magical powers he was able to free himself from this ridiculous situation. In revenge for this mockery, he extinguished all fires in Rome and, thanks to his magical powers, created such a situation that only the king's daughter was able to give fire from her body orifices. Each person had to fetch this fire himself at the Forum. Another version relates that the Romans had to fetch their fire from a prostitute.
An almost nude courtesan sits on a high pedestal, her lap is smoking. At her feet a Roman is about to light a lamp with the fire of the woman. Behind him others are holding up more lamps and candles.
M.R.

Winzinger, 1963, n° 155.

143 - Horatius Cocles - Cat. 119

Copperplate engraving.
With monogram, c. 1520/30.
65×38 mm. B. 29, H. 35, Wz. 156.
Regensburg, Museen der Stadt Regensburg.

This engraving, which appears to be more Italian than Danube and which indicates Altdorfer's study of Italian themes and pictorial models, depicts the Roman hero Horatius Coctes. Stories tell that in the year 507 B.C., Horatius Publius, called the one-eyed Cocles, prevented the Etruscan King Porsenna from capturing Rome by defending the Tiber bridge single-handed until it collapsed. Thereupon Horatius jumped into the water and swam to the Roman shore. On the lower edge of the picture the engraving shows a part of the bridge, in the background a war camp with tents is descernable. While jumping, Horatius, dressed in a helmet and armor, holds his large sword, to which is connected an octagonal parry-bar, with its tip pointing upwards. R.B.

Winzinger, 1963, n° 156.

144 - Judith with the head of the Holofern - Cat. 120.

Copper engraving.
With monogram, ca. 1520/30.
64×39 mm. B.1, H.1. Wz. 158.
Paris, Bibliothèque Nationale, Cabinet des Estampes. ECN 153.

With a lightly striding stance Judith presents the head of the Holofern cruelly impaled on a sword. The biblical story of the book of Judith is here reduced to a single depiction of the Old Testament heroine with her distinguishing attributes, the sword and the head. Such a graphic rendering of the theme is iconographically unusual.
As with the copper engraving of Dido Wz.159 (cat. 14) the noticeable striding posture of the figure of Judith is attributable to Zoan Andrea's engraving "Four dancing girls" B.18. This print for its part imitate Mantegna's painting "Parnassus" in the Louvre. M.R.

Tietze, 1923, p.176. Winzinger, 1963, n° 158.

145 - Dido - Cat. 121.

Copper engraving.
With monogram and titled "Dido". Ca. 1520/30.
64×38 mm. B.42, H.48. Wz. 159.
Paris, Bibliothèque Nationale, Cabinet des Estampes.
ECN 1472.

Dido, daughter of Mutto the king of Tyre, fled to Lybia from her brother Pygmalion who had killed her brother out of covetousness. There she founded the stronghold of Carthage (Virgil, Aeneid I,340-366).
She fell unhappily in love with Aeneas whos had arrived at Carthage on his wanderings. When she was deserted by him she took her life out of sorrow at this loss. She had a funeral pyre ereted out of the treasure left behind by the Trojans and she stabbed herself on top of it with Aeneas' sword (Virgil, Aeneid IV, 646-665).
In this little engraving the scene of the action is represented by means of blazing flames and rising clouds of smoke behind Dido.
Winzinger attributes Dido's unusually dance-like posture to a model picture. As with the copper-engraving of Judith (cat. 120) this Dido also seems to be indebted to the engraving of "Four dancing girls" by Zoan Andrea. Altdorfer also used this print as the model for a drawing.
M.R.

Winzinger, 1963, n° 159.

148 - Crouching Venus - Cat. 124

Copperplate engraving.
With monogram, c. 1525/30.
61×41 mm. B. 33, H. 40, Wz. 166.
Regensburg, Museen der Stadt Regensburg.

149 - Hercules and the Muse - Cat. 125

Copperplate engraving.
With monogram, c. 1520/25.
66×45 mm. B. 28, H. 30, Wz. 160.
Museen der Stadt Regensburg.

Hercules, a hero of Greek mythology, was made immortal by the gods after accomplishing his twelve deeds. He was allowed entrance into Olympus and was given the goddess Hebe as a wife. In this copperplate engraving Hercules, who can be identified by his symbol, the lionskin hanging over his arm, is depicted at the stage when he has already become immortal. The horn of plenty in his hand, the laurel wreath on his head, indicate that he is a hero rewarded by the gods. He is accompanied by a muse with a lyre, the muse of love lyrics. This is probably meant as a reference to the love between Hercules and the goddess Hebe.
Altdorfer, who repeatedly studied the works of the Italian Renaissance artists for his late, small-format engravings, probably used an Italian model for this work. R.B.

Winzinger, 1963, n° 160.

150 - Neptune on a sea-snake - Cat. 126.

Copper-engraving.
With monogram, ca. 1520/25.
26×46 mm. B.30, H.36, Wz.162.
Paris, Bibliothèque Nationale, Cabinet des Estampes.
ECN 1459.

Neptune, the god of the seas, with his trident lies on the scaly body of a sea monster. A narrow piece of cloth flaps frivolously around his body.
This little engraving probably goes back to an Italian model, an engraving or a niello. However, nobody has yet been able to find a definite model for it. M.R.

Winzinger, 1963, n° 162.

116 - The Small Crucifixion - Cat. 92

Copperplate engraving.
With monogram, c. 1512/15.
61×40 mm. B. 7, H. 8, Wz. 120.
Regensburg, Museum der Stadt Regensburg.

Compared with the turbulent scene of the big Crucifixion (Cat. 104, fig. 128, Wz 134) which is rich in figures and bold in the interlacing of the figures with the landscape, Altdorfer in this earlier, small Crucifixion seems to renounce almost all attempts at depicting emotion and mood.
The group around the cross seems to be standing more in front of than in a landscape. Mary and John are placed under the arms of the cross in the foreground. The remaining space above their brightly radiating nimi is filled with four angel heads. Only behind this narrow stage does a landscape, which is sketched out on a small scale, unforld. M.R.

Winzinger, 1963, n° 120.

121 - The Judgement of Paris - Cat. 97

Copperplate engraving.
With monogram, c. 1515/18.
60×40 mm. B. 36, H. 37, Wz. 131.
Regensburg, Museum der Stadt Regensburg.

In three engravings of the same format and probably made concurrently, in St George, Pyramus and Thisbe (Wz. 132) and this rendition of the Judgement of Paris, Altdorfer reverts to themes he had already depicted at an earlier date in larger-sized woodcuts. In comparison with the earlier version of the Judgement of Paris. Altdorfer in this engraving dispenses with the rich landscape and the light effects fo the woodcut. In front of a precipice with a gate cut into the rocks, which gives a view over rich flora, Paris has fallen asleep next to a spring. Mercury is kneeling beside him, as though requesting him to pass his judgement. The three goddesses are preparing themselves for the contest. Hera is standing at the spring behind Paris. Aphrodit is directing Cupid's attention to the judge and Athena, who can be recognized by the Gorgon, watches her adversary. M.R.

Winzinger, 1963, n° 131.

130 - The "Beautiful Mary" on the Throne - Cat. 106

Copperplate engraving.
With monogram, c. 1519/20.
60×40 mm. B. 13, H. 14, Wz. 137.
Regensburg, Museum der Stadt Regensburg.

In the celestial sphere, Mary is sitting on a Renaissance throne with a high base, whose front is decorated with Altdorfer's large monogram plaque. She is surrounded by angels playing music. The throne, flanked by pillars on both sides, with a broad upper double-moulding and a floral border is reminiscent, on the one hand, of the framing utilized by Altdorfer in his woodcuts of the Beautiful Mary, and the other, it also anticipates frames which were in fact executed by. Altdorfer at a later date, as for example the portal of the conference room in the Town Hall of Regensburg. Hans Mielich reproduced this portal in a miniature on parchment 1536 so that a picture of it has been preserved. The connection between this copperplate engraving and the image of the Beautiful Mary, the object of many pilgrimages, lies in the clothing of the throned figure, the headscarf trimmed with stars, the byzantine iconography. M.R.

Tietze, 1923, p. 191. — Winzinger, 1963, n° 137. Winzinger, 1975, n° 93

131 - Solomon's Idol Worship - Cat. 107

Copperplate engraving.
With monogram, c. 1519.
61×41 mm. B. 4, H. 4, Wz. 136.
Regensburg, Museum der Stadt Regensburg.

Solomon, who, at an advanced age was seduced by his numerous wives to worship strange gods and for this punished by God, is depicted standing in a church. One of his lovers points out a female idol in a niche of the altar. It is most probably meant to be Astarte, discussed in the Book of Judges (11,5), who was worshipped as a celestial and earthly goddess and thus represented the pagan counterpart to Mary. This copperplate engraving might be understood as a reference to the "false" worship of the Jews in Regensburg. It belongs with the engraving Christ Drives Away the Money-Changers (Cat. 109, fig. 133), which is of the same size. M.R.

Winzinger, 1963, n° 136. — Cat. Luther und die Folgen für die Kunst, 1983/84, n° 11.

132 - Beautiful Mary in Landscape - Cat. 108.

Copper engraving.
With monogram, ca. 1519/20.
56×35 mm. B.12, H.13, Wz. 140
Paris, Bibliothèque Nationale, Cabinet des Estampes.

Mary sits in a landscape with the Christ child on her lap making a gesture of benediction. The brightly gleaming haloes shine upon the middle of the picture so that only a tree on the right and a few shrubs and a church on the right-hand edge can be distinguished.
Mary's clothing is closely related to that on the wood-cut "Beautiful Mary of Regensburg" Wz.89 (cat. 106). Here too she wears a spangled shawl over her head and shoulders; it has broad double braiding and frayed sleeves. Without doubt this little print was intended to be used on pilgrimages, for the pilgrims who from 1519 onwards travelled to see the famous miraculous image of the "Beautiful Mary". Michael Ostendorfer's wood-cut Wz.245 gives a convincing impression of the pilgrimages to Regensburg. M.R.

Winzinger, 1963, n° 140.

147 - The fight for the nymph - Cat. 123.

Copper-engraving.
With monogram, ca. 1520/25.
60×40 mm. B.38, H.45, Wz 164.
Paris, Bibliothèque Nationale, Cabinet des Estampes.
ECN 1468.

An old Silenus is on the point of seducing a kneeling nymph who has fallen asleep. He is caught in the act by a youth who threatens him with a cudgel. Startled the old man turns towards his attacker and tries to ward off the blows by using a branch.
This engraving goes back to an Italian model. It reproduces in a different way Marcantonio Raimondi's engraving B.279. In his version Altdorfer forges the landscape which in Raimondi's work leads way off into the background and gives the scene a backloth of thick bushes. In the model the odl Satyr's intentions are more obvious. The seducer is horned and depicted ithyphallically. M.R.

Winzinger, 1963, n° 164.

122 - Mary with her Child and St. Anna at the Cradle - Cat. 98

Copperplate engraving.
With monogram, 1515/20.
62×56 mm. B. 14, H. 15, Wz. 128.
Brunswick, Herzog Anton Ulrich-Museum.

In a bare room, defined by the contained figures who shine with their own light, Mary brings the Baby Christ to his cradle, which has just been prepared by St. Anne. The holy women are shown engaged in everyday activities. The artist captures the mood of intimate mutual affection among the three figures. Only the glowing nimbi indicate that these saints are extraordinary people.
The simple wooden cradle already appears in the work of Altdorfer at an earlier date, namely laterally inverted in one of the border drawings in the prayer book of the Emperor Maximilian, and can be traced back to the child's cradle in the Ambrose panel, which is part of Michael Pacher's altar of the Church Fathers. M.R.

Tietze, 1923, p. 178. — Winzinger, 1963, n° 128. — Cat. *Luther und die Folgen für die Kunst,* 1983/84, n° 119.

133 - Christ Drives Away the Money-Changers From the Temple - Cat. 109

Copperplate engraving.
With monogram, c. 1519.
60×40 mm. B. 6, H. 7, Wz. 138.
Regensburg, Museen der Stadt Regensburg.

The scene is located in a vaulted hall with pointed arches. In the foreground of the picture, Christ is storming up to two money-changers, kneeling over their purses which are bursting open. In the background, other figures are standing or fleeing. The clothes of the by-standers remind one of the persons in the etching of the entrance hall of the synagogue, of 1519. The reason for this engraving, the theme of which is unusual for Altdorfer, may have been the expulsion of the jews from Regensburg in 1519. Like the temple, which Christ wanted to tear down and erect anew within three days (John 2.19), the synagoge was torn down and replaced in a great hurry, at first with a wooden church meant to house the image of the *Beautiful Mary* (said to be endowed with the power of working miracles). Winzinger points out the similarities between the temple and the architecture of the entrance hall of the synagoge. M.R.

Tietze, 1923, p. 178. — Winzinger, 1963, n° 138, p. 28, p. 42.

134 - Mary looks for the Twelve Year Old Christ in the Temple - Cat. 110

Copperplate engraving.
With monogram, c. 1519/20.
60×40 mm. B. 24, H. 6, Wz. 139.
Regensburg, Museen der Stadt Regensburg.

As in many of his depictions of Mary, Altdorfer has used the byzantine Lukas-Madonna, with a head and shoulder cloth adorned with stars as a model for this reprensentation of Mary. This Lukas-Madonna was greatly worshipped in Regensburg at his time. R.B.

Winzinger, 1963, n° 139.

142 - Violin-Player - Cat. 118

Copperplate engraving.
With monogram, c. 1515/25.
60×40 mm. B. 54, H. 70, Wz. 141.
Regensburg, Museen der Stadt Regensburg.

Winzinger, 1963, n° 141.

152 - Pair of lovers led in triumph by sea-gods - Cat. 128

Copper engraving.
With monogram, c. 1520/25.
46×80 mm. B. 31, H. 44, Wz. 163.
Paris, Bibliothèque Nationale, Cabinet des Estampes. ECN 1460.

Altdorfer borrowed the two sea-horses and their riders from a niello by Peregrino da Cesena (Hind, 1936, n° 194), though he arranged them the other way round.
What in Peregrino's work was a carriage with Neptune standing in it here becomes a triumphal procession for a couple crowned with laurel. The girl, perhaps a nymph, holds the skull of an animal in her raised left hand. The figure which has been added on the right with one of his legs in fetters and the bearded man with a fish behind them are both absent from the model.
Unlike the niello this engraving does away with any representation of landscape and gives the scene a background of parallel hatching which is continued unchanged into the water. Owing to the overlapping of the figures at the edges this piece has the effect of being an excerpt from a larger work. M.R.

Winzinger, 1963, n° 163

154 - Entrance Hall of the Synagoge in Regensburg - Cat. 130

Etching.
With monogram and inscription: *Porticus Synagogae/Judaicae Ratisponen/Fracta. 21. Die. Feb. Ann. 1519.*
164×118 mm. B. 64, H. 83, Wz. 174.
Berlin, Kupferstichkabinett, SMPK. Inv n° 75-1896.

The fate of the Jewish synagogue in Regensburg is intimately linked with Albrecht Altdorfer in person and his function as member of the Outer Council of the city. One to the economic decline of the once wealthy city of Regensburg and the rising indebtedness of the Christians to the Jews, the good relationship which had existed for centuries between the two groups turned into a hatred for the Jewish community. Supported by a generally propagated antisemitic movement and religious fanaticism, the city council announced the expulsion of the Jews and the demolition of the synagogue.
This happened on February 22, 1519, immediately after the death of Emperor Maximilian, the protector of the Jewish population. Altdorfer belonged to the chosen members of the council who informed the Jews that they had to leave the Synagoge immediately and the city within five days. Two hours later, the demolition of the medieval synagoge commenced. One day before, on February 22, 1519, Altdorfer made two etchings, each with a view of the synagoge, using a prosaic, realistic manner of depiction. The etching in question, depicting two religious men in typical Jewish costume hurrying to the service, bears the date of that day, the other etching has inscribed on it the comment "according to God's just judgement" *(iusto dei iudicio).*
R.B.

Winzinger, 1963, n° 174. — Cat. *Kunst der Donauschule,* 1965. n° 150.

155 - Interior of the Synagoge of Regensburg. - Cat. 131

Etching.
With monogram and inscription *ANN. DNI. D. XIX/IUDAICA RATISPONA/SYNAGOGA. IUSTO/DEI. IUDICIO. FXNDIT (V) S/EST EVERSA.*
170×125 mm. B. 63, H. 82, Wz. 173.
Museen der Stadt Regensburg.

Winzinger, 1963, n° 173. (cf. cat. 130).

MAXIMILIAN I THE PRAYER-BOOK OF EMPEROR

Emperor Maximilian's plan to have a printed prayer-book produced, with border illustrations in the style of Flemish livres d'heures, probably dates back to the year 1508. In that year King Maximilian had been proclaimed Emperor of the Holy Roman Empire with the pope's approval in the cathedral of Trient. As 1508 was the year in which the Augsburg printer Johannes Schoensperger was appointed court printer, it seems likely that the idea of commissioning a special prayer-book coincided with the coronation of the Emperor.

However, the work on the prayer-book progressed very slowly as was the case with the other literary and artistic projects of this ruler. This was perhaps partly because, in accord with Maximilian's wishes, new type characters had to be designed, cut and cast for the printings which he had planned. Wolfgang Spitzweg, who had previously worked in the chancellery of Emperor Friedrich III in the new town of Vienna, was involved in the design of the so-called prayer-book type.

In October 1513 the emperor received the first copy of the prayer-book printed on parchment; it was sent to him from Augsburg by the humanist Dr. Konrad Peutinger, the emperor's adviser in his literary projects. The remaining copies of the edition were completed on 27th December 1513. From then on Peutinger sent parts of a copy to different artists who had been chosen to decorate the borders of the text with pen-and-ink drawings. Of the 157 pages of the edition Dürer received 56, i.e. more than a third. Albrecht Altdorfer received half of them.

Three went to Hans Burgkmair, seven to Hans Baldung Grien, six to Lukas Cranach and eighteen to Jörg Breu. The rest remained empty; some pages are lost.

It seems that the border drawings executed by Dürer, alternately in reddish, green and pale violet ink, served as models for the other illustrations. Dürer's highly imaginative decorations, composed of pictorial and ornamental elements, are only loosely connected to the text; occasionally a drawing is actually in direct contrast to the text, in other cases he illustrates the text with considerable humour. Of all the collaborators on the prayer-book it was Albrecht Altdorfer who followed Dürer's example the closest - both formally and spiritually - in the parts of the book decorated by him. On the other hand the illustrations done by a colleague from his studio reveal a rather stiff and unoriginal artist. In terms of artistic quality only the few drawings by Lukas Cranach come anywhere near to those of Dürer and Altdorfer.

Nothing is known for certain about the use to which the emperor intented the prayer-book and illustrations to be put. It is now generally supposed that the prayer-book was designed for the use of the chivalrous order of St. George, founded by Maximilian's father,

Emperor Friedrich III, and revived by Maximilian. As for the preparation of the border drawings, here too we have to content ourselves with looking at the process normally employed by Maximilian and his advisers in comparable projects.

First the emperor has a painter prepare rough drafts. After he had expressed his wishes and suggested revisions they were given to one or several other artists for improvement. Only when the second step had been approved by the prince were they passed on for their final execution, as in the triumphal procession for example, ending in their transfer onto the wood-blocks (fig. 175 to 182). In the case of the illustrations for the prayer-book, however, it is not possible to decide whether we are looking at the first drafts or the final version itself. The lack of unity in the different artist's treatment of their material suggests that the second possibility is unlikely. The system of decoration should surely be more consistent. In the case of Breu and Baldung we have the impression that they had no clear idea as to how they were to decorate the borders.

The prayer-book was divided into two parts between 1598 and 1600. The pages now numbered 1 - 56 and 63 - 68 were acquired by Duke Maximilian of Bavaria, pages 57 - 62 and 69 - 157 came into the possession of Cardinal Granvella, the minister to King Philip II of Spain. Whereas the first part, with the drawings by Dürer, has remained in Munich until the present day, the descendants of Granvella sold their part to the future abbot of the Benedictine monastery at Besançon. In 1827 the book came into the possession of the Bibliothèque Municipale of Besançon from the last librarian of the monastery. F.A.

SELECTION: 32 illustrated pages.
I. Albrecht Altdorfer: I to XX, and XXII (21 p.).
II. Jörg Breu: XXI and XXIII (2 p.).
III. Albrecht Altdorfer (in the style of): XXIV and XXV (2 p.).
IV. Lukas Cranach the elder: XXV to XXXII (7 p.).

tia · Pro ſanctis: vt ſupra · Ad
ſextã antiphona · Ne timeas
Maria · Capitulum ·
Abit ei dominᵘˢ ſedem
Dauid patris eius: et
regnabit in domo Jacob in
eternum: et regni eius nõ erit
finis · Deo gratias · Verſ̃ · Be
nedicta tu in mulieribus · Re
ſponſoriũ · Et benedictus fru
ctus ventris tui · Pro ſanctis ·
Ad nonam antiphona · Ec
ce ancilla domini · Capituliũ
Ecce virgo · Verſic · Angelus

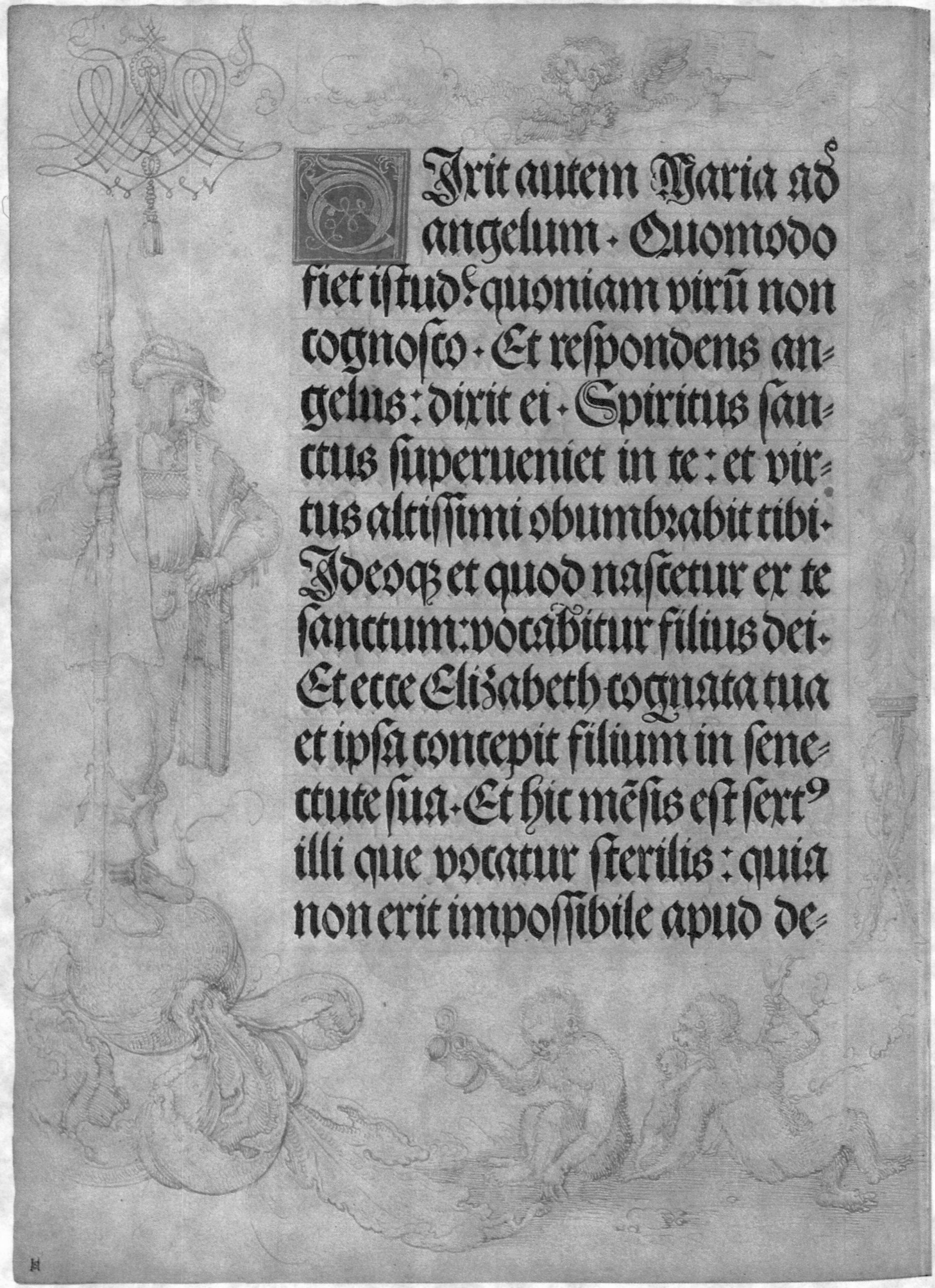

Irit autem Maria ad
angelum · Quomodo
fiet istud? quoniam virũ non
cognosco · Et respondens angelus: dixit ei · Spiritus san-
ctus superueniet in te: et virtus altissimi obumbrabit tibi·
Ideoqz et quod nascetur ex te
sanctum: vocabitur filius dei·
Et ecce Elizabeth cognata tua
et ipsa concepit filium in sene-
ctute sua· Et hic mẽsis est sert⁹
illi que vocatur sterilis: quia
non erit impossibile apud de-

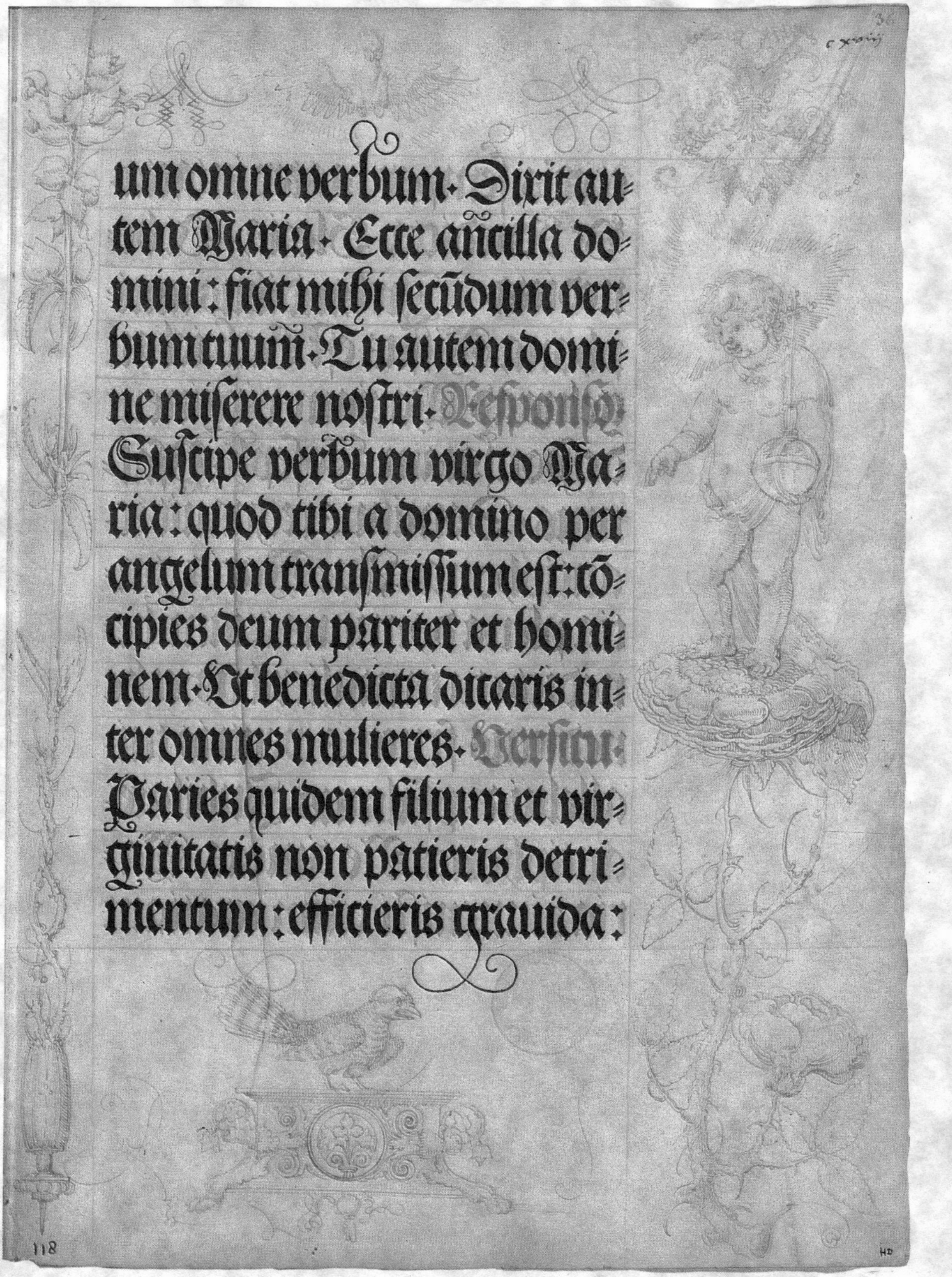

um omne verbum · Dixit au
tem Maria · Ecce ancilla do
mini : fiat mihi secundum ver
bum tuum · Tu autem domi
ne miserere nostri · Responso
Suscipe verbum virgo Ma
ria : quod tibi a domino per
angelum transmissum est : con
cipies deum pariter et homi
nem · Et benedicta dicaris in
ter omnes mulieres · Versicu
Paries quidem filium et vir
ginitatis non patieris detri
mentum : efficieris gravida ·

III

A. Altdorfer

118

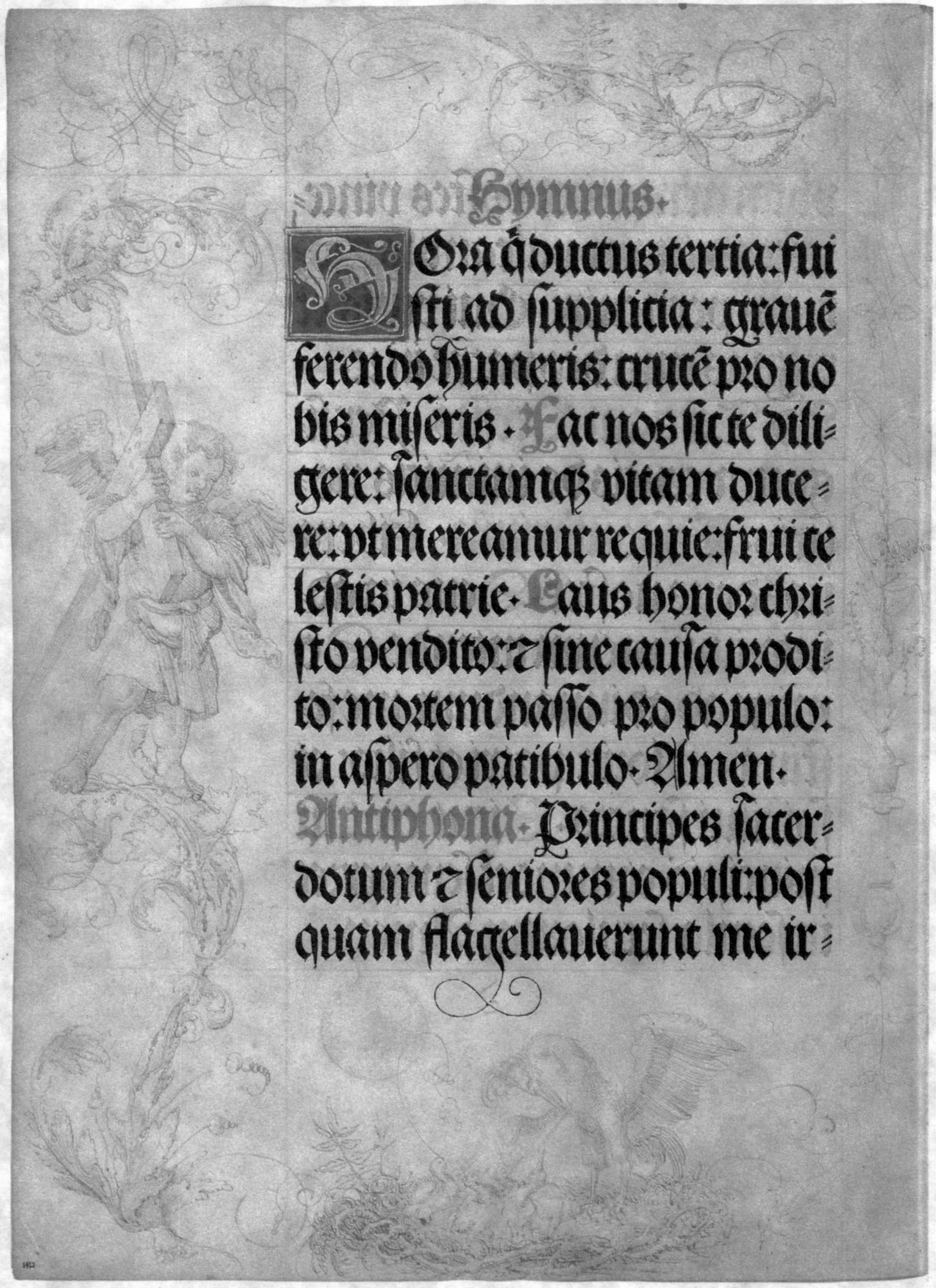

HOra ꝗ ductus tertia: fui
sti ad supplicia: grauē
ferendo humeris: crucē pro no
bis miseris · Fac nos sic te dili
gere: sanctamꝗ vitam duce=
re: vt mereamur requie: frui ce
lestis patrie· Laus honor chri
sto vendito: ⁊ sine causa prodi=
to: mortem passo pro populo:
in aspero patibulo· Amen·

Antiphona· Principes sacer=
dotum ⁊ seniores populi: post
quam flagellauerunt me ir=

IV
A. Altdorfer

ruerunt in me dicentes: crucifige crucifige eum.

Psalmus.

Attende anime mee: et
libera eam: propter inimicos meos eripe me. Tu scis
improperium meum: et confusionem meam: et reuerenti
am meam. In conspectu tuo
sunt ostes qui tribulant me:
improperium expectantes cor
meum et miseriam. Et susti
nui qui simul contristaretur:
et non fuit: qui consolaretur

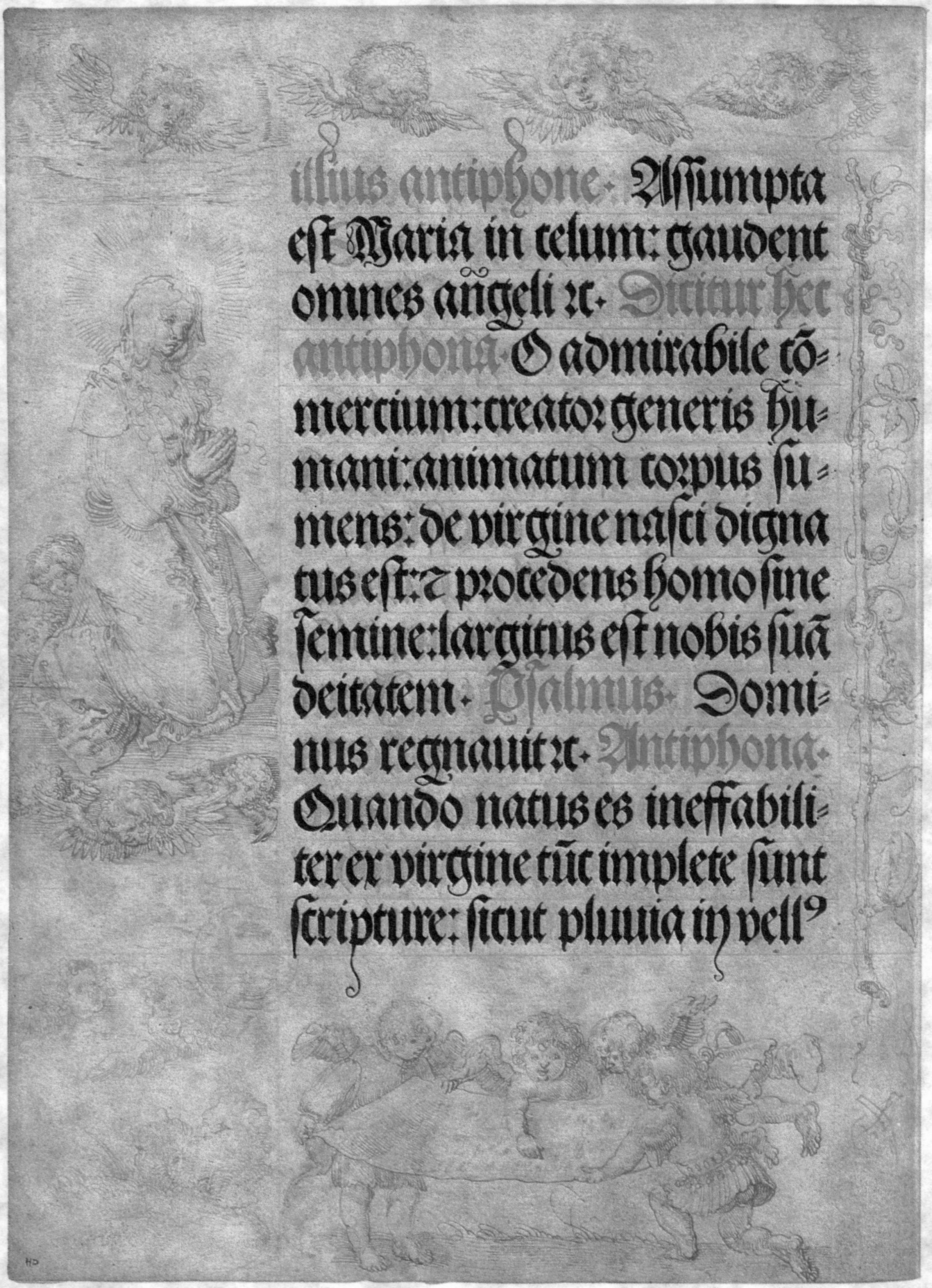

illius antiphone· Assumpta
est Maria in celum: gaudent
omnes angeli ꝛc· Dicitur hec
antiphona· O admirabile co̅
mercium: creator generis hu
mani: animatum corpus su
mens: de virgine nasci digna
tus est: ꝛ procedens homo sine
semine: largitus est nobis sua̅
deitatem· Psalmus· Domi
nus regnauit ꝛc· Antiphona·
Quando natus es ineffabili
ter ex virgine tu̅c implete sunt
scripture: sicut pluuia in vell⁹

VI
A. Altdorfer

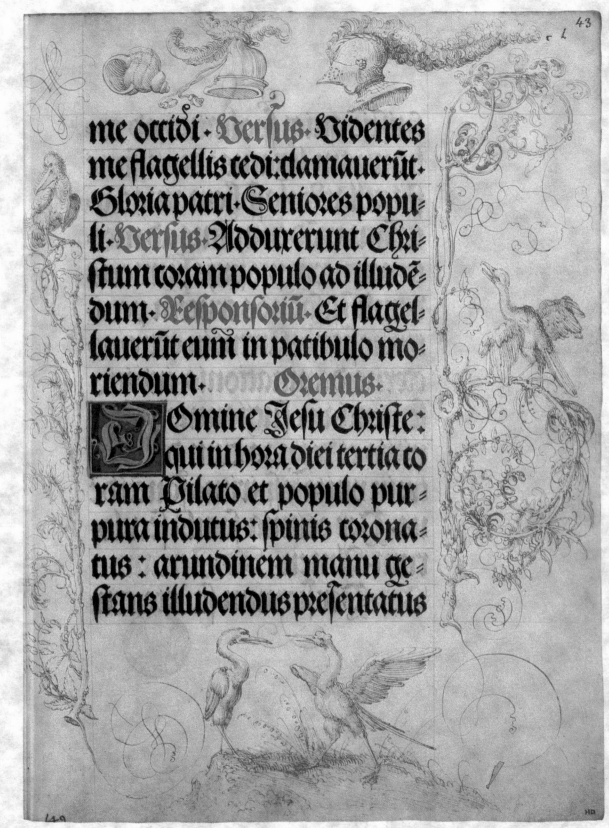

me occidi · Verfus · Videntes
me flagellis tedi: clamauerūt ·
Gloria patri · Seniores populi · Verfus · Adduxerunt Chri-
stum coram populo ad illudē-
dum · Responsoriū · Et flagel-
lauerūt eum in patibulo mo-
riendum · Oremus ·
Omine Jesu Christe:
qui in hora diei tertia coram Pilato et populo pur-
pura indutus: spinis corona-
tus: arundinem manu ge-
stans illudendus presentatus

Aspiciamus in auctorē fidei et consummatorem Jesum: qui proposito sibi gaudio sustinuit crucem confusione contempta. Deo gratias. Versus. Foderunt manus meas: et pedes meos clauis. Responsoriū. Perforātes lancea latus meum. Et pedes Gloria patri. Foderunt Versus. Diuiserunt sibi vestimenta mea. Responsoriū. Et super vestem meā miserunt sortem. Oremus.

VIII

A. Altdorfer

cis de inimicis nostris· Respō
sorium· Libera nos deus no
ster· Deus in adiutoriū me
um intende· Domine ad ad
iuuandum me festina· Glo
ria patri· Sicut erat in princi
pio rc· Hymnus·

Eutem p nobis subijt:
et stans in illa sitijt: Ie
sus sacratis manibus: clauis
fossis z pedibus· Honor et bñ
dictio: sit crucifixo filio: qui suo
nos supplico: redemit ab exi
tio· Laus honor Christo ven

IX
A. Altdorfer

dito: et sine causa prodito: mor
tem passo pro populo in aspe
ro patibulo Amen · Antipho
na · Attendite vniuersi popu
li et videte dolorem meũ: quia
pro vobis crucifixus sum ·
Psalmus ·
Ircũdederunt me ca=
nes multi conciliũ ma
lignantium obsedit me · Fo
derunt manus meas ⁊ pedes
meos: dinumerauerũt oĩia
ossa mea · Ipsi vero considera
uerunt et inspexerunt me: di

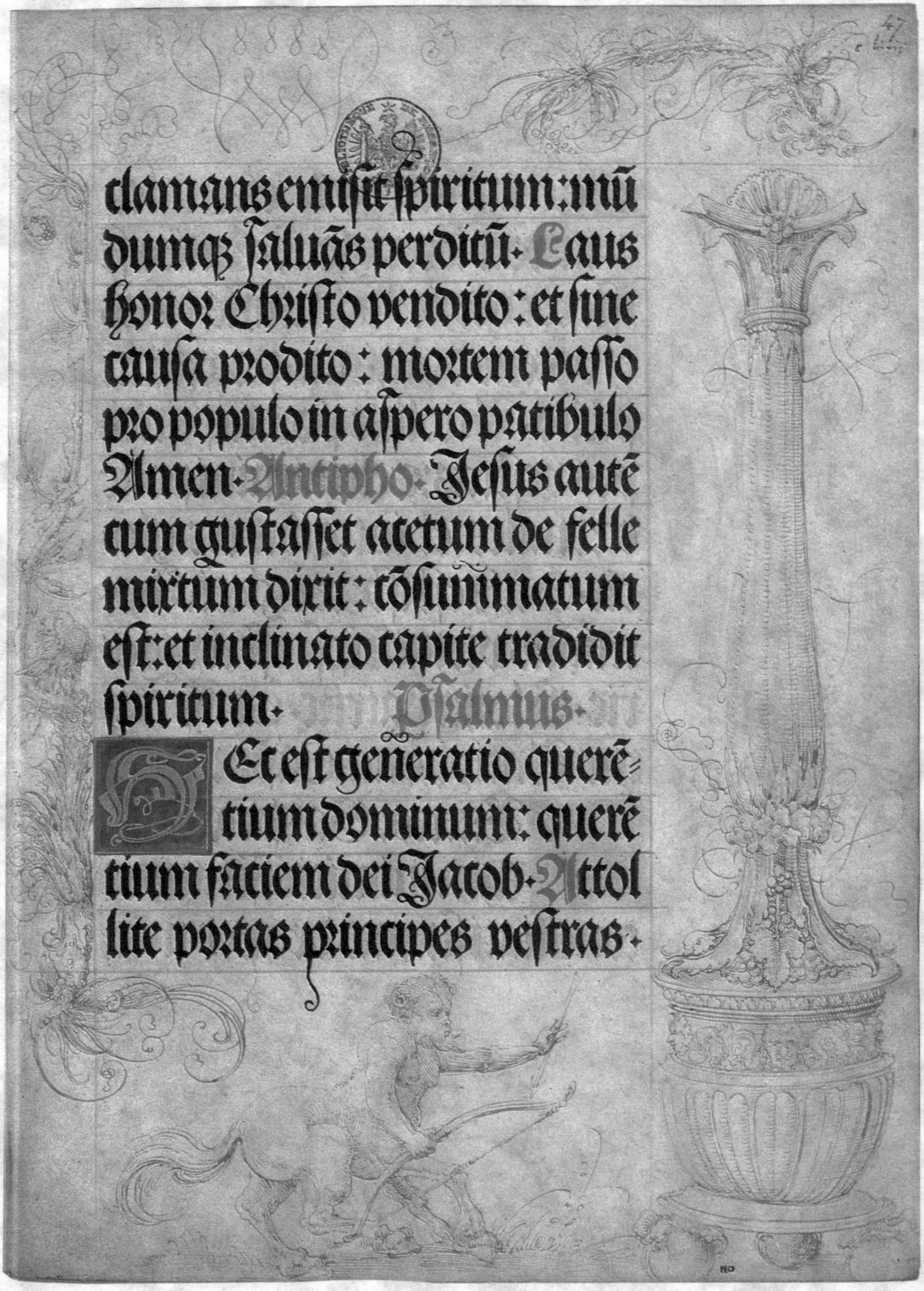

clamans emisit spiritum: mū
dumqʒ saluās perditū· Laus
honor: Christo vendito: et sine
causa prodito: mortem passo
pro populo in aspero patibulo
Amen·Antipho·Jesus autē
cum gustasset acetum de felle
mixtum dixit: cōsummatum
est: et inclinato capite tradidit
spiritum· Psalmus·

Et est generatio querē
tium dominum: querē
tium faciem dei Jacob·Attol
lite portas principes vestras·

Astigãs castigauit me
dominus: et morti non
tradidit me. Aperite mihi por
tas iusticie ingressus in eas: tõ
fitebor domino: hec porta do
mini iusti intrabunt in eam.
Confitebor tibi quoniam ex=
audisti me: et factus es mihi
in salutem. Lapidem quem
reprobauerũt edificantes: hic
factus ẽ in caput angeli. A do
mino factum est istud: et est
mirabile in oculis nostris.
Hec dies quam fecit dominⁿ:

XII

A. Altdorfer

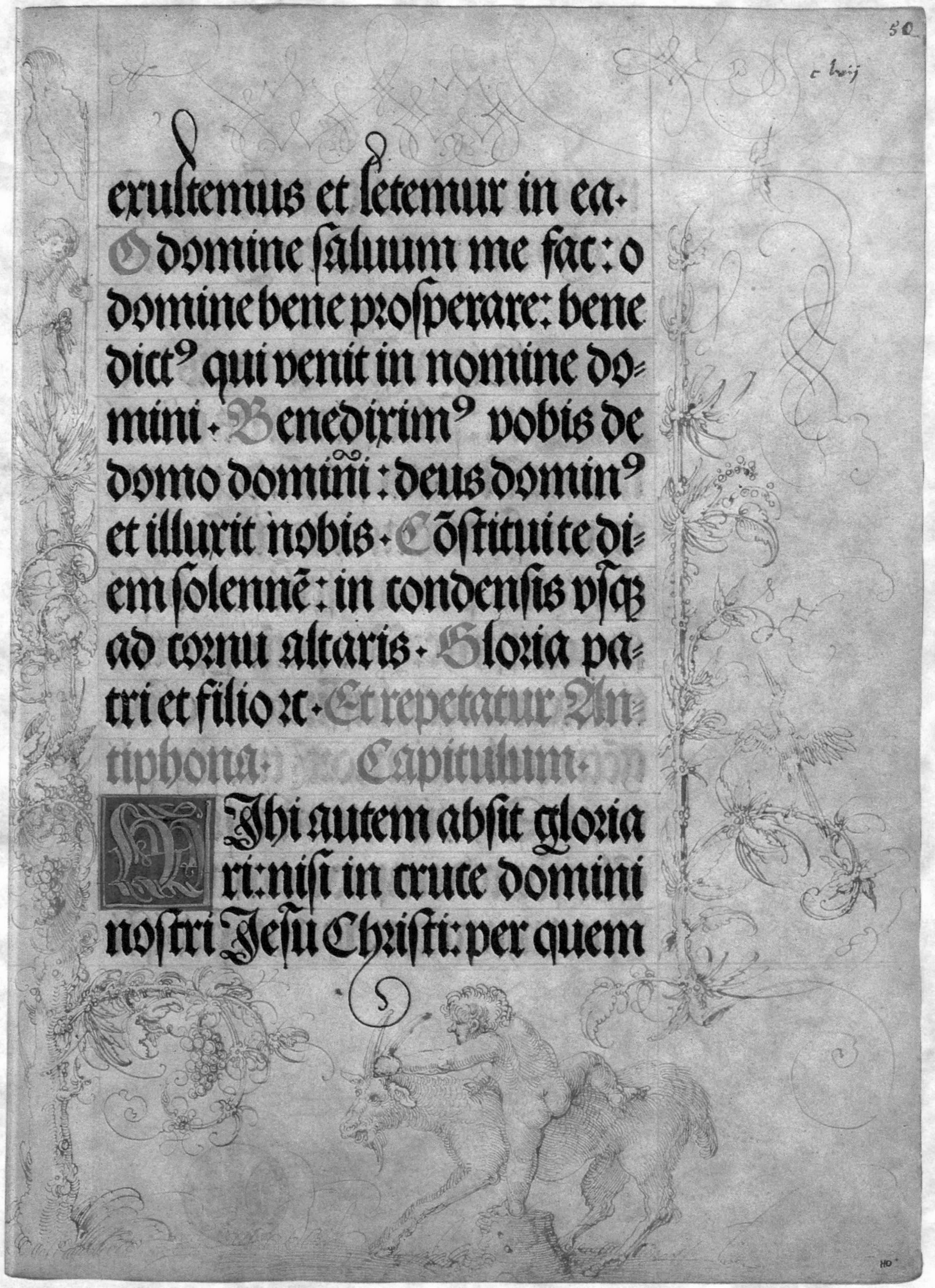

exultemus et letemur in ea·
O domine saluum me fac: o
domine bene prosperare: bene
dict⁹ qui venit in nomine do
mini · Benedirim⁹ vobis de
domo domini: deus domin⁹
et illuxit nobis · Constitui te di
em solenne: in condensis vsq3
ad cornu altaris · Gloria pa
tri et filio xc · Et repetatur An
tiphona: Capitulum·

Ihi autem absit gloria
ri: nisi in cruce domini
nostri Jesu Christi: per quem

XIII
A. Altdorfer

tuit sitientem iam sepeliat : vt
defunctum· Canticum·
Magnificat anima mea
dominum · Et exulta=
uit spiritus meus : in deo sa=
lutari meo· Quia respexit hu=
militatem ancille sue : ecce eni
ex hoc beatam me dicet omnes
generationes· Quia fecit mi=
hi magna q̄ potens est: et sctm̄
nome eius· Et misericordia ei
us a progenie inprogenies: ti
mentibus eum· Fecit potenci
am in brachio suo: dispersit su

XIV

A. Altdorfer

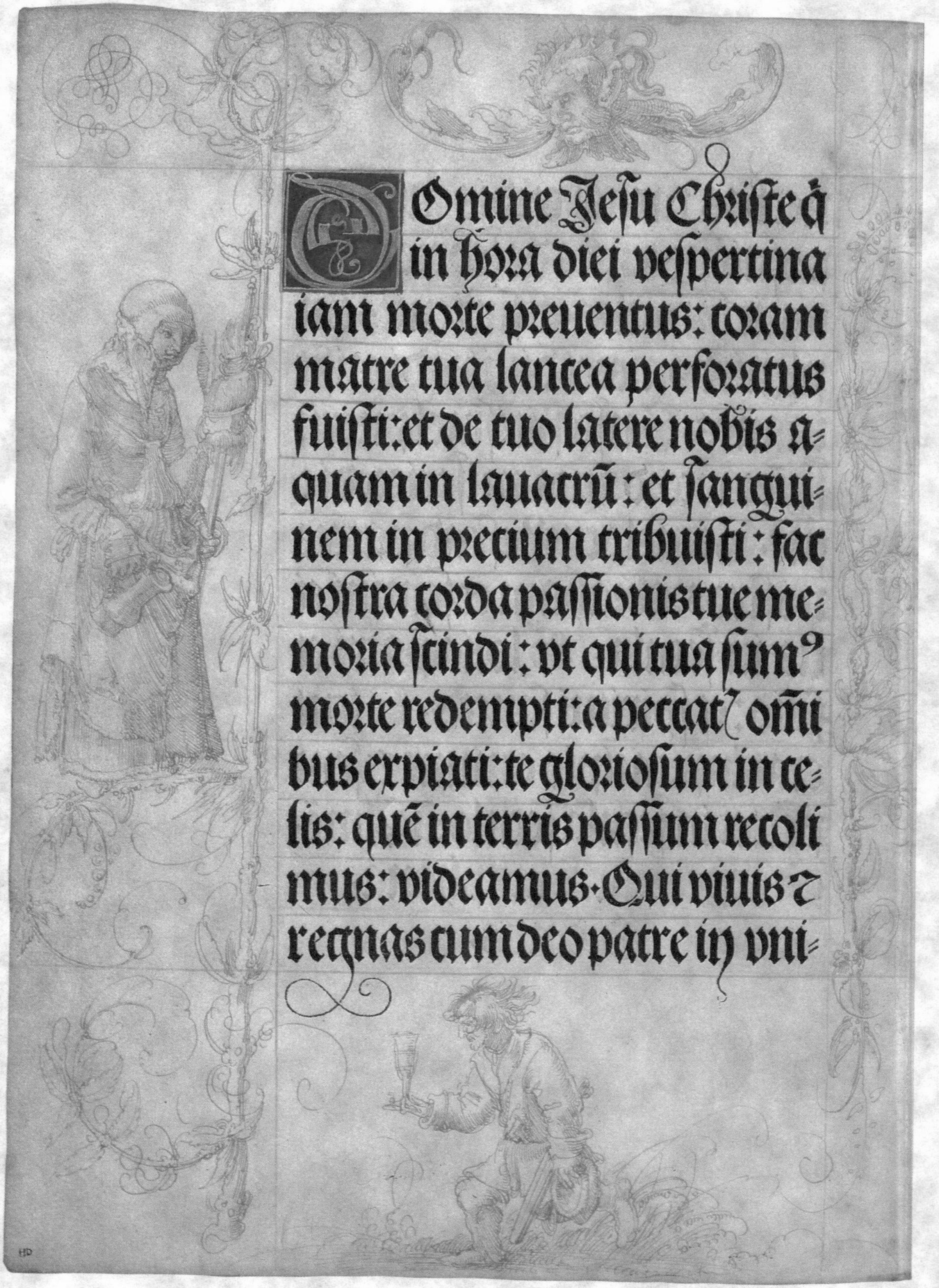

Omine Jesu Christe q̃
in hora diei vespertina
iam morte preuentus: coram
matre tua lancea perforatus
fuisti: et de tuo latere nobis a
quam in lauacru̇: et sangui
nem in precium tribuisti: fac
nostra corda passionis tue me
moria scindi: vt qui tua sum⁹
morte redempti: a peccat̃ omi
bus expiati: te gloriosum in ce
lis: que̅ in terris passum recoli
mus: videamus·Qui viuis ⁊
regnas cum deo patre in vni-

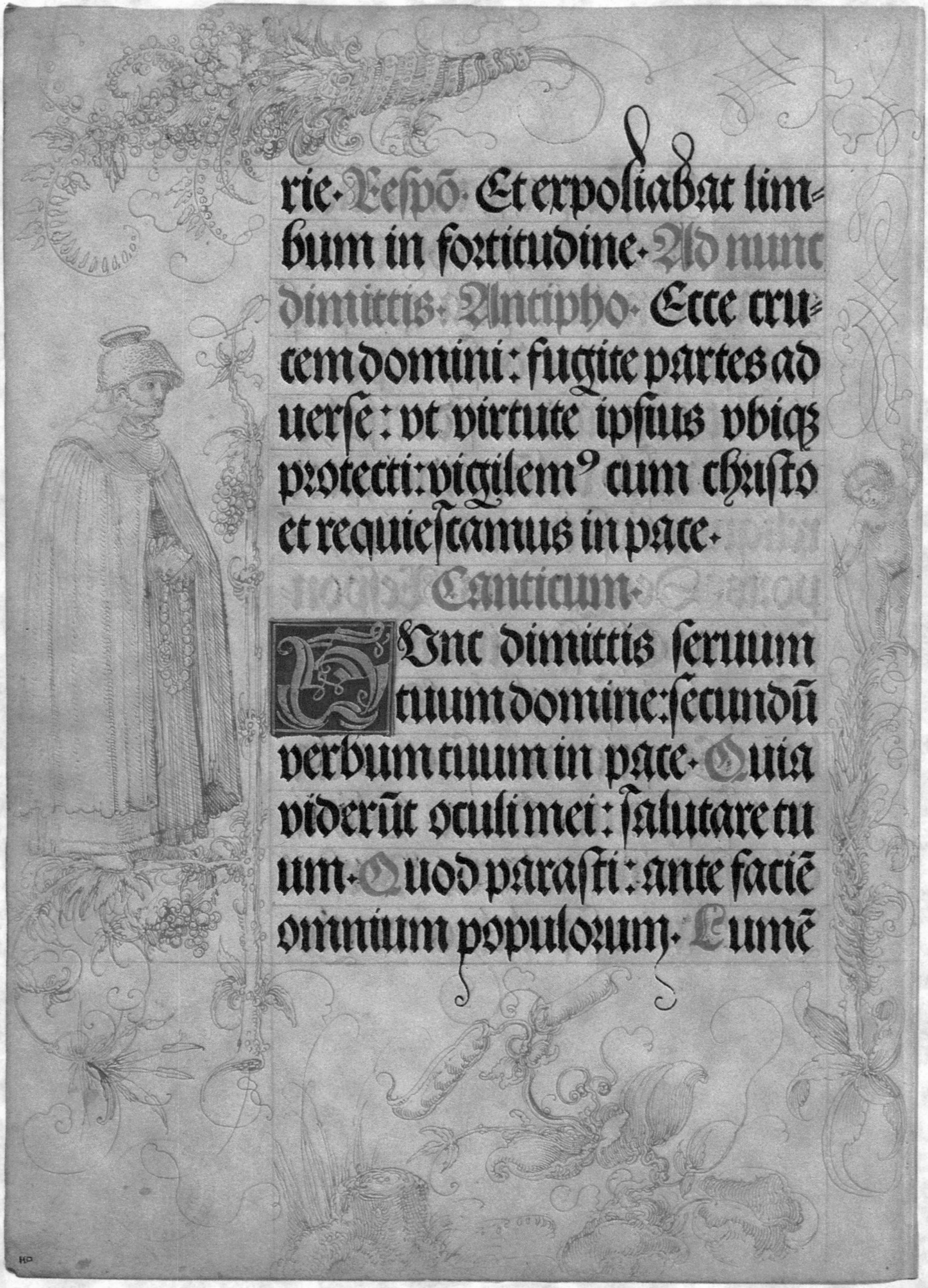

rie·Vespō· Et exploiabat lim=
bum in fortitudine· Ad nunc
dimittis· Antipho· Ecce cru=
cem domini: fugite partes ad
uerse: vt virtute ipsius vbiqʒ
protecti: vigilem⁹ cum christo
et requiescamus in pace·

Canticum·

Vnc dimittis seruum
tuum domine: secundū
verbum tuum in pace· Quia
viderūt oculi mei: salutare tu
um· Quod parasti: ante facie
omnium populorum· Lume

in secula seculorum Amen.
Antipho. Tulit Joseph corpus Jesu: et inuoluit illud in
sindone munda: et posuit eum
in monumento.
Psalmus.
Squo domine obli-
uisceris me in fine: vsq
quo auertis faciem tuam a me.
Quamdiu ponam consilia in
anima mea: dolorem in corde
meo per diem. Vsquo exal-
tabitur inimicus meus super
me: respice et exaudi me domi

et eleuamini porte eternales
et introibit rex glorie. Quis est
iste rex glorie? dominus fortis
et potens dominus potens in
prelio. Attollite portas princi
pes vestras: z eleuamini porte
eternales: et introibit rex glo
rie. Quis est iste rex glorie? do
minus virtutu ipse est rex glo
rie. Gloria patri zc. Et repeta
tur Antiphona. Capitulum.

Fratres: Gaudete quia
cum inimici essemus re
conciliati sumus deo per mor

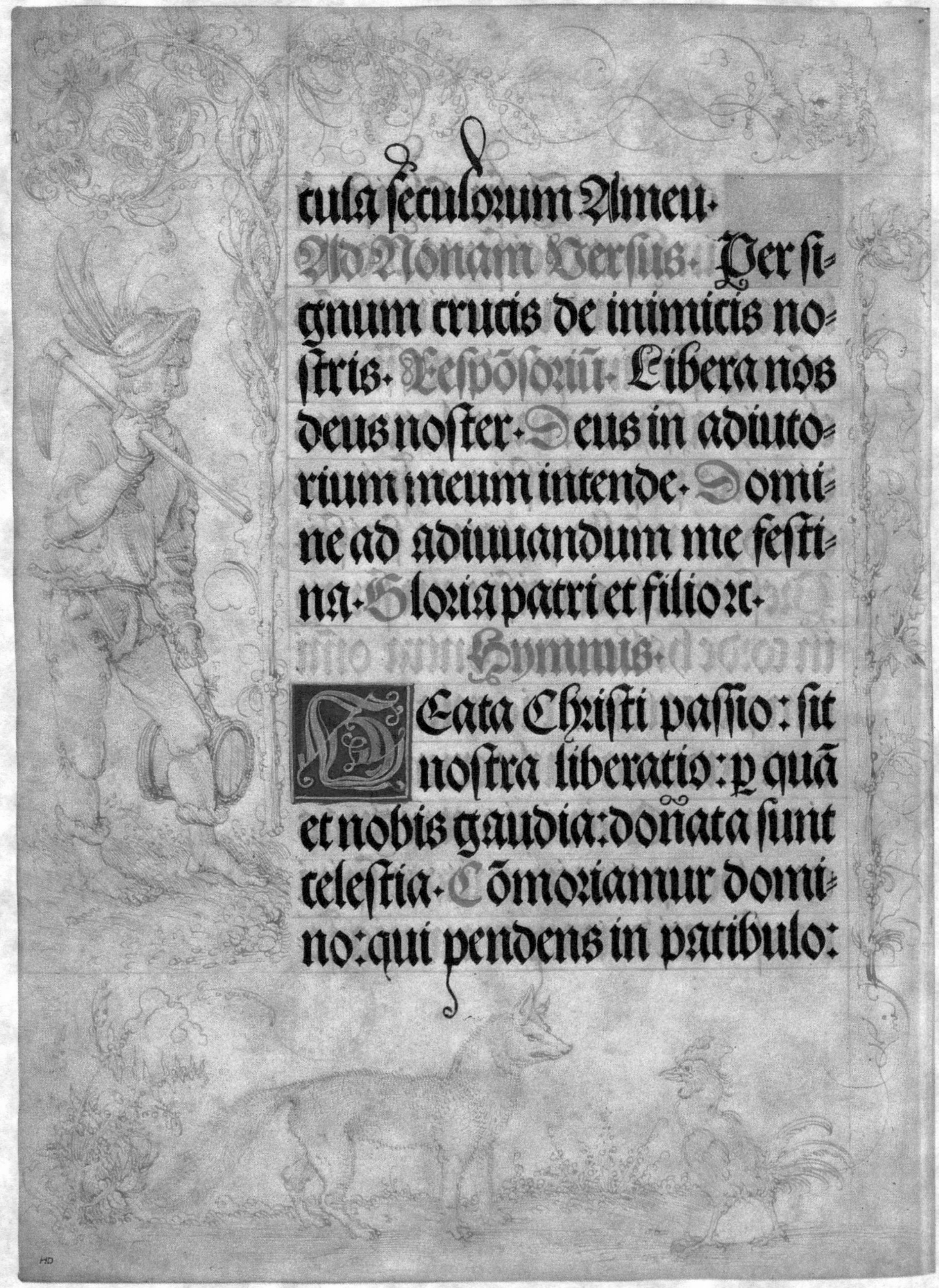

cula feculozum Amen.
Ad Nonam Verfus. Per fi-
gnum crucis de inimicis nostris. Refpōfoziū. Libera nos
deus nofter. Deus in adiuto-
rium meum intende. Domi-
ne ad adiuuandum me festi-
na. Gloria patri et filio rc.
Hymnus.

Beata Christi paffio: sit
nostra liberatio: p quā
et nobis gaudia: doñata funt
telestia. Cōmoriamur domino: qui pendens in patibulo:

mihi mundus crucifixus est:
et ego mundo · Deo gratias ·

Hymnus

Qui pressura mortis du-
ra: soluisti nexus crimi
num: Nos ad pacem: duc vera
cem: iesu corona virginum. In
flagellis potum fellis: bibisti
amarissime: Pro peccatis perpetra
tis eterne rex altissime. Nostre
genti recolenti: morti tue suppli
cum: Da virtutem: et salutem:
Christe redemptor omnium·
In amara crucis ara: fudisti

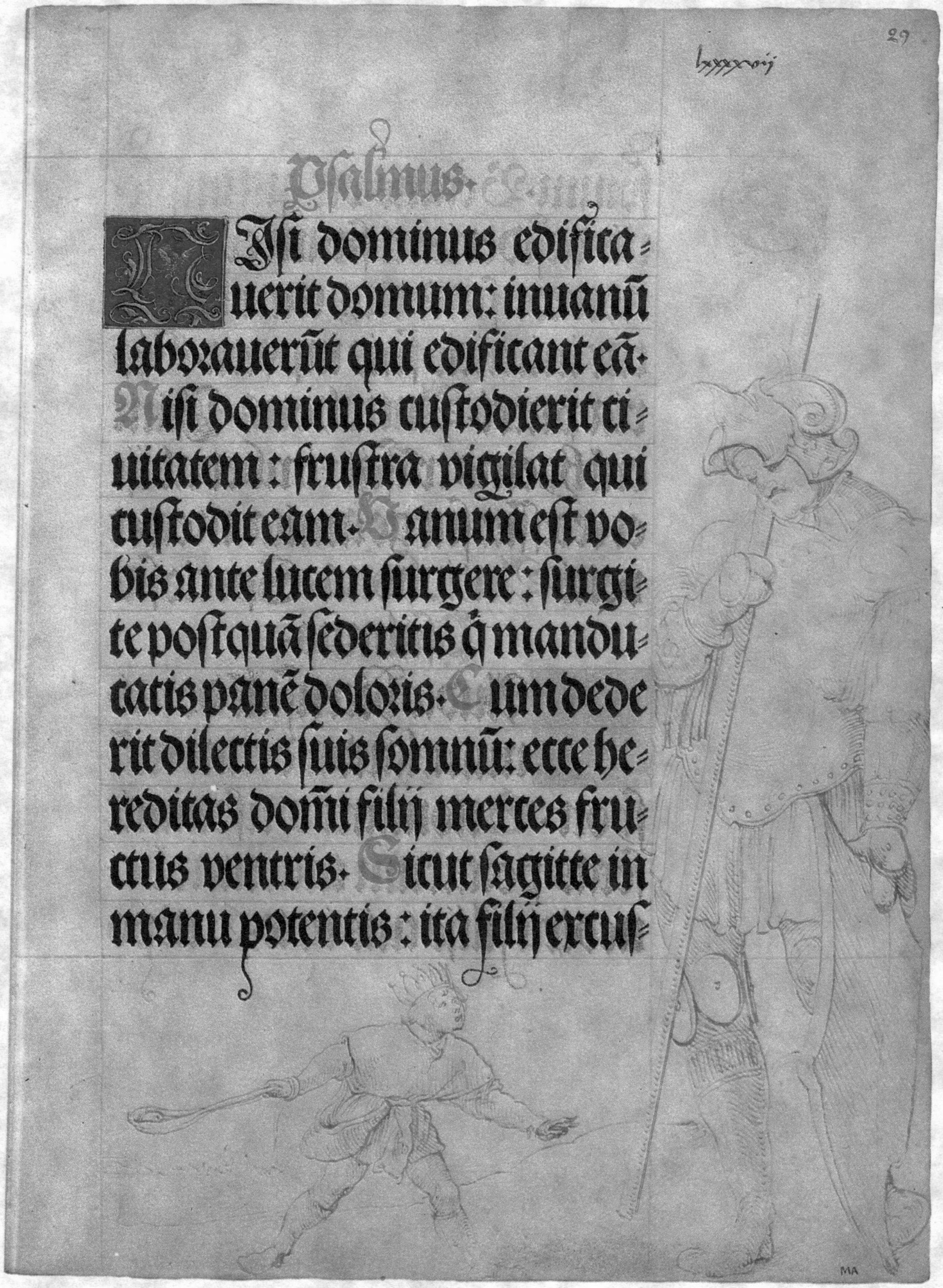

Psalmus·

Isi dominus edifica=
uerit domum: inuanū
laborauerūt qui edificant eā·
Nisi dominus custodierit ci
uitatem: frustra vigilat qui
custodit eam· Uanum est vo
bis ante lucem surgere: surgi
te postquā sederitis q̃ mandu
catis panē doloris· Cum dede
rit dilectis suis somnū: ecce he
reditas domͥi filij mertes fru
ctus ventris· Sicut sagitte in
manu potentis: ita filij excus

MA

et non inueni · Et dederunt in
escam meam fel: et in siti mea
potauerunt me aceto · Glo=
ria patri et · Repetatur Anti=
phona · Principes sacerdotū
et seniores populi: postquam
flagellauerunt me: irruerunt
in me dicentes: crucifige cruci=
ge eum · Capitulum ·
Christus factus est pro
nobis obediens vsqz ad
mortem: mortem autem cru=
cis · Deo gratias · Responsoriū
Seniores populi clamauerūt

mihi quia incolatus meus p̄
lōgatus est: habitaui cum ha
bitantibus cedar: multum in
cola fuit anima mea· Cū his
qui oderunt pacē: eram pacifi
cus: cum loquebar illis impu
gnabāt me gratis· Gloria pa
tri et filio· Psalmus·

Leuaui oculos meos in
mōtes: vnde veniet au
rilium mihi· Aurilium meū
a domio: qui fecit celum et ter
ram· Non det in commotio
nem pedem tuum: neq̃ dor

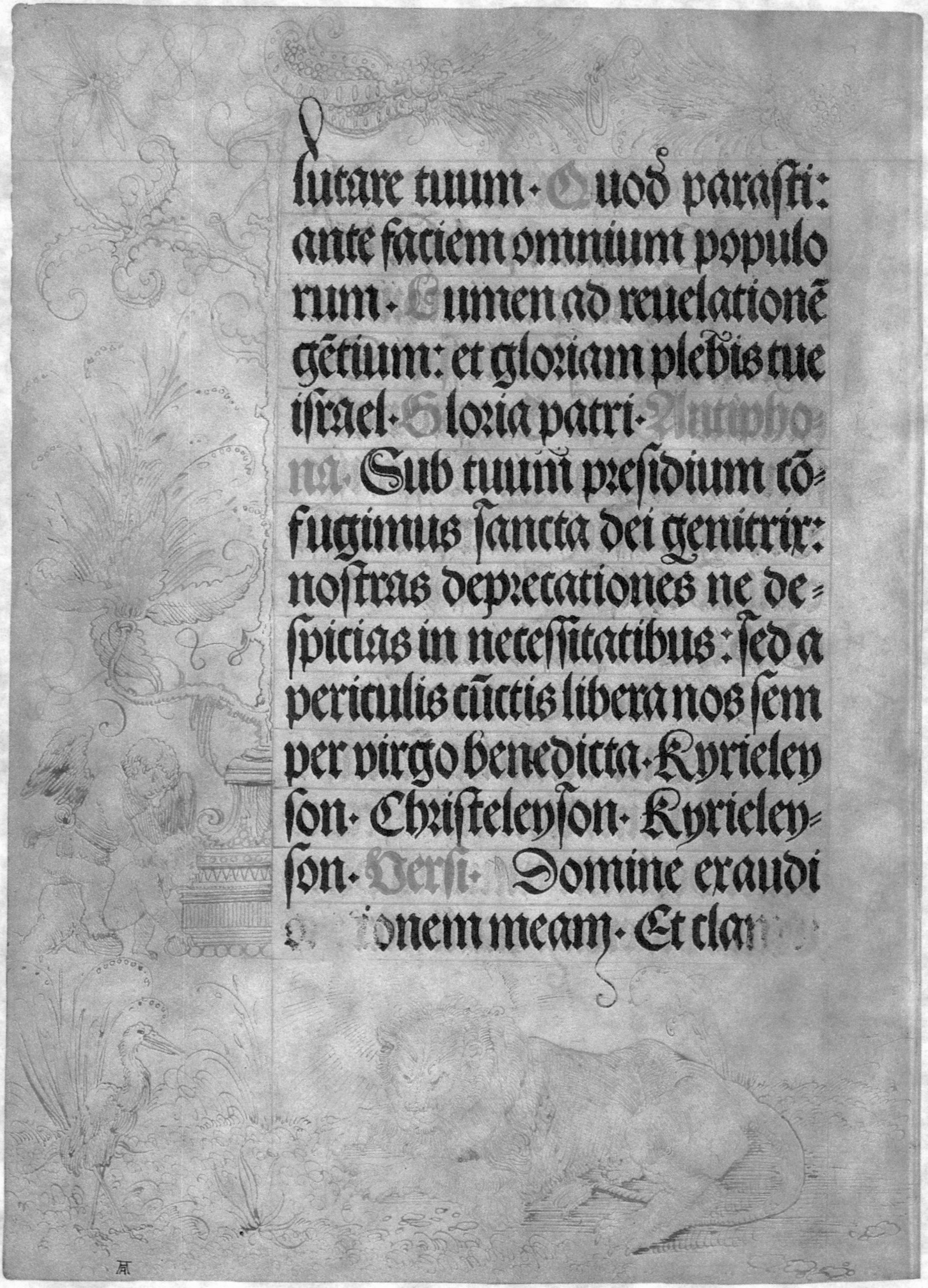

lutare tuum · Quod parasti:
ante faciem omnium populo
rum · Lumen ad reuelationē
gētium: et gloriam plebis tue
israel · Gloria patri · Antipho
na · Sub tuum presidium cō
fugimus sancta dei genitrix:
nostras deprecationes ne de=
spicias in necessitatibus: sed a
periculis cūctis libera nos sem
per virgo benedicta · Kyrieley
son · Christeleyson · Kyrieley
son · Versi · Domine exaudi
tionem meam · Et cla

XXIV
A. Altdorfer (école d'.)

fum effici mereretur : ſpiritu
ſancto cooperante preparaſti:
da vt cuius commemoratio
ne letamur: eius pia interceſſi
one ab inſtātibus malis : et a
morte perpetua: ⁊ ab omī tri
bulatiōe liberemur · Per eun
dē chriſtū dīm noſtrū · Amē ·
Anime omnī fideliū defun
ctorū: p miſericordiā dei requi
eſcant in pace Amen ·

Pſalmus ·

Eus miſereatur noſtri
et beŋedicat nobis: illu

in virtutibus eius: laudate eũ
secundũ multitudinem ma-
gnitudinis eius· Laudate eũ
in sono tube: laudate eum in
psalterio et cythara· Laudate
eum in tympano et choro: lau
date eum in cordis et organo·
Laudate eum in cymbalis be
nesonãtibus: laudate eum in
cymbalis iubilationis: omis
spiritus laudet dñm· Gloria·
Antiphona· Pulchra es et de-
cora filia hierusalem: terribi-
lis vt castroz acies ordinata·

letabuntur in cubilibus suis.
Exultatioes dei in gutture eo
rum: et gladij ancipites i ma
nibus eorum. Ad faciendam
vindictam in nationibus: in
crepatioes in populis. Ad al
ligandos reges eorum in con
pedibus: et nobiles eorum in
manicis ferreis. Ut faciant in
eis iudicium conscriptum: glo
ria hec est oibus sanctis eius.
Laudate dominum in sanct
eius: laudate eu in firmamen
to virtutis eius. Laudate eum

Capitulum

Iderūt eam filie syon
et beatissimam predica-
uerunt: et regine laudauerūt
eam. Deo gratias Hymnus.
Gloriosa domina excel
sa super sydera: qui te
creauit prouide lactas sacrato
vbere. Quod eua tristis abstu
lit: tu reddis almo germine: in
trent vt astra flebiles: celi fene
stra facta es. Tu regis alti ia
nua: et porta lucis fulgida: vi
tam datā per virginē gentes

XXVIII

Lucas Cranach

Sicut locutus est per os san-
ctorum: qui a seculo sunt pro-
phetarum eius. Salutem ex
inimicis nostris: et de manu
omnium qui oderunt nos.
Ad faciendam misericordiam
cum patribus nostris: et me-
morari testamenti sui sancti.
Jusiurandum quod iurauit
ad Abraham patrem nostrum:
daturum se nobis. Ut sine ti-
more de manu inimicorum
nostrorum liberati: seruiam9
illi. In sanctitate et iusticia co

trix Maria virgo perpetua:
templum domini sacrarium
spiritus sancti: sola sine exem
plo placuisti domino nostro
Hiesu christo: ora pro populo:
interueni pro clero: intercede
pro deuoto femineo seru. Ky
rieleyson. Christeleyson. Ky
rieleyson. Versi. Domine ex
audi orationem meam. Re
sponsorium Et clamor meus
ad te veniat. Oratio.
Eus qui de beate Ma
rie virginis vtero: ver

Oratio·

Protege domine populum tuu et apostolorum tuorum Petri et Pauli: et aliorum apostolorum patrocinio confidentem: perpetua defensione conserua· Per·

De sanctis Oratio·

Omnes sancti tui quesumus domine nos vbiqz adiuuent: vt dum eorum merita recolimus: patrocinia sentiamus: et pacem tuam nostris concede temporibus: et ab

XXXI

Lucas Cranach

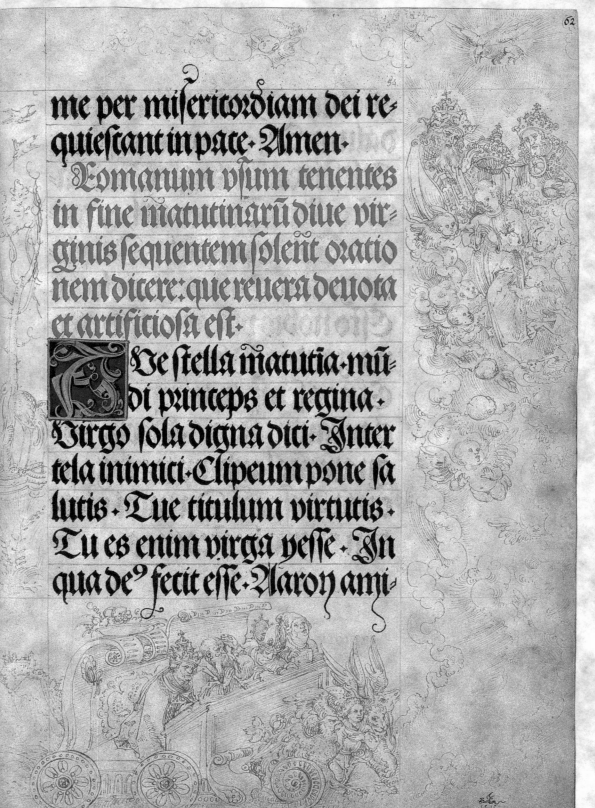

me per misericordiam dei re-
quiescant in pace·Amen·
Romanum vsum tenentes
in fine matutinarū diue virginis sequentem solent oratio
nem dicere:que reuera deuota
et artificiosa est·
Ve stella matutia·mū-
di princeps et regina·
Virgo sola digna dici·Inter
tela inimici·Clipeum pone sa
lutis·Tue titulum virtutis·
Tu es enim virga yesse·In
qua de⁹ fecit esse·Aaron ami

246 - Mary and Child - Cat. 162 Bis

ERHARD ALTDORFER

Few dates in the life of Erhard Altdorfer are known for certain. He was born in Regensburg around 1480, probably only a few years after Albrecht Altdorfer in whose will he was expressly mentioned as his brother. On account of the similarity in style of their work it is assumed that he spent some time in Albrecht's workshop during the years around 1506. In 1512 he entered the service of Duke Heinrich the Peacemaker of Mecklenburg and was court painter and master builder at the court of Schwerin from then until his death circa 1561. It is understood from various documents and registers in Schwerin that he was given a house by the Duke, was well paid and was always held in high esteem. R.B.

246 - Mary and child - Cat. 162 bis

Pen and ink drawing in black, highlighted in white on red grounded paper.
c. 1520/30.
Initialled by Albrecht Altdorfer and later dated 1533.
On the back — Christ on the Cross with John and a Thief.
199×149 mm.
Berlin, Kupferstichkabinett, SMPK. KdZ 2026.

Mary, her naked child on her lap, is sitting in the middle of a landscape with trees and houses in the background. She is holding a pomegranate, the symbol of her purity.
This way of depicting Mary, popular since the time of Dürer, is marked in this instance by some remarkably realistic touches. In particular, Mary's life-like, girlish appearance with her long, flowing curls and her full, round face make her look like an ordinary person.
The drawing was formerly thought to have been done by Albrecht Altdorfer, though it is now generally attributed to his brother Erhard Altdorfer, who, being artistically less independent than Albrecht, was given the inspiration for this work by his brother. Later as court painter for the Duke of Mecklenburg, he was influenced by Lucas Cranach the Elder. Cranach's influence can be seen in the portrayal of the child and — on the back of the drawing — in the figure of Christ on the cross. R.B.

Friedländer and Bock, 1921, p. 5 — Winzinger, 1952, n° 149 — Stange, 1964, p. 91.

249 - Landscape with large spruce tree - Cat. 165

Pen and black ink, highlighted in white on green grounded paper.
Unsigned, 1530.
306×195 mm.
Copenhagen, Statens Museum for Kunst.

This large, impressive print was correctly attributed to Erhard Altdorfer by Friedländer. It shows even more clearly than the wood engravings the influence his training in the Austro-Bavarian region still had on his work, even when he was in the North. The development can be traced from the drawing entitled "John on Patmos" (c. 1510, Wz. 148) to a print produced about ten years later and then to the work in question. F.A.

Friedländer 1923, p. 155. — Winzinger, 1952, n° 151.

247 - Standing female figure - Cat. 163

Pen and black ink, highlighted in white, grounded in yellowish brown
Undated, c. 1508/10.
117×78 mm. Wz. 144.
London, University College.

248 - The decapitation fo John the Baptist - Cat. 164

Pen and dark brown ink
c. 1506
109×113 mm. Wz. 143.
Regensburg, Museen der Stadt Regensburg.

A backwall of large square blocks and unpatterned floor create a narrow room, with no visible walls at the sides, which has a stage-like effect. The executioner, sword in hand, is standing with his legs apart over the headless body. He is passing the head to Salome who is waiting to the right with a platter in her hand. Two women are having a conversation behind her.
The restrained, slightly rigid lines of the print indicate that this is the work of Erhard Altdorfer. The extremely fine and detailed nature of the drawing led Winzinger to the correct conclusion that this was a draft for an engraving. This composition of figures is reflected in a drawing (East Berlin) and three paintings (Vienna, Padua, Florence). These figures are combined with a landscape background in a drawing in the Smith College Museum of Art, very similar to that of Cat. 132 to 139). It is possible that all these variations were inspired by one of Albrecht Altdorfer's missing paintings. B.B.

Winzinger, 1952, n° 143. — Cat. *The Danube School* 1969/70, n° 66. — K. Packpfeiffer, *Studien zu Erhard Altdorfer*, Diss. Phil., Vienna 1978, n° 13, pp. 73-76, 160f

247 - Standing female figure - Cat. 163

248 - The Decapitation of John the Baptist - Cat. 164

248 Bis - Saint Anne - Erhard Altdorfer - c. 1509/10 - Bright brown background - 170×123 mm - Frankfurt - Städelesches Kunstinstitut.

249 - Landscape with large spruce three - Cat. 165

250 - Mountainscape with tree on the left - Cat. 166

Signed etching.
1520 or a little later.
117×161 mm. B. 71, H. 2.
Berlin, Kupferstichkabinett, SMPK, Inv. n° 83-1889.

This landscape is Erhard Altdorfer's only remaining etching. He concentrated mainly on wood engraving. If it were not for the initials in the top right-hand corner which prove this is Erhard's work, it could be attributed to Albrecht (Bartsch). There are, in fact, similarities in style between this and Albrecht Altdorfer's landscape etchings. For example, the mountain valley leading into the distance between steep slopes and the spruce at the front edge of the picture with its double trunk, as well as the hooked type of hatching, bear a strong resemblance to Albrecht Altdorfer's work, of which the observer needs to have prior knowledge. The resemblance is also apparent in the inclusion of other motifs, such as the spruce trees which are only par-

tially visible, the cloud formation and the mill. Out of all his works Erhard Altdorfer shows most affinity with the style of the Danube School in this and other landscapes. On the other hand, Lucas Cranach the Elder's influence is more apparent in his portrayal of figures. R.B.

Winzinger, 1963, n° 244. — Cat. *The Danube School*, 1969/70, n° 39. Packpfeiffer, 1978, p. 23.

250 - Mountainscape with tree on the left - Cat. 166

251 - Landscape with View of the Sea - A. Altdorfer - c. 1525 - 206×312 mm - Vienna, Albertina.

MASTER OF THE HISTORIA

The Master of the Historia, formerly also often called Master of the Vita, was, along with Albrecht Altdorfer and Wolf Huber, one of the most important exponents of the Danube School. His title was taken from the manuscript of the "Historia of Frederici III and Maximilian I", the text of which he illustrated with pen and ink wash drawings. The Historia were written in Regensburg in 1513/14 and were probably illustrated around 1514/16. The Master must therefore have been in Regensburg at that time. The miniatures for Emperor Maximilian of the triumphal procession

also suggest this. Many bear the stamp of the Master's work and were painted in Albrecht Altdorfer's workshop around 1515. The painted winged altar in Pulkau (Austria) is also one of the Master's major works, and has earned him the additional title Master of Pulkau.

R.B.

252 - Landscape with watermill - Cat. 168

253 - Noblewoman with retinue out riding - Cat. 169

254 - The adoration of the three kings - Cat. 170
Pen and ink drawing in black, highlighted in white on reddish-brown grounded paper.
Dated 1512.
218×164 mm.
Berlin, Kupferstichkabinett SMPK. KdZ 113.

The New Testament story of the three kings who followed a star to Bethlehem to pay homage to the newly-born Messiah has been placed in a contemporary setting. Mary and child are sitting in front of the city gates, sheltered by the city wall. Joseph is standing next to her, while the first king, kneeling before the child, offers his gift. The other kings and an escort in riding habit follow him.
For a long time the drawing was considered to be one of Albrecht Altdorfer's works, though the pronounced white highlighting and the

drawings bear close relation to Altdorfer's. The small heads of the figures, the thick parallel hatching and the physical effect of depth are marks of the Master's style. R.B.

Friedländer and Bock, 1921, p. 4 — Winzinger, 1952, n° 128 — Oettinger, 1957, n° 112.

255 - The Decapitation of Saint Katharine - Cat. 171
Pen and black ink
c. 1510

kind of pen-strokes used would appear to disprove this. It is assumed that this is a copy of one of Altdorfer's drawings, probably done by the Master of the Historia who trained with Altdorfer and whose

150×125 mm. Wz 134
Vienna, Akademie (2528).

254 - The adoration of the three Kings - Cat. 170

255 - The Decapitation of St. Catherine - Cat. 171

LUKAS GRANACH THE ELDER

Lukas Granach the elder, one of the sons of the painter Hans Maler, was born in 1472 in the Upper Franconian Town of Kronach, which belonged to the bishopric of Bamberg. He began his apprenticeship in his father's workshop and in 1501 he set out for Vienna. It is impossible to ascertain where he went during his years as a travelling apprentice before he arrived at Vienna. The young Cranach must have been decisively influenced by the humanist spirit of the university of Vienna under the Emperor Maximilian, with such famous teachers as Konrad Celtis and Johann Cuspinian. His successful activity in that town, where he produced among other works a series of woodcuts for the printer Johannes Winterburger, lasted until 1503/04. In 1504 Cranach began to sign his works with the initials LC. Further travels took him via Nuremberg to Wittenberg where in 1505 he succeeded Jacopo de Barbari as court painter to the Elector Friedrich of Saxony and where he received a fixed salary. From this point onwards he added the coat of arms of the Saxon Electorate to his works. Right up to his death in 1553 Cranach lived under the protection of the Saxon Elector as a respected and wealthy citizen. He ran an extensive workshop, travelled far and wide often on political missions, and for a long time held the office of mayor of Wittenberg. Lukas Cranach the elder's paintings and graphic works were considerably marked, both thematically and iconographically, by his personal acquaintance with members of the university which was founded in 1502; these included Martin Luther, Philipp Melanchton, Cardinal Albrecht of Brandenburg and numerous members, of the aristocracy. R.B.

257 - The Thief on the Cross - Cat. 172

257Bis - Crucifixion - Cat. 172Bis, p. 358.

258 - The Thief on the Cross - L. Cranach - Pen-and-ink - Berlin, K., SMPK.

257 - The Thief on the cross - Cat. 172

Black chalk, highlighted in white, on red grounded paper.
c. 1502.
215×128 mm.
Berlin, Kupferstichkabinett, SMPK n° Inv. 4451.

The collection of the Kupferstichkabinett in Berlin includes two drawings of the two thieves bound to the cross, one of which (the drawing of the thief turned to the left) is included in this catalogue. These drawings, originally attributed to Matthias Grünewaldt, but now generally considered to be the work of Lucas Cranach the Elder, are studies on the theme of Calvary, with which the artist was preoccupied during his early creative years.
Both prints show the dying man writhing in physical torment as a result of the torture of the cross. He has surrendered to his fate and, perhaps already dead, with his head hanging down, he struggles against the cross and his bonds. With this direct portrayal Cranach achieves an expressiveness of an intensity that he achieves in none of his other Calvary scenes, not even his engraving of 1502 which bears close relation to this drawing. The emphasis on the expression of human feeling and its importance within a picture are present to this extent only in Cranach's early works and have had a far-reaching effect on the development of the Danube style. R.B.

Rosenberg, 1960, n° 3 — Jahn, 1972, p. 30/31 — Anzelewski, in: Cat. *Dürer und seine Zeit*, 1967/68, n° 64. — Cat. *Lucas Cranach, 1973*, n° 34.

260 - Sacred Heart - Cat. 174

Wood engraving.
Signed and dated 1505.
380×284 mm. B. 76, H. 69.
Paris, Bibliothèque Nationale, Cabinet des Estamps, ECN 878.

Holy Mary and St John are kneeling in the middle on a patch of grass on the nearside bank of a river, with Sebastian and Rochus behind them. Four angels are hovering above them, carrying a shield bearing a large heart which is half engulfed by flames. Christ is hanging on a tau-shaped cross, which is surrounded by a banner, within the heart. This may possibly be a devotional picture which served, along with prayer, to ward off the plague*. The heart is a symbol of "unio mystica", the mystical union of man and Christ, and of the heart, uplifted by prayer, and the Sacred Heart. The work is therefore deeply rooted in the mystical thinking of the late Middle Ages, which dates from the time of Augustin and Bonaventura and was widespread among the Order of Augustinian Cannons and at the electoral court in Wittenberg. Lukas Cranach was probably commissioned to do this engraving during his first year as court painter. In his iconography Cranach largely followed the tradition of the late Middle Ages for portraying the Sacred Heart. He expands on the earthly theme in the lower half of the picture where a landscape, which includes a hunting-lodge, can be seen. This completes an element which is curious in form as well as in content.

* This would explain the presence of the saints Sebastian and Rochus, and the tau-shaped cross, all of which served to ward off the plague.
R.B.

Koepplin/Falk, 1976, n° 7.

260 - Sacred Heart - Cat. 174

262   The temptation of St. Anthony - Cat. 176
Wood-cut.
Signed and dated 1506.
400×268 mm. B.56, H.76,II.
Paris, Bibliothèque Nationale, Cabinet des Estampes.
ECN 884.

The representation of the saint hovering in the air, surrounded by demons tormenting him, can be traced back to Schongauer (Minott 54). However, whereas Schongauer has the group of figures forming the centre of the print and details of rocky landscape restricted to the bottom right-hand corner, Cranach sets the scene against a complete landscape. The right-hand side is taken up by an oversized tree in front of a wooded hill. The rocky slope on the left contains the hermit's cave. A deep river-landscape with a castle completes the picture. Above the horizon the saint hovers in empty space. It is impossible to imagine such an emphatic contrast between the turbulent scene and the calm landscape devoid of people without the example of Dürer's wood-cuts of the Apocalypse (e.g. the 24 elders, B.63, Michael fighting with the dragon, B.72). The composition of the strong angel (B.70) is a particularly good comparison. Pleydenwurff's wood-cut of the Antichrist from the Schedel world chronicle represents a similar battle in mid-air (cf. Koepplin/Falk, 1976, no.399). Finally the fall of Simon Magus as depicted by, among others Dürer (Winkler 219), forms a related circle of themes. B.B.

Jahn, 1955, p. 19f - Koepplin/Falk, 1976, no.398.

263 - Saint George - Cat. 177

Wood engraving.
Signed and dated 1506.
378×277 mm. B. 67.
Paris, Bibliothèque Nationale, Cabinet des Estamps ECN 891.

This very large wood engraving brings to mind contemporary paintings, such as Dürer's Paumgartner Altar on the side panels of which
saintly knights, standing like statues, formed the centre of the middle
painting. In this work too St George, flanked by angels carrying parts
of his armour, is represented as a statue. He is taken out of the legend
which is depicted in the small pictures of the distant background landscape. The gaze of the young knight, who has a fashionable hairstyle
and a disc-shaped aureole, is fixed on a distant object which is explained
by the flag he is holding. St George was the patron of the George order
of Knights, founded in 1468-69 by Emperor Freidrich III and summoned to join the crusade against the Turks by Emperor Maximilian in
1503. Certainly this is how Lucas Cranach portrayed the figure of St
George, whose self-assured and individual appearance is determined by
the spirit of Humanism. R.B.

Koepplin/Falk, 1976, n° 11

264 - Riding couple with two dogs - Cat. 178
Wood-cut.
Signed and dated 1506.
172 × 123 mm. B.117, H.114, III.
Paris, Bibliothèque Nationale, Cabinet des Estampes. ECN 908.

An elegantly dressed couple ride slowly through a landscape with a fortress on a rocky hill, the man in the saddle, the woman sitting behind him riding side-saddle. The man leads two dogs with a leash.
The quality of this print lies in the balanced distribution of ornamental, richly structured elements and contrasting empty space. Thus, for example, Cranach achieves the clear, beautiful effect of the rump of the horse and the lush bushes on the right in front of the light middleground. B.B.

Koepplin/Falk, 1974, no.19.

264 - Riding couple with two dogs - Cat. 178

265 - Saint Christopher - Cat. 179
Painted wood engraving.
Signed, 1506.
283×193 mm. B. 58.
Paris, Bibliothèque Nationale, Cabinet des Estampes, ECN 887.

Like many of his contemporaries, Lucas Cranach portrayed the popular legend of the giant, St Christopher. He was the patron saint of travellers and was called upon to ward off the plague and quick death.

Cranach's portrayal of the saint who, burdened by the child Jesus, is laboriously making his way to the river-bank, is splendid and highly expressive. He probably had Dürer's wood engraving of Sampson's fight with the lion in mind (c. 1496, B. 2). The mighty figure, wrapped in a big cloak, fills the entire width of the picture and, as he climbs the steep side of the bank, moves towards the observer. St Christopher seems to pause as he listens to Jesus on his shoulders. Jesus, in the centre of the picture, has his hand raised above his head towards heaven in a gesture of blessing.

The new technique of painted wood engraving, which Cranach applied for the first time in those years, gives the work a life-like, three dimensional effect. The so-called clair-obscur technique is a printing process requiring two wooden plates. The engraved plate with the raised, black-inked lines is used as usual, while the second plate is covered with paint and a more deeply inlaid drawing which comes out white in print. The wood engraving is thus enriched and has the quality of a painting, like the light-dark drawings which were very popular at that time. R.B.

Koepplin/Falk, 1976, n° 402. — Cat. *Kunst der Reformationszeit*, 1983, n° A 26.

267 - The Judgement of Paris - Cat. 181

Wood engraving.
Signed and dated 1508.
366×254 mm. B. 114, H. 104.
Paris, Bibliothèque Nationale, Cabinet des Estamps. ECN 902.

The legend of the judgement of the King's son, Paris, belonged to those themes which gained avid interest in Germany following the spread of Humanism and the Renaissance, and which, moreover, were popular in learned and noble circles. The choice of Paris (he was elected to choose the most beautiful of three goddesses), which subsequently led to the disaster of the Trojan War, was didactically and morally compared with the choice made by Hercules. He correctly opted for virtue at the cross-roads. The Judgement of Paris was often performed as a play before the princes. Because of the allusion to eroticism and the presence of the Goddess of Love, Aphrodite, the theme was also associated in an allegorical way with princley courtships and marriages. In Berlin's "Skulpturengalerie" (SMPK) there is a stone relief produced in 1529 by Doman Hering, in which Paris has the facial features of the electoral prince, Ottoheinrich of Pfalz. This relief closely resembles Cranach's wood engraving.
Lucas Cranach's innumerable protrayals of the Judgement of Paris, which he did while court painter for Friedrich of Weisen in Wittenberg, should be considered against the intellectual background of that time. In this wood engraving, later followed by a number of paintings, he combined the ancient scene with a landscape of this homeland as did Albrecht Altdorfer. Here the people are an integral part of the natural landscape, while those in his paintings, which have rather a courtly character, have moved to the foreground and the landscape is merely a backdrop. R.B.

Cat. *The Danube School*, 1969/70, n° 13 — Koepplin/Falk, 1976, n° 528.

268 Adam and Eve - Cat. 182

Wood engraving
Initiated LC and serpent, also dated 1509.
333×229 mm - B1
Paris, Bibliothèque Nationale, Cabinet des Estampes, ECN 829.

Before this wood engraving by Cranach the animals had never played such an important role in works illustrating the Fall of Man. However, Cranach was always famous for his animal drawings and was taken on court hunts by the electoral princes, which gave him an opportunity to sketch. Even so, the lion must be based on a drawing by another artist. The model for the stag in the front left of the engraving is taken from a missing drawing in Dessau.
Like the masters of the Danube School, Cranach tends to emphasise the landscape or other supplementary details (in this case the animals), while attributing less importance to the actual theme of the engraving.

Keopplin/Falk 1974, Fig. 2, n° 573.

269 - Saint Chrysostomus - Cat. 183

c. 1509
B. VII. I
Paris, Bibliothèque Nationale, Cabinet des Estampes, ECN 825.

268 - The fall of man - Cat. 182

269 - St. Chrysostomus - Cat. 183

270 - Rest during the Flight - Cat. 184

271 - The rest on the flight to Egypt with angels dancing a roundel - Cat. 185

270 - Rest during flight - Cat. 184
Wood engraving.
c. 1509.
285×185 mm. B. 3, H. 7.
Paris, Bibliothèque Nationale, Cabinet des Estampes. ECN 832.

The Madonna, seated in front of an oak tree in the middle of the picture, is feeding her child. To the left Joseph approaches from behind the tree, leading a grazing donkey. To the right cherubs are drawing water and drinking at a watering-place. Behind another cherub is beating a branch on a willow tree. Above, on one of the branches of the oak tree, cherubs are playing musical instruments.
In its structure and in the richness of form this compostion bears a relation to the Fall of Man which was produced in the same year. B.B.

Koepplin / Falk, 1976, n° 375.

271 The rest on the flight to Egypt with angels dancing a roundel - Cat. 185
Wood-cut.
With winged snake.
Ca. 1510/15.
338×236 mm. B.4, H.8.
Paris, Bibliothèque Nationale, Cabinet des Estampes. ECN 833.

On a grassy bank in front of an oak against which Joseph is leaning sits Mary with the child. Angel putti dance around the bank, holding hands and forming a circle. In the tree two putti are stealing young birds from a nest.
There are two striking differences between this and cat. 157. The landscape appears more arid, ther is less floral variety, the graphic texture of the print is more restrained. The less rich vegetation could, however, be explained by the fact that other elements are here superimposed on the iconography of the Rest on the Flight. Whereas in the other work Joseph with the ass, the suckling, the water-place all refer to the biblical event, in this one only the image of troubled Joseph has remained. On the other hand, the Madonna on the grass bank originates from the circle of themes of the *Hortus Conclusus.* The puttis' round dance is probably not really essential to the iconography; it appears in Altdorfer's Birth of Mary (Ca. 1520, Munich, Alte Pinakothek), perhaps inspired by this Granach print, and it appears of course as a round dance of angels already in Botticelli's mystic Birth of Christ (ca. 1500, London, National Gallery). The motif of putti as nest-robbers comes from book illustrations (Erhard Reuwich's title-page to Bernhard von Breydenbach's Peregrinationes in Terram Sanctam, Mainz 1486, and Dürer's title page for Konrad Celtis' Quattuor libri amorum, Nuremberg 1502). In view of its frequent and varied use it is unlikely to have any specific meaning. B.B.

Winkler, 1961, p. 149-163 - *Koepplin/Falk, 1976, n° 376.*

272 David and Abigail - Cat.-186
Wood-cut.
Signed and dated 1509.
243×172 mm. B.122, H.3.
Paris, Bibliothèque Nationale, Cabinet des Estampes. ECN 830.

A woman sits beside a tree, a little dog jumping up at her. She holds a vessel in her lap and gives a water-bottle to a knight standing on the right, armed with a sword and halberd.
This represents an episode from the Old Testament in I Samuel, 25. Hard-hearted Nabal refused David his hospitality. In a rage the latter decides to get his right by force; however, Nabal's beautiful, clever wife Abigail prevents him from doing so by giving him the refreshment he had asked for. God lets Nabal die, and David marries the widow. In the typology of the "Speculum humanae salvationis" this scene pre-figures Mary's intercession to the angry Christ. B.B.

Koepplin/Falk, 1976, no.457.

272 - David and Abigail - Cat. 186

Christ on the Mount of Olives, the Arrest, Christ before Caïphas, Flagellation, the Laying in the tomb, Resurrection
Wood engravings from the Passion series of 14 prints
The Arrest is initialled and dated 1509.
250×172 mm.

Whether the book entitled *Passio D.N. Jesu Christi, venustissimis imaginibus eleganter expressa ab illustrissimi Saxoniae ducis pictore Luca Cranagio Anno 1509* ever, in fact, appeared in Wittenberg, has recently been disputed. Nevertheless, the plates, which even at this time seem to be damage and cracked at the edges, were reused to produce these prints. Three of the prints are framed with passe-partouts, used frequently in Cranach's workshop (e.g. Holy Mary with the baby Jesus and her mother, Anna, B. 68, Jahn, 1955). This proves that printing would still have been done in his workshop, probably up to the 1540's.

273 - The Arrest - Cat. 187
B. 8, H. 11.
Paris, Bibliothèque Nationale, Cabinet des Estampes. ECN 837.

Malchus, sitting on the floor, has had one of his ears cut off by Peter who is standing in the front right of the picture. Christ, harrassed by the henchmen, is sewing the ear back on. In the background is the scene of the youth who fled so late that the henchmen tore off his cloak (Mark 14, 51). This could also be based on Dürer's copper engraving from the Passion series (B. 5). Otherwise the turbulent composition of figures is most closely related to Jan Joest's High Altar (1505-08, Kalkar, St Nikolai).

Koepplin/Falk, 1976, n° 311.

II. Der verrheter Judas hatte jnen ein zeichen gegeben vnd gesagt / Welchen ich küssen
werde / der ists / den greiffet. Matth. xxvj.

III. Ich habe frey öffentlich geredt fur der Welt/ Ich habe allezeit geleret in der Schule vnd
in dem Tempel/ da alle Jüden zusamen komen etc. Johan. xviij.

VI. Die straff ligt auff jm/ auff das wir friede hetten/ Vnd durch seine wunden sind wir
alle geheilet. Esaie liij.

274 - Christ before Caiphas - Cat. 188
B. 10, H. 12.
Paris, Bibliothèque Nationale, Cabinet des Estampes. ECN 838.

On Christ's declaration that he is the Son of God, the High Priest Caiphas tears off his robe. According to ancient legal practice the throwing down of gloves is an oath and signifies excommunication.

Koepplin/Falk, 1976, n° 313.

275 - Flagellation - Cat. 189
B. 12, H. 15.
Paris, Bibliothèque Nationale, Cabinet des Estampes. ECN 841.

Koepplin/Falk, 1976, n° 315.

276 - The laying in the tomb - Cat. 190
B. 19, H. 22
Paris, Bibliothèque Nationale, Cabinet des Estampes. ECN 848.

The inspiration for this composition with the tomb parallel to the picture apparently comes from the Netherlands. It can be compared with Quentin Massy's Seven Sorrows of Mary (1505, Brussels) Dirk Bout's picture of the cloth used by Veronica to wipe Christ's face (London, National Gallery) and with another portrayal of the laying in the tomb from Cranach's area (Kreuzlingen, Kister's collection). The Master HS used Cranach's engraving as a model for a small relief in 1516 (Berlin, SMPK). B.B.

Koepplin/Falk, 1976, n° 322.

XIII.   Er ift begraben wie die Gottlofen / vnd geftorben wie ein Reicher. Efaie liij.

278 - The Resurrection - Cat. 192
Bright blue in colour. B. 20, H. 23.
Paris, Bibliothèque Nationale, Cabinet des Estampes. ECN 849.

This print painted in one colour with a brush achieves an effect similar to that of painted wood engraving. This technique is often found in Cranach's early prints (cf Koepplin/Falk, 1974, n° 14, 15). At the same time Cranach was experimenting with the technique of colour printing. B.B.

Koepplin/Falk, 1976, n° 310-323, p. 570-576.

2.

Christ as Saviour, St. Andrew, St. John the Baptist
Wood engravings.
From a series of 14 with Christ, the 12 apostles and Paul.
c. 1510/15.
Paris, Bibliothèque Nationale, Cabinet des Estampes.
ECN 831-853-855.

Unlike Niklaus Manuel Deutsch, Cranach stands his figures on thin strips of ground. They are framed at the sides by naturalistic twig design used for title page framework, emulating Erhard Reuwich. The imaginative playfulness with touches of the grotesque might also stem from the book illustration, as, for example, in the portrayal of John: the shrubs flanking him are as vigorous as they are bizarre; as if they were balustrades they bear a basket where cherubs play and a pot from which grass and oak leaves spill. Only in the depiction of the Saviour is there no framework at the sides: he is accentuated by an aureole with cherubs around his head.

279 - St. John the Baptist - Cat. 193
302×182 mm. B. 27, H. 35. ECN 855.

Altdorfer probably had this print in mind for his drawing Wz. 48, dated 1517.

Koepplin/Falk, 1976, n° 442.
Winkler, 1961, p. 149-163 — Koepplin/Falk, 1976, n° 438-451.

280 - St Andrew - Cat. 194
312×187 mm, B. 25, H. 33. ECN 853

Koepplin/Falk, 1976, n° 440.

281 - Christ as Saviour - Cat. 195
In ochre, blue-grey and red.
329×184 mm. B. 23, H. 31. ECN 851

Koepplin/Falk, 1976, n° 438.

279 - St. John the Baptist - Cat. 193

280 - St. Andrew - Cat. 194

281 - Christ as Saviour - Cat. 195

282 - The death and assumption of the virgin Mary - Cat. 196

Prophen.

Seraphin.

Cherubin.

Patriarchen.

Thron.

Zwelffboten.

Dominaciones

Marterer

principatus

Junckfrawen

283 - Coronation of Mary - Cat. 197

282 - The death and assumption of the virgin Mary - Cat. 196

Wodd-cut.
Ca. 1510/15.
397×283 mm. H.73a.
Paris, Bibliothèque Nationale, Cabinet des Estampes. ECN 881

Koepplin/Falk, 1976, n° 395.

283 Coronation of Mary - Cat. 197.

Wood-cut.
Ca. 1510/15.
397×281 mm. H.73b.
Paris, Bibliothèque Nationale, Cabinet des Estampes. ECN 882.

Inscriptions from bottom to top; Left: *Angelus, Archangel (us), Virtutes, Potestates, Principatus, Dominaciones, Throni, Cherubin, Seraphin;* right: *Kindlen (children), Eelewth (married couples), Witwen (widows), Beichtiger (confessors), Junckfrawen (virgins), Marterer (martyrs), Zwelffboten (apostles), Patriarchen, Propheten.*

These two prints are united formally and in terms of content, and they belong together in the catalogue. They are to be read from bottom to top and represent with remarkable thoroughness the legendary events of the death of Mary and her assumption into heaven. The framed rectangular fields in the first print contain the terrestrial events: the bottom line in the middle - Mary weeps with yearning for her son; on the outer left - an angle announces her imminent death and brings her a palm branch from paradise, which is to be carried in front of her bier. Next to it - St. John, miraculously brought along, receives the palm branch; on the outer right - the other apostles congregate, also by some miracle. Above it - the death of Mary, the soul of the departed is received in heaven by Christ; outer left - the apostles bear Mary to her grave, a high priest wants to overturn the bier and his hands become withered. In the middle - the apostles standing around the empty grave from which Mary has just risen. Above it the assumption is depicted twice in a shaft of clouds and with accompanying angels and putti. At the very top is a frontal view of the coronation; Christ and God the father sit on either side of Mary, each holding with one hand the crown over the head of the Kneeling.woman. The dove of the Holy Ghost hovers above them, to the right and left groups of angels are in attendance.
Mary's ascent to heaven is flanked on both sides by groups of half-figures and banks of cloud with are marked with inscriptions. The 9 choirs of angels on the left lead Mary in her ascension to heaven - in accord with the Legenda Aurea which follows the homilies of St. Gerard in this detail. The very oddly arranged group of saints on the right poses some problems. Apostles (Zwelffboten), martyrs and confessors (Beichtiger) as well as virgins all belong to the normal repertoire of the Litany, though prophets and patriarchs are much more rare, as are widows. But the category of married couples is a total exception to this; it is true that there are saintly married couples (Henry and Kunigunde for example), but they could not appear together in the Litany which insists on the separation of families. Moreover, these married couples are a direct contradiction of Mark 12,25. The group of children is just as unusual: the only children usually mentioned in the Litany are the innocents, the victims of the Bethlehem infanticide, yet they are placed between apostles and martyrs in the hierarchy. Specific features of identifiable saints are completely absent from the exceptional groups.
By filling the surface with secondary figures and masses of cloud the artist has created a uniform carpet-like effect. In this respect the print had an influence on monumental works such as the Marian altars of Mauer and those from Zwettl (now in Adamov, URSS). B.B.

Koepplin/Falk, 1976, n° 395/sq.

284 - The sermon of John the Baptist - Cat. 198

Coloured wood-cut.
Signed and dated 1516.
335×236 mm. B.60, H.85.
Paris, Bibliothèque Nationale, Cabinet des Estampes. ECN 893.

Non-coloured prints from the pure line-block have also been preserved. The graphic density and the completeness of the cut of the lines, in the shady areas of the little wood for example, or in the Baptist's halo, hardly allow the chiaroscuro to come into its own in the coloured plate. One can therefore suppose that it was originally intended to be a black and white print.
The scene is set at the edge of a wood. John stands behind an improvised barrier between two trees, his right hand raised in an oratorical gesture. Standing and sitting in front of him on the open field are about two dozen listeners of different ages and sexes, including several mothers with their children.
The iconography of John, preaching behind a barrier made out of a branch, can be found in a plate by Rueland Frueauf (ca. 1499, Klosterneuburg) and later in a pulpit carving ascribed to Benedikt Dreyer (ca. 1533, Zarrentin). B.B.

Koepplin/Falk, 1976, no.420 - cat. (Art of the Reformation period) Kunst der Reformationszeit, 1983, no.A 25, E 53 - cat. Luther und die Folgen für die Kunst, 1983, no.104. (Luther and the consequences for art).

285 - The third tournament - Cat. 199

Wood-cut.
Signed and dated 1509.
292×416 mm. B.125, H.118.
Paris, Bibliothèque Nationale, Cabinet des Estampes. ECN 912.

The whole page is filled with a mass of knights riding against each other with lances. The picture is charaterised by magnificent helmet plumes and caparisons as well as the intertwined straight lines of the lances. The background is made up of trumpeters, and an audience of knights and women behind a parapet. Prominence combatants is given to the two foremost galloping towards each other in parallel lines; the caparison of the knight on the right is decorated with the letter G. The striking motif of the hovering lance reappears in one of Dürer's woodcuts for the Freydal (B.app.36).
The print is believed to represent in idealised from the 1508 Wittenberg tournament. B.B.

Koepplin/Falk, 1974, n° 111.

286 - The German Tournament: "Anzogen race" - Cat. 200

Wood engraving.
c. 1516/17.
236×324 mm. B. app. 37, H. 120.
Paris, Bibliothèque Nationale, Cabinet des Estampes. ECN 914.

The print was counted earlier among Dürer's wood engravings which were to illustrate an unprinted edition of Emperor Maximilian I's *Freydal* which remains in manuscript form. On one of these on the right (B. app. 36) the figure of the fallen knight appears again. However, Cranach dramatises considerably Dürer's rather pale version of the battle by showing the opponent losing his saddle too and his spear or splinters from it spinning in the air. In the codex *Freydal* miniatures, Philip of Rechberg wears a helmet in a race against the Emperor which is decorated with a shoe like the knight on the left of the print (see Q.V. Leitner (Ed.), Freydal, Vienna 1880-82, p. 220). The composition does not match Cranach's engraving. P. 41 and 224 are closer). The "A" on the shield and saddle cloth of the adversary on the right could refer to "Austria" and be applied to Maximilian. B.B.

Koepplin/Falk, 1974, n° 115.

285 - The third tournament - Cat. 199

286 - The German Tournament: "Anzogen race" - Cat. 200

287 - Saint Anne - L. Cranach - 610×400 mm - Munich, Alte Pinakothek.

288 - The Crucifixion - L. Cranach - 1380×990 - Munich, Alte Pinakothek.

253- Noblewoman with retinue out riding - Cat. 169
Pen and black indian ink, highlighted in white, on paper grounded in greyish-yellow
Dated 1516.
208×157 mm.
Berlin, Kupferstichkabinett, SMPK KdZ 82.

The print shows a riding scene. A noblewoman is riding out of the castle gates. She is splendidly dressed, complete with feathered hat. Her armed retinue follows on foot. In the background the houses, church and fountain of a little village can be seen nestling into the rockface. The drawing was originally thought to have been done by Albrecht Altdorfer, but nowadays is attributed to the Master of the Historia. The thin and thick pen strokes and the painted effect of the Indian ink are characteristic of his style. The Master may have been familiar with Albrecht Altdorfer's drawing of the *Falcon Huntress* which has a similar motif. R.B.

Friedländer and Bock, 1921, p. 5. — Winzinger, 1952, n° 135. — Cat. *Kunst der Donauschule,* 1965, n° 238.

252 - Landscape with watermill - Cat. 168
Pen and ink drawing in black and India ink, highlighted in white on reddish-brown grounded paper.
c. 1520/25
208×153 mm.
Berlin, Kupferstichkabinett, SMPK. KdZ 92.

In this drawing a watermill is standing in front of mountains which fade into the distance. A bridge, on which the tiny figure of a fisherman can be perceived, stretches from the watermill over the stream to the bank in the foreground, where there is a willow tree with a thick trunk and feather-like branches. Two tall trees with drooping branches form the border of the left edge of the picture. They are pushed so far to the fore that they appear to leave the field of the picture and the observer has the impression of standing next to the trees and looking at the landscape.
The fairy-tale mood produced by the trees and the romantic charm of the drawing are found frequently in the Master of the Historia's work. His direct contact with Albrecht Altdorfer is particularly apparent in this sensitive portrayal of nature, which has only recently been attributed to him. R.B.

Friedländer and Bock, 1921, p. 5. — Winzinger, 1952, n° 140 — Benesch and Auer, 1957, p. 130 — Stange, 1964, p. 114.

WOLF HUBER

As with almost all artists of those times, biographical details of Wolf Huber's life come to light mainly from his dated works. It is thought that Wolf Huber was born around 1480 in Feldkirch in Vorarlberg and was perhaps the son of "Hanns Huber, painter in Feldkirch" mentioned in 1491. His early works indicate a possible meeting with Lukas Cranach the Elder in Vienna shortly after 1500. It was probably during these years that he also met his contemporary Albrecht Altdorfer. It is clear from a contract dated 1515 for the painting of the altar of St. Anne in Feldkirch that Huber was already living in Passau at this time and owned a workshop. As court painter and master builder to the Prince's bishop, Huber held

a respected post and was well rewarded for the varied tasks he carried out. He died, according to the inscription on his gravestone, on 3 June 1553. R.B.

289 - Foothills of the Alps - Landscape - Cat. 201

Pen and brown ink with water colours.
With monogram and dated 1522 which has been changed later to 1532.
211×306 mm.
Berlin, Kupferstichkabinett, SMPK. KdZ 2061.

This piece of work is doubtless one of the most beautiful of Wolf Huber's landscapes which through him and Albrecht Altdorfer became a quite new and artistic independent genre, soon having numerous followers. Huber explored Nature's shapes in many earlier detailed studies depicting for example a single tree or a clump of trees. The often objectively realistic style of such studies contrasts with our example where the impression of nature is conveyed by colour. The contrast between light and dark, between the pastel shades in the background and the dark earthy colours of the foreground and the delicate red light from the sky lends the picture a delightful touch of romantic magic. The clouds in the sky, streaked with red light, also add to the feeling that one is being reminded of the alpenglow, that fascinating natural phenonomen lasting but a few minutes at sunset with which Wolf Huber must surely have been familiar from his homeland. And yet the artist was less concerned in this drawing with depicting the actual phenonomen objectively than he was with creating the landscape with the eyes and feelings of the observer who is seized by this unique vision. R.B.

Heinzle, 1953, n° 91 and fig. 40. — Stange, 1964, p. 100 and fig. 170. — Winzinger, 1979, n° 69.

290 - Landscape with a Footbridge - Cat. 202

Pen in black, first sketched in watercolors. On the back a sketch of a tree in black pen.
c. 1519/20.
Berlin, Kupferstichkabinett, SMPK. KdZ 1692.

A low bush at the right edge of the picture indicates the bank of a river, over which there is a wooden footbridge. In the distance, houses with pointed gables and towers, and a church rise up from behind the fields and trees lining the opposite river bank.
This pen drawing, formerly attributed to Albrecht Altdorfer and today, due to Winzinger, to Wolf Huber, is a particularly impressive example of the artist's examination of the artistic problem of landscape rendition. Compared to earlier drawings, Wolf Huber has by now mastered perspective, spatial depth, light conditions and color. The footbridge, covering the whole drawn angle of view and heavily foreshortened at the other end, directs the view across the wide river to the opposite bank, to the church and the village. Because the horizon line runs along the lower part of the picture, the impression emerges of a gently rolling countryside, disappearing in the distance. The delicate gray-blue tones of color of the background seem like a veil of haze, which emphasizes the distance of the village, whereas the willow and bush, due to the clarity of their colors and the broader penstrokes, move tangibly into the foreground. B.B.

Friedländer and Bock, 1921, p. 45. — Winzinger, 1979, n° 65.

290 - Landscape with a Footbridge - Cat. 202

291 - Landscape with Big Tree - Cat. 203

Pen in brown. Upper edges of the drawing have been rounded off.
With the date 1523.
151×220 mm.
Berlin, Kupferstichkabinett, SMPK. KdZ 1270.

In several of his drawings Wolf Huber is concerned with tree shapes, merely indicating the background landscape with a few soft strokes. The gnarled tree trunk in the foreground, which the pictorial framing captured only up to the first branches, appears to the viewer to be well advanced in years, although the true height remains unclear. Next to it stands a younger and a very young tree. With a secure execution of the drawn line, the artist has captured the living corporality of the tree and its outward appearance, marked by age and weather. This drawing

is to be understood as a very realistic sketch made from nature. B.B.

Friedländer and Bock, 1921, p. 56. — Heinzle, 1953, n° 98, Ill. 44. — Stange, 1964, Ill. 178. — Winzinger, 1979, n° 70.

291 - Landscape with big Tree - Cat. 203

292 - Landscape - Wolf Huber - Pen-and-ink - Munich, Graphische Sammlung

293 - Landscape - Hirschvogel - Oxford, Ashmolean Museum.

294 - Lanscape with Castle - W. Huber - 1515 - Pen-and-ink - Munich, Graphische Sammlung.

295 - Landscape with Castle - Cat. 205

296 - Landscape with Tree - W. Huber - 1530
Pen-and-ink - Munich - Graphische Sammlung.

293 - Castle Landscape - Cat. 204
Grey-brown pen and ink. Wz 2.
176×134 mm. No signature or date.
Oxford, The Ashmolean Museum.

It is not easy to understand why Winzinger has placed this and the Berlin print of similar theme before the Nurenberg study of the Mondsee, 1510. As dated pictures show, the involved and detailled style is found in Huber's work only some years later. F.A.

Halm 1930, n° 33. — Heinzle n° 3. — Winzinger 1979, n° 2.

295 - Landscape with castle - Cat. 205
Light brown pen and ink. c. 1503/5.
191×130 mm.
Berlin, Kupferstichkabinett, SMPK. KdZ 97.

The drawings of Wolf Huber (the most outstanding representative of the Donau School apart from Albrecht Altdorfer) constitute a very important part of his work. Their theme for the most part is landscape with which he was preoccupied. The first example of this is dated 1502. The Berlin landscape drawings also belong to these earliest days. The unsteadily jagged and crinkly lines of the fields, often with only vague outlines which are reminiscent of Altdorfer's style, still have an unpolished effect. But with regard to the picture's structure and the style, the essential features of Huber's landscapes are already suggested. Huber creates with few devices an idea of volume. The tree at the righthand edge of the picture is placed on a level with the observer. The horizon in the lower half of the picture makes the hilly landscape appear far away and the eye wander into the distance. R.B.

Friedländer and Bock, 1921, p. 57. — Heinzle, 1953, n° 3. — Stange, 1964, p. 98. — Cat. *Dürer und seine Zeit*, 1967/68, n° 135. — Winzinger, 1979, n° 3.

302 - Mountain landscape with bridges - Cat. 209
Pen and brown ink.
210×160 mm. Wz 4.
No signature or date.
Oxford, The Ashmolean Museum.

With regard to its date, the same can be said of this perhaps unfinished drawing as of Winzinger's n° 2 (Cat. 204). The thick and even strokes which shape the foreground make it hard to gain an overall view of the composition and we are scarcely aware that our gaze is led through an arch in the rock on the right. The radiant sky is a further indication that the drawing was completed after 1510. F.A.

Halm 1930, n° 114. — Winzinger 1979, n° 4.

297 - Landscape - W. Huber - 1518 - Pen-and-ink - Munich, Graphische Sammlung.

Pen and black ink with grey wash.
210×330 mm. Wz. 109.
Signed W.H. and dated 1552.
London, University College.

This spacious landscape from Huber's last creative period is an extraordinarily impressive composition as Winzinger has rightly recognised. But it can hardly have been drawn without preceding studies in nature. One has attempted to identify the rock fortification in this drawing as the defile Fragstein in Prätigau which seals off the Landquart valley from the Upper Rhine. The fortification consisted of the converted grotto under the overhanging rock and of a wall stretching to the bank with a gate so that the valley was barred to enemy access, a high rockface falling right to the water on the other bank. As Fragstein was only roughly a day's journey south of Feldkirch, the supposed study might have been drawn during one of Huber's stays in his home town, and might therefore be dated 1532 at the latest. Should the Fragstein conclusion not be accurate, the only one Austrian rock fortification

that it might be is the Puxer Loch in Steiermark for there also an advance fortification can be found and a church or chapel in the vicinity.
F.A.

E. Poeschel: Eine Bündner landschaft von Wolf Huber, in *Anzeiger für schweizerische Altertumskunde 35*, 1933, p. 142 ff. — Heinzle, n° 168. — Winzinger, 1979, n° 109.

Wolf Huber (?)
Pen and black ink.
Dated 1528 and inscribed on the right at the top: *das ist das erst.*
220×310 mm.
Braunschweig, Herzog Anton Ulrich Museum. N° Z 41.

The unity of space apparent in other landscapes is very much lacking
in this drawing. The flaws in the picture's structure have given rise
again and again to doubt in the literature as to who drew it. The drawing is thus frequently held to be the work of an apprentice while Winzinger has classed it recently as Wolf Huber's. It does seem probable
that Huber marked the date 1528. However, if this landscape's two-
dimensional effect is compared with the liberally and vivaciously defined lines and the depth of earlier works, to attribute it to Huber is probably dubious. R.B.

Heinzle, 1953, n° 122. — Cat. *Kunst der Donauschule, 1965*, n° 296. — Winzinger,
1979, n° 80.

300 - Landscape - Cat. 208
Pen.
Grenoble, Musée de Grenoble, Inv. MG1465

301 - Castle - W. Huber - 1542 - Basel - Kupferstichkabinett der öffentlichen Kunstsammlung.

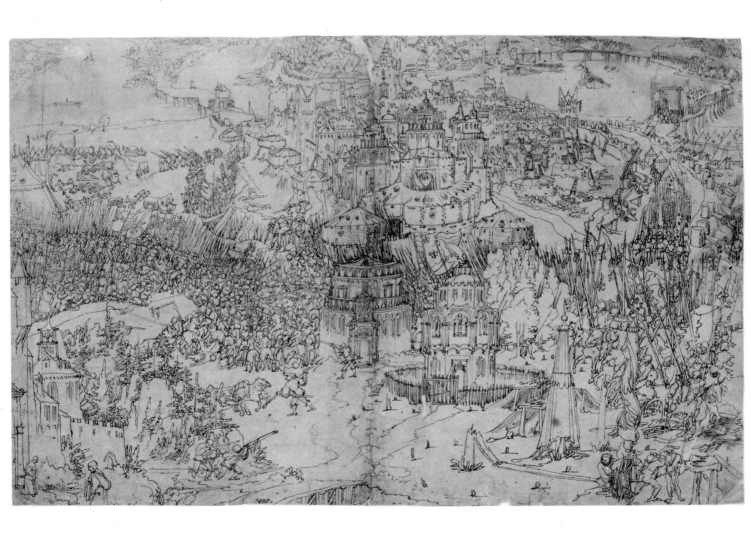

302 - Mountain landscape with Bridges - Cat. 209   303 - The Battle of Pavie - W. Huber - Munich.

304 - The Annunciation - Cat. 210

Brown pen and ink with grey-brown wash.
1514
123×90 mm. Wz. 27.
Copenhagen, Statens Museum for Kunst.

The positioning of the figures in this picture reveals that Huber had in mind Dürer's corresponding wood engraving from "Marienleben" (Mary's Life) of 1504 (B. 83). Huber modifies the somewhat arbitrary spatial structure of Dürer's composition to a Gothic church interior. The nave extends into the distance and is outlined precisely; a lively game with light and shade arises from the use of the wash. Comparing this with Altdorfer's *Church Interior* shows how two artists with similar drawing techniques can differ in their conception of space. F.A.

Winzinger, 1979, n° 27.

305 - Transfiguration of Christ - Cat. 211

Pen in black, gray wash.
With name sign and date 1526.
191×150 mm.
Berlin, Kupferstichkabinett, SMPK. KdZ 11732.

This signed and dated drawing belongs to a series of drawings which were done by Wolf Huber in the years 1525/26, probably as sketches for paintings. In these drawings one can notice the landscape receding in favor of the human figure, which is outlined with clear and secure pen strokes. This, in comparison with earlier drawings, expressive drawing style can be recognized again and again, above all in Huber's later drawings (see cat. 212). Limited primarily to figure drawings, these scenes appear to be dramatically animated. With the help of the gray wash, additional accentuation is placed on light and shadow, thus dividing the angle of view into two halves.
In the upper half, in the light sphere, floats the transfigured body of Christ, which has been sketched with only a few lines and is corporally hardly tangible, while the seemingly three-dimensional figures of the apostles are blinded by the light and, seeking shelter, turn their faces to the shadowy earth. R.B.

Heinzle, 1953, p. 21. — Stange, 1964, p. 103. — Cat. *Dürer und seine Zeit,* 1967/68, n° 139. — Winzinger, 1979, n° 75.

306 - Christ at the Mount of Olives - Cat. 212

Pen in black, gray wash, highlighted in white on red-brown-pigmented paper.
c. 1545/50
275×190 mm.
Berlin, Kupferstichkabinett, SMPK. Kdz 8478.

If one compares the drawing, so strikingly modern in its expressivity, with the signed rendition of the transfiguration of Christ preceding it in the catalogue, there can be no doubt about its attribution to Wolf Huber.
In this late drawing Huber has described the scene at the Mount of Olives using extremely sparse means along with the highest degree of mastership. The figures and the landscape have been briefly outlined with a few generous penstrokes. The details have not been developed thoroughly in all their particularities, but rather limited to the most essential aspects and only sketched out in so far as they are significant as carriers of the mood. This is particularly noticeable in the Christ figure, which is completely non-three-dimensional and flat, and receives its expressive power exclusively from the highly dynamic contourline. Wolf Huber was not concerned with depicting the external event, but rather tried to grasp the spiritual sentiments, tried to express the fear and solitude Christ underwent before his death at the Mount of Olives. R.B.

Friedländer and Bock, 1921, p. 57. — Heinzle, 1935, p. 91, n° 166. — Winzinger, 1979, n° 103.

304 - The Annunciation - Cat. 210

305 - Transfiguration of Christ - Cat. 211

306 - Christ at the Mount of Olives - Cat. 212

307 -Saint George - Cat. 213.
Wood-cut.
With monogram and date 1520.
204×152 mm. B.7. Wz. 271.
Paris, Bibliothèque Nationale, Cabinet des Estampes. ECN 1524.

This large print dated 1520 is the earliest of the thirteen surviving wood-cuts by Wolf Huber, and the only one bearing a date. The artist only produced comparitively few works in this medium, even if we take into account that some prints may have been lost in the course of time, the second decade of his creative live. They are all distinguished by common stylistic features which are seen at their best in this depiction of St-George. The landscape does not form the background to the action as it does in other works of the artist; instead it reflects the turbulence of the action and plays an essential part in creating the atmosphere. The people do not seem very life-like and are woven into the natural surroundings rather like figures in a tapestry - particularly the small figure of the princess who, according to the legend, was to be sacrified to the dragon. The great energy of the representation is achieved not least by graphic means, the density and diversity of the almost equally broad strokes of the lines. This print is one of the most significant achievements in the medium of the wood-cut. R.B.

Heinzle, 1953, n° 60. - Cat. The Danube School, 1969/70 n° 85. Winzinger, 1979, n° 271 and p. 48f.

307 - Saint George - Cat. 213.

308 -Saint Christopher - Cat. 214.

Wood-cut.
With monogram, ca. 1518/20.
120×94 mm. B.6. Wz 269.
Paris, Bibliothèque Nationale, Cabinet des Estampes. ECN 1523

Wolf Huber frequently reproduced Saint Christopher carrying the Infant Jesus across a rushing river. In the earlier depictions of this scene St. Christopher is seen as a slim knightly figure moving in a restrained manner. Here however Huber depicts him, in accordance with the legend, as a coarse, strong man of gigantic stature. The natural surroundings are violently agitated, with gnarled trees and whirling water completely characteristic of the Danube School. A gale seems to be shaking the whole landscape, puffing up St. Christopher's cloak and driving thick clouds across the sky in which the sun continues to shine brightly. The style of drawing and above all the formation of the sky with turbulent clouds on the left and the sun in a crown of rays are also found in Huber's wood-cut representing the crucifixion of Christ (cf. cat. 217). R.B.

Heinzle, 1935, p. 83, n° 138. - Winzinger, 1979, n° 269. - Cat. The Danube School, 1969/70, n° 87.

309 - Pyramus and Thisbe - Cat. 215

Wood engraving.
c. 1513/15.
119×92 mm. B. 9, Wz. 266.
Berlin, Kupferstichkabinett, SMPK. Inv. n° 361-7.

Like Albrecht Altdorfer, Wolf Huber took up the tragic love story of Pyramus and Thisbe many times. The dead body of Pyramus, his features contorted like a mask, is depicted in a greatly narrowed perspective so that one's gaze falls on his bent and apparently enormous leg. As he was doing this, Huber probably had in mind two of Albrecht Altdorfer's wood engravings — those of Pyramus and Thisbe and Jael and Sisera, both completed around 1513. He has combined these versions of a figure laid at an angle well into the picture with its legs turned forwards. Thisbe is wearing a delicate garment shaping her body which is tied beneath the breast in Ancient Greek style and slit at the side to the thigh drawing attention to her leg. The girl's figure is modeled on a Mantegna engraving of four dancing maid-servants which also influenced two of Aldorfer's works. The predilection of the Danube school's main masters for Andre Mantegna's graphic work, which is verified by a number of other examples, demonstrates especially clearly their lack of affinity with Italian Renaissance art. In dramatic expression, and also by the way the landscape is formed, this wood engraving is comparable with the preceding catalogue item. R.B.

Heinzle, 1953, n° 34 and Fig. 76. — Cat. *Kunst der Donauschule*, 1965, n° 322. — Cat. *The Danube School*, 1969/70, n° 88. — Winzinger, 1979, n° 266.

308 - Saint Christopher - Cat. 214.
309 - Pyramus and Thisbe - Cat. 215

310 -Adoration of the magi - Cat. 216.

Wood-cut.
With monogram, ca. 1512/13.
118×92 mm. B.2, Wz 263.
Paris, Bibliothèque Nationale, Cabinet des Estampes. ECN 1519

This is one of four wood-cuts representing scenes from the chidhood of Christ. As they all have the same format, similar style of composition and structure they obviously belong together. It is conceivable that Wolf Huber planned a larger sequence of wood-cuts illustrating the story of the childhood of Christ or that some prints from such a sequence, similar to those of Dürer and Altdorfer, have since been lost. These four depictions are closely related to the paintings for the St. Anne altar in Feldkirch for which Huber concluded a contract in 1515 - to such an extent that they can in any case be regarded as a preliminary stage for this important work. R.B.

Heinzle, 1953, p. 77, n° 118 - Winzinger, 1963, n° 263 - Cat. Kunst der Donauschule, 1965, n° 325. - Cat. The Danube School, 1969/70, n° 90.

313Bis - Crucifixion - Cat. 217Bis

c. 1525
Pen-and-ink sketch - 320×215 mm.
Provenient : Charles Ricketts and Charles Shannon.
The Fitzwilliam Museum Cambridge (2076)
(Wolf Huber)

311 - Christ's Crucifixion - Cat. 217

Wood engraving.
Signed, c. 1516.
122×93 mm. B. 5, P. 10, Wz. 267.
Paris, Bibliothèque Nationale, Cabinet des Estamps, ECN 1522.

On a hill the roughly sawn wooden cross towers up aslant in the distance. Christ hangs there crumpled with his head bowed forward. His face is turned towards John at the foot of the cross who gazes at him with plaintive gestures. Some distance away, Mary, her head bowed, mourns quietly to herself. A mass of heavy dark clouds draws together over the scene and begins to make the sun on the horizon look dismal. Wolf Huber has heightened the drama of this event in the way he has composed his wood engraving. The emotional tension created by the dialogue between the deeply moved figure of John in the middle at the picture's front and Christ is reflected in the turbulence of the natural surroundings, the mass of clouds blocking out the sunshine. The powerful outlines and thick hatchings complement this strong expression of emotion. The motif of the crucifix aslant which determines the scene's profound impact goes back to Dürer's work *Tafelbild der Sieben Schmerzen Mariae* (panel of Mary's Seven Sorrows) of 1495/96 (Dresden, Gemäldegalerie). Huber was probably acquainted with Cranach's so-called Schleissheim Crucifixion of 1503 (Munich, Alte Pinakothek), where this motif is taken up and conveyed in a dramatically intensified form. R.B.

Heinzle, 1953, n° 43, and fig. 77. — Cat. *The Danube School*, 1969/70, n° 86. — Winzinger, 1979, n° 267.

310 - Adoration of the magi - Cat. 216.

311 - Christ's Crucifixion - Cat. 217

312 - Flogging - W. Huber - 1540 - Oil on limewood - 898×673 mm - St Florian.

313 - The Arrest of Christ - W. Huber - 1530 - Oil on limewood - 605×677 mm - Munich, Alte Pinakothek.

313 Bis - Crucifixion - Cat. 217 Bis

314 - Christ on the Mount of Olives - W. Huber - c. 1530 -   Oil on limewood - 607×677 mm - Munich, Alte Pinakothek.

315 - Lamentation - W. Huber - 1524 - 1060×870 - Paris - Musée du Louvre.

GEORG LEMBERGER

Georg Lemberger was born around 1490 in Landshut; he was probably the brother of the wood-carver Hans Leinberger. We do not know when he left his home town and where he stayed during his apprenticeship and his period as a journeyman. From his style of drawing we can assume that he came into early contact with Wolf Huber's workshop in Passau. Meanwhile there is also no doubt that he contributed to the "Triumphal Procession of Emperor Maximilian I" between 1513 and 1515 in Albrecht Altdorfer's work shop in Regensburg. In 1523 Lemberger got the freedom of the city of Leipzig. He left Leipzig in 1532 on account of his evangelical faith. He probably moved to Magdeburg then and died there in about 1540. R.B.

316 - Double Bass Player - Cat. 218

Georg Lemberger (?)
Copper engraving.
c. 1515.
87×68 mm. H.I. 71.
Paris, Bibliothèque Nationale, Cabinet des Estampes.
ECN 1479.

317 - Mercenary and camp follower - Cat. 219

Pen and black ink.
c. 1515/20.
Falsely initialed "HS" later.
211×160 mm.
Berlin, Kupferstichkabinett, SMPK. KdZ 1075.

There is much discussion as to who produced this rare copper engraving of a musician wreathed with laurels who only wears a cloak knotted over his left shoulder.
On the back of the Berlin exemplar there are traces of Albrecht Altdorfer's *St Hieronymus Reading* (Cat. 105), which suggests a connection with him. However, the Double Bass Player bears no initials like all other of Altdorfer's copper engravings. Winzinger takes the head from this engraving (the rest of which was probably inspired by an Italian model) and compares it with a bearded head from a sketch of eight men's heads in Stockholm which he attributes to Georg Lemberger. The very similar shaping of nose and beard would seem to support his idea that the engraving is also Lemberger's. M.R.

Winzinger, 1963, Appendix n° 27. — Winzinger, 1964, p. 81-90.

Mercenary and camp follower were part of the everyday life in those unsettled times around 1500 when Germany was ravaged by wars and atrocities. Both figures were often depicted in art of that time as representatives of professions. The drawing is attributed to Georg Lemberger of whom there is still little record as an artist. Influenced by Altdorfer and Huber, he was a Bible illustrator mainly. It is supposed that he stayed at Albrecht Altdorfer's workshop between 1513 and 1515 when the battle scenes were completed for Emperor Maximilian's triumphal procession. Lemberger's contribution can be seen in the bearer figures. His turbulent drawing style with lines that often only barely, though aptly, grasp the essential part of the drawing reveal typical features of the late Danube style. R.B.

Friedländer and Bock, 1921, p. 57. — Oettinger, 1959, p. 35. — Winzinger, 1952, n° 152. — Cat. *Kunst der Donauschule*, 1965, n° 172. — Winzinger, 1979, n° 215.

317 - Mercenary and Camp Follower - Cat. 219

319 to 322 The Four Evangelists - Cat. 220 to 223

Wood engraving.
c. 1523.
148×94 mm.
Berlin, Kupferstichkabinett. SMPK. Inv. n° 550-9 to 553-9
Regensburg, Museen der Stadt Regensburg.

In Leipzig Georg Lemberger was commissioned many times to produce wood engravings for various editions of Luther's Bible. The landscape engraving of the four evangelists was completed in 1523 for the octavo edition of the Old and New Testaments published in Wittenberg by the Lotther Brothers. Lemberger's Danube School background and above all his contact with Albrecht Altdorfer's workshop finds expression in the highly imaginative landscape which reaches into the distance and in the choice of certain motifs like the hills in the background or the single trees at the picture's edge with branches hanging down like drips. The muddled, heavily lined scene and the aureoles of rays bring to mind some of Wolf Huber's wood engravings. R.B.

Grote, 1933, p. 15 ff. — Cat. *The Danube School*, 1969/70, n° 95.

323 - Moses and the Burning Bush - Cat. 224

Wood engraving.
Before 1536.
118×137 mm. H. 72, Schramm 443.
Berlin, Kupferstichkabinett, SMPK.

The wood engraving is one of a series of 106 illustrations for the Old Testament which were printed first of all in Johannes Bugenhagen's Low German Bible translation in Magdeburg (Melchior Lotther) in 1536 and used again in 11 further editions until 1561.
The scene could have been inspired by a similar one from Holbein's Icones, fol. BIVv, which although it only appeared in print in 1538, had already been used for a Zurich Bible. It is true that Lemberger combines several scenes in one picture here: in the foreground Moses is sitting and taking off his shoes as God instructs him (Moses 2, 3, 5) while his flock of sheep graze behind. He appears in the distance again with his crook which is changing into a serpent (Moses 2, 2-4).
Here a whole wood is burning, not just a bush. The fiery aureole around God's apparition can be compared with similar motifs in Altdorfer's work. On the other hand, the rough drawing style is reminiscent of Wolf Huber. B.B.

Grote, 1933, p. 22-26.

318 - Saint Christopher - G. Lemberger - Wz. 153 - Basel - Kupferstichkabinett der Offentlichen Kunstsammlung.

319 to 322 - The Four Evangelists - Cat. 220 à 223

323 - Moses and the Burning Bush - Cat. 224

HANS LEU THE YOUNGER

Hans Leu the Younger, son of the Zurich painter Hans Leu, was born around 1490. The style of his drawings leads one to assume that he met Wolf Huber and stayed at Dürer's workshop in Nurenberg aroud 1510. Leu must at least have made Albrecht Dürer's acquaintance personally because Leu sends his regards to Dürer in a letter to Provost Felix Frey in Zurich dated 6 December 1523. It can be proved that he was in Zurich from 1514 where one year later he became a master painter. He painted altars and murals, drew leaded outlines and made wood engravings. On 24 october 1531 he fell in the battle on the Gubel while fighting with Zwinglis.

324 - The Mourning of Christ - Cat. 225

Pen and black ink, highlighted in white on red grounded paper.
c. 1512
214×156 mm.
Berlin, Kupferstichkabinett, SMPK. KdZ 4056.

Grief-stricken, Jesus' mother, Mary and Mary Magdalene are bending over Christ's body which has been taken down from the cross. John, Jesus' favourite disciple, and Joseph of Arimathia stretch up their arms violently in lamentation.
In its style, in its pathos and by the hilly landscape, the drawing shows the Danube influence. It could be the work of Hans Leu, a less important artist who, as he was learning from other's models, probably also came into contact with Albrecht Altdorfer's art. Often apparent in Hans Leu's drawings are the very summary and violent style, the slight effect of depth and the figures moved right to the front edge of the picture. R.B.

Friedländer and Bock, 1921, p. 5. — Winzinger, 1952, n° 124.

325 - St. Sebastian - Cat. 226

Pen and black brown ink. 1514.
213×160 mm.
Berlin, Kupferstichkabinett. SMPK. KdZ 5555.

The print corresponds almost directly to a drawing in Nurenberg (Germanisches Nationalmuseum, Hz 33) bearing Hans Leu's monogram and the date 1512 (or 17?). Both prints are about the same size, however, the Nurenberg one is more deeply cut, above all on the left and on the lower edge. The Berlin print is considered to be the copy. This theory is supported not only by weak points in the lanscape, for example the uniform hatching on the stretch of water on the right which in the Nurenberg print suggests the landscape's reflection with more effect, but also some discrepancies, for example the gap in the crossbow shaft where there is a wedge in the Nurenberg print and the artificial zig-zag on the right branch which in the Nurenberg print is a split in the wood. Neither does the style correspond completely to Leu's who uses powerful strokes for the shade. Last of all, the way the date is written and its position are not typical of him. However, the artist of the Berlin print has not only made and extraordinarily careful and exact copy but he is very skilful in adapting to his model's characteristic style and shaping, as for example in the quality of the main figure which does not lie far behind Leu, and this is an indication that the drawing is the work of someone from Leu's workshop. B.B.

Bock, 1921, p. 63. - F. Zink, Cat. of the National Museum of Nuremberg, *Die deutschen Handzeichnungen*, vol. 1, Nuremberg 1968, n° 138, p. 172-174.

327 - St George - Cat. 227

Wood engraving.
1516
219×159 mm. H. 4.
Berlin, Kupferstichkabinett, SMPK.

Differing from Cranach, Leu shows the saint on horseback as he battles with the dragon. To the right praying under a tree, the princess awaits her release.
The overall composition together with the structure of the landscape backdrop, with layers of rock and mountain segments one on top of the other, and finally the way the mountains and vegetation have been depicted refer directly to Altdorfer's St. George (Cat. 95). And yet the effect here is somewhat more sober and more easily surveyed than in the latter; Leu avoids the abstractedly representational and strongly ornamental forms. For example, the mountains in his work are not so needle-pointed as in Altdorfer's. He is more concerned with the pure representation of physical conditions than with Altdorfer's graphic two-dimensional models, whatever the common theme may prove.
B.B.

Cat. *Meister von Albrecht Dürer*, 1961, n° 240.

328 - St. George - Cat. 228

Pen and black ink, highlighted in white on yellow-brown grounded paper.
c. 1513.
209×138 mm.
Berlin, Kupferstichkabinett, SMPK. KdZ. 816.

The Danube influence on the Zurich painter, Hans Leu, is shown clearly by the picture's composition and drawing style in this representation of the knight George on horseback killing the dragon with his long sword. The technique of light and dark shading on tinted background is an indication that Hans Leu came into contact with Albrecht Altdorfer's work, while the landscape's form, the trees with their hanging branches and their position at the very edge of the picture, the single willow tree stump, reveal a leaning towards Wolf Huber's landscape scenes. R.B.

Friedländer/Bock, p. 63, n° 816. — Debrunner, 1941, p. 21. — Cat. *Meister um Albrecht Dürer*, 1961, n° 236.

439

325 - St. Sebastian - Cat. 226

326 - Christ in Gethsemane Hans Leu le Jeune - Basel.

327 - St. George - Cat. 227

328 - St. George - Cat. 228

"IW" MONOGRAM

The monogram appears on two wood engravings of which one is dated 1515. It is a W with a small hook which is crossed through with a horizontal stroke. The stroke can be read as an I lying on its side or as a doubling or abridging sign. In the second case the monogram might be taken as WW or WB and could be connected with the Mühldorf painter Wilhelm Weinholt or Beinholt who died in 1521. Winzinger identifies him as the Master of Mühldorf, an important and previously anonymous panel painter of the Danube School who was given his title after two altar wings in Altmühldorf.

329 - Madonna on the Crescent of the moon - Cat. 229

329 - Madonna on the crescent of the moon - Cat. 229

Wood engraving.
Initialled and dated 1515.
190×128 mm. B. 1, G. 938, G./St. 1550-1.
Berlin, Kupferstichkabinett, SMPK.

The depiction of Mary as the Woman of the Apocalypse standing on the crescent of the moon surrounded by an aureole is one of the most popular picture themes of the late Middle Ages. Here, however, she is notably not portrayed in a priestly way, strictly from the front, as most often, but slightly turned to give an almost three-quarter view of her. Her slenderly turned to give an almost three-quarter view of her.

Her slenderly proportioned, slim-waisted figure curves backwards and forwards like a letter S. The drapery behind appears to envelope her. The shaping of the cloth is brought alive by the contrast between the falling or flat surface which is uncreased and the bulging folds. The contrast between the beautifully outlined figure of Mary and the unwieldy stiff baby Jesus is surprising as are also the squat-looking cherubs' busts in the corners.

All these artistic devices are reminiscent of sculptures by Hans Leinberger from Landshut.B.B.

F. Winzinger, Unbekannte Werke des Meisters von Mühldorf, in: *Zeitschrift des deutschen Vereins für Kunstwissenschaft 22,* 1968, p. 13-28.

330 - The Apostles take their leave - Cat. 230

JÖRG BREU THE ELDER

Jörg Breu the elder was born in Augsburg around 1480 and painted and drew for wood-cuts and stained glass. From 1502 onwards he was an independent master in Augsburg where he is believed to have run a large workshop. Before that he probably stayed in Austria and later travelled to Italy and then to Strasbourg in 1522. Jörg Breu died in his home town in 1537. His workshop was kept going by his son Jörg Breu the younger.

330 - The apostles take their leave - Cat. 230

Pen and ink drawing in black.
Unsigned, 1525/30.
197×235 mm.
Berlin, Kupferstichkabinett SMPK, KdZ 4448.

At the end of the four gospels Christ instructed the apostles to go out into the world and spread the new teachings to the people. This was represented in German art by the scene of the apostles taking their leave. Since the mid-15th century this scene had been given special prominence in Franconia and Austria. It shows the apostles ready to leave, embracing each other or already setting off in different directions. This theme gave artists the opportunity to paint as varied a landscape as possible.
Although Jörg Breu's drawing belongs to a later creative period the background landscape does display many elements which are reminiscent of the Danube School. In contrast to the free structure of the landscape, the simple form and even lines of the apostles are typical of Augsburg art. F.A.

Friedländer and Bock, 1921.

331 - The battle of Pavia - Cat. 231.

Wood-cut on two blocks.
380×528 mm. cut. H.53, G.356.
Paris, Bibliothèque Nationale, Cabinet des Estampes.
ECN 1043

The battle of Pavia must be seen as one of the most significant battles of the 16th century. King François I of France besieged the town which was being defended by the imperial troops of Charles V. The French established themselves in the zoological gardens near the town, the walled area on the wood-cut. In the night of 24.2.1525 a hole was broken in the wall of the zoological gardens and the imperial troops marched on to the Mirabello Castle, François I's quarters. The emperor's troops, which were the weaker in the beginning, were reinforced by 800 Spanish marksmen who fought freely in small groups with a new battle technique. Soon the French and imperial cavalry stood face to face. François I was taken prisoner after a duel with Count Nicolaus of Salm.
Jörg Breu's wood-cut, of which there are three copies, gives in the first instance a bird's eye view of an extensive landscape with the sun rising behind it. On the left lies Pavia on the Ticino, behing it the Alps. In the foreground the imperial cavalry enters the zoological gardens and becomes involved in a skirmish in the middle of the garden. Sporadically marksmen fire into the crowd. The two sides are indicated by means of banners. In the background, beside the tower building appears a horse with a caparison decorated with fleurs-de-lis. In the crowd beyond it there is a sign with the inscription "Captio Regis", indicating the capture of King François I. M.R.

Dogson, Campbell, Beiträge zur Kenntnis des Holzschnittwerks.
Jörg Breus. In. Jahrbuch der Königlich preussischen Kunstsammelungen XXI, 1900, p.192-214 - Stöcklein, Hans, Die Schlacht bei Pavia. In, Buchner,/Feuchtmayr, Oberdeutsche Kunst der Spätgotik und Reformationszeit, Augsburg, 1924 p. 230-239.

Dit is ōbeleth end stad va pauie
von frā aſt? Conninck vā Brākiērt
en deṅ ſlach des ſeluē Conīc inz des
k eyſais karol? heyr. Der franſoyse
nederlage, en des Connies van viāc
rijckſ? gheuangenuſſe ghe ſuede. Int
Jaer. M.CCCCC.XXV. deṅ xxiiij.
dach febuarn.

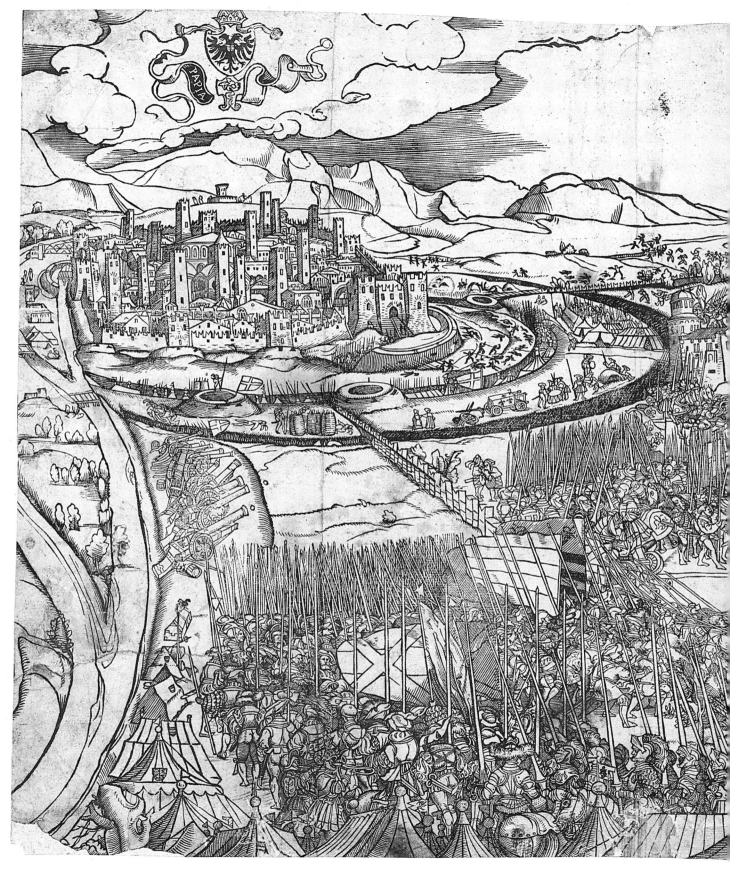

MICHAEL OSTENDORFER

Michael Ostendorfer was born between 1490 and 1495 and died in 1559 in Regensburg. It cans be proved that he was there from 1520 as a painter and designer of wood engravings especially for book illustrations. It is possible he was at Altdorfer's workshop with which he must have already had contact when he took part in the building of the chapel "Schöne Maria" (beautiful Mary). Owing also to few further commissions in Regensburg, reformed in 1542, he was completely impoverished during the last years of his life.

332 - The pilgrimage to holy Mary in Regensburg - Cat. 232

Wood engraving in two parts.
Initialled. c. 1519/20.
580×391 mm. G. 967, G./St. 923. Wynen 55.
Regensburg, Museen der Stadt Regensburg.

Depicted is the last great pilgrimage of the late Middle Ages which happened in Regensburg in 1519 following a pogrom. The ostensible cause was the alleged wondrous healing by the grace of Mary of a craftsman injured when the synagogue was pulled down. However, that the citizens had massive economic interests in the pilgrimage is recorded in our wood engraving which was itself probably mlade to propagate this movement: in the midst of the old ghetto ruins a provisional church made out of wood has been built; the panel painting of holy Mary in the interior (Wz. 41) which can be seen through the door and the flag on the tower were delivered by Altdorfer in this same year and the sculptor Heydenreich's statue of Mary was put up in front just as quickly. Here she is standing as the focus of the throng of pilgrims' excessive worship. From the point of view of form, the groups of figures in the picture are reminiscent of Altdorfer's crowd scenes on the last panels of the Florian legend, for example in the martyrdom scene or in the source of miracles. (Wz. 34, 36). Even the type of figures and heads correspond to those on Altdorfer's graphic prints produced at the same time. B.B.

Wynen, 1961, n° 55, p. 115-117, 292-294 — Cat. *From a Mighty Fortress*, 1983, n° 184 — Cat. *Martin Luther und die Reformation in Deutschland*, 1983, n° 78 — Cat. *Kunst der Reformationszeit*, 1983, n° B82 — Cat. *Luther und die Folgen für die Kunst*, 1983, n° 5.

333 - Sketch for a tabernacle - Cat. 233

Woodcut on two blocks.
Initialed and dated 1521.
934×200 mm. G. 969-970, G st. 925, Wynen 57.
Regensburg, Museen der Stadt Regensburg.

This tabernacle used for the taking of the consecrated host — a circular recess fitted with latticed bars, supported by pillars and torch-bearing angels — rests on a raised pedestal. Above this, shielded in an octagonal "casing", surrounded by columns, is a free interpretation of the scene; and again, above this, a relief or painting illustrating the gathering of the manna, framed by an arch with angels bearing cartouches on either side, completes the structure where Mary and John both appear on a crucifix. The clear style of the figures, lively and animated, is for Wynen reminiscent of Hans Leinberger's style. B.B.

Wynen, 1961, n° 57, pp. 123-125, 295 ff.

334 - Our Lady of Regensburg - Cat. 234

Woodcut. Wz. 245.
c. 1520.
Regensburg, Museen der Stadt Regensburg.

Contrafactur der Kirchen zu Regenspurg / welche zu der schönen Maria genannt
worden / mit Beschreibung und Verzeichnuß / der wunderbarlichen und zuvor nie erhörten Wallfahrt /
so im Jahr 1519. daselbst geschehen.

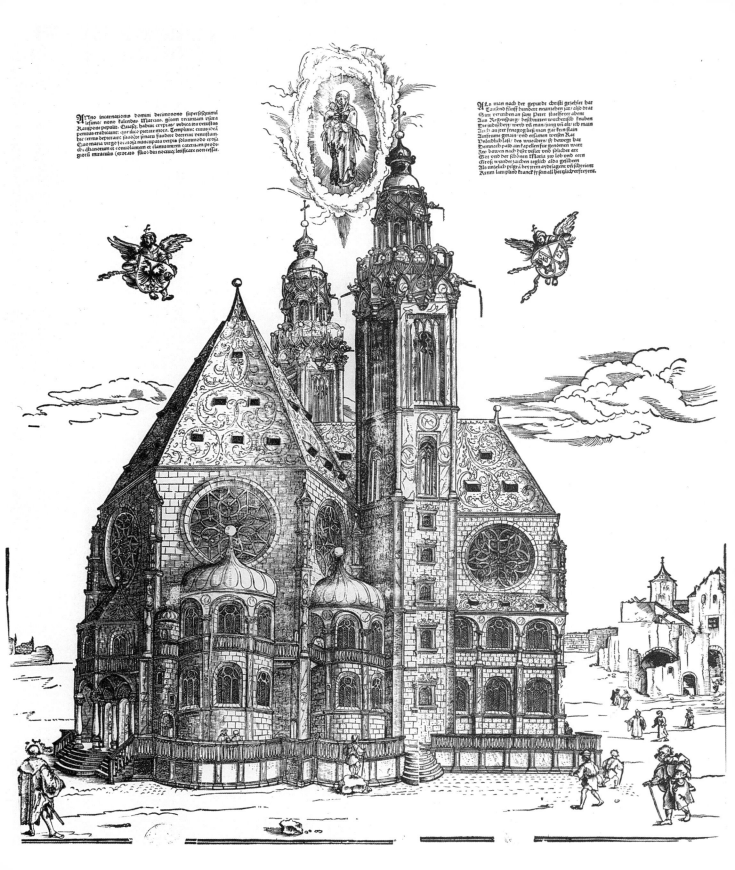

HANS LEINBERGER

The sculptor, Hans Leinberger, was probably born towards 1480/1485 at Landshut in Bavaria, where he lived from 1513 to 1530. But, as his master altar in the collegiate church of Moosburg testifies, he seems to have worked there at a prior date. This altar was donated in 1511 and erected in 1514. Leinberger was in the service of Duke Ludwig X of Bavaria but also executed the bronze statue of Count Albrecht of Habsburg for the funeral monument of Emperor Maximilian at Innsbruck.

336 - Virgin with child ("Shöne Maria") - Cat. 236

Bas relief with some of the original colour remaining.
Lindenwood. H. 663 mm, W 290 mm.
c. 1520/1525.
The lower parts as well as the borders of the mantle have been lost.
Regensburg, Museen der Stadt Regensburg.

337 - St. Peter - Cat. 237

This work in wood, discovered in 1981 and presented here for the first time, is indeed that of the master of Landshut: the form as well as the excellent artisitc quality testify to this. What stands out here is the contrast in the formal principle which unites the sculptural character of the figure, its relaxed posture and the peaceful lines of the undulating movements of the garment. This bas-relief is very close, both stylistcally and chronologically speaking, to that of the Madonna at the church of St. Cassian at Regensburg (c. 1520). The garment shows a direct correspondence with the concept of the body as seen through the eyes of the Renaissance; it falls simply and smoothly with sober lines. The bas relief most likely dates from the end of Leinberger's middle period, that is, between 1520 and 1525, when the cult of the Virgin Mary ("Schöne Maria") of Regensburg reached its peak. The charming theme of the infant Jesus embracing Mary, which took its inspiration from the portrayals of the "Glykophilusa" (Affectionate) in the byzantine art, seemed particularly well-suited to the lifelike image Leinberger held of the Virgin Mary. This is already present in his majestic sand-stone Madonna conserved at Berlin and subsequently the statuettes which are now at Berlin and Munich.

Following Altdorfer's example, Leinberger also several times illustrated the theme of the Virgin Mary, which was extremmly popular towards the end of the Middle Ages, or as they are called Luke's Madonnas dressed in byzantine-style costume, wearing a wide-brimmed hat and bordered cloak, and this long before the pilgrimage to Regensburg (1519); (examples being the figure which appears in the centre of the main altar at Moosburg, and his bronze statuettes at Berlin executed around 1515/1516). Next, in 1519, he received a commission from the city of Regensburg but of this only the correspondance remains; and then the Madonna of St. Cassien, and in both cases his works are directly linked to the Regensburg cult and the holy image of Virgin Mary that Albrecht Altdorfer had painted for this purpose. The formal inspiration of the latter creat ion, along with the close link with the drawing Altdorfer made in Berlin, clearly show the relation between Leinberger and Altdorfer, whose artistic contribution to the Regensburg pilgrimage had been exceptionally important. As city counsellor he had certainly been involved in the two contracts by which the city of Regensburg commissioned from Leinberger two statuettes (1519/1521) that were to appear on the altar of the temporary chapel built to commerorate this pilgrimage.

This artistic exchange which must have continued throughout the life of the two masters, goes back, however, much further: it finds its greatest expression in the correspondance between two chef-d'œuvres — Altdorfer's altar for the church at St. Florian and the main altar at Moosburg, which was executed by Leinberger. It bears excellent witness to the intimate relationship between the sculpture and painting of the Danube School. The master of Landshut occupies an eminent place in the art of Austro-Bavarian woodcarving in the 16th century, and his influence in this domain has been lasting. W.P.

Georg Lill: Hans Leinberger, Munich 1942 — Alfred Stange: Albrecht Altdorfer, Hans Leinberger und die bayerische Kunst ihrer Zeit; In: alte und moderne Kunst, 10jg., 1965, n° 80, pp 14-19. — Anton Legner: Akzente der Donauschulplastik; In: Werden und Wandlung — Studien zur Kunst der Donauschule. Linz 1967, pp. 152-155 — Alfred Schädler: Zur künstlerischen Entwicklung Hans Leinbergers. In: Müncher Jahrbuch der bildenden Kunst, 3 F., Vol. XXVIII, k 977, pp. 59-90 — Achim Hubel: Die "Shöne Maria" von Regensburg; In 850 Jahre Kollegiastift zu den heiligen Johannes Evangelist in Regensburg 1127-1977. Munich — Zurich 1977, pp. 199-231.

MASTER H.L.

The master who in 1526 completed the main altar of Brisach Cathedral and who signed himself HL, has been identified with a monogrammist who signed these initials on almost all of 25 engravings and 9 woodcuts. Thus far the monogramme has not been able to be identified and there is as yet no cosensus as to the artist's stylistic origins: there would seem to be some link with the main altar at Mauer, near Melk (Lower Austria). As there exist woodcuts dated 1511/1522 — and in several cases the date has been altered to 1533 — his date of birth has been estimated as being around 1480-85 and his death prior to 1533 or rather with his move to the Netherlands before 1533 owing to the outcome of the difficult situation brought on by the Reformation. R.B.

338 - St. Christopher - Cat. 238

337 - Saint Peter - Cat. 237

Engraving.
Initialed and dated 1522.
174×102 mm. LoBnitzer 16, Schindler B1 A21.
Berlin Kupferstichkabinett SMPK.

The Saint is standing on a mound of earth. Behind him is a knarled tree trunk. Extreme bottom right, a corner of landscape is visible with a figure on a bridge. In the left foreground, at the edge of the picture, there is a small expanse of water with a hoop net.

Peter himself is characterised by an enormous volume of fabric which constitutes his cloak and which hangs over his right arm forming two billows, one to the front and one behind. The material almost divides the figure into two halves. The legs and right hip are seen from the front, the upper half of the body, which emerges from the garment, is turned to the right, whilst the head is bent forward towards us. The apostle is holding an open book in his left hand, with his right hand he leans upon a staff which at first sight appears to be a T-shaped staff like that of Saint Anthony, but when the keybit located at the upper extremity becomes apparent, the object can then be identified as a man-sized key.

In fact, by an interplay of proportions, the life-sized bunch of keys which is hooked onto the top of the staff, makes Peter's key appear twice as big. There are other iconographic features which are equally disturbing: for an apostle, sandals and trousers in such a state of disrepair are hardly fitting. A sheathed dagger hangs between his legs. This engraving is a highly personal synthesis of the "German manner" and the "Latin manner". B.B.

Sommer, 1936, p. 250 — Baxandall, 1980, p. 141 ff. — Schindler, 1981, n° A 21, p. 52 — Liebmann, 1982, p. 388.

338 - Saint Christopher - Cat. 238

Woodcut.
Initialed, c. 1515/20.
196×141 mm. B. 2, H. 10, LoBnitzer 26, Schindler B3.
Paris, Bibliothèque Nationale, Cabinet des Estampes. ECN 2622.

Saint Christopher is standing in the water, legs astride; his movements are awkward and give an impression of clumsiness. The Infant Jesus seen from behind is climbing onto his shoulders and is vigorously pressing a terrestrial globe onto the giant's head; the latter is crying out and lifting his right hand in search of aid. His head and upper body are bent over to the side under the pressure and his left knee is giving way. The cloth of his cape and the tails of his garment are floating in large undulations, which emphasize the suddeness of the movement. The dramatic intensity of this moment of deep despair, prior to the revelation of God, is quite remarkable. Generally, iconography portrays Christopher in the Infant's Grace at the moment of benediction; here, the pagan giant is depicted at the very moment when it is clearly and painfully made known to him that he is carrying on his shoulders a burden "greater than the whole world". Seen from this point of view, the emphasis is on the effect of the shock rather than on the imminent revelation. The pathetic language of the forms is marvellously adapted to this deliberate choice of theme; it is entirely centred on the figures, whilst the landscape in the background receives a cursory and unsubtle treatment.

Iconographic parallels are to be found in sketches, by Niklaus Manuel for example (cf. Cat. Niklaus, Manuel Deutsch, 1979, n° 201, fig. 128). Altdorfer certainly conceived the legend in the same terms, as the prints Wz. 21, 22, 38 testify. In print Wz. 21, St Christopher has even lost his balance and is slipping backwards into the water. B.B.

Sommer, 1936, p. 249 — Schindler, 1981, n° B3, p. 90-92, 99.

339 - Saint Sebastian - Cat. 239

Woodcut.
Initiated, c. 1525.
225×152 mm. B. 22, LoBnitzer 29, Schindler B 9.
Berlin, Kupferstichkabinett, SMPK.

The Saint is standing, tied to a slender oak tree, in a space which is delimited by the walls of a ruined house. Three large arrows have pierced his forhead, his arm and his leg. The figure is presented as a well-balanced whole, with the head falling over to the left and the mouth contorted. The loin cloth around the hips also floats out towards the left in the form of a shell and originates from behind the figure, who is holding the upper fold in his right hand. There are very apparent differences if one compares this nude figure with the "man of sorrows" (Cat. 238 Bis); the outlines and body shading are more measured, more expressive, the function of the limbs is more obvious and the stable part of the subject is better-balanced. A sketch of a male nude exists on the back of a wing of the Niedorrotweiler retable (Krummer-Schroth, 1971, reprod. 23) and bears a striking resemblence to this print. The protrusion of the jaws, the contours of the shoulders and the overall style is so similar that the comparison with the Niedorrotweiler retable, which was dated belatedly, is unavoidable. B.B.

Krummer-Schroth, 1971, p. 86 — Baxandall, 1980, p. 121 — Schindler, 1981, n° B 9, p. 95-99.

342 -Two amorettes with the pea-pod - Cat. 242.

Copper engraving.
With monogram and date 1519.
In a later state changed in 1533.
92×73 mm. B.8, H.34, LoBnitzer 23,I, Schindler A15,I.
Paris, Bibliothèque Nationale, Cabinet des Estampes. ECN 2628.

In a pea-pod wound into an oval garland interspersed with flowers like a garland of roses two winged putti with feathered arms are playing with a gigantic pea-pod in ecstatic delight. The putto behind grasps into it with his right hand while he swings a chain with his other hand. The putto in the front is already biting into a pea. The background is made up of horsemen on a bridge.

457

338 Bis - Christ, the Man of Sorrow - Cat. 238 Bis

This puzzling scene has still not been satisfactorily explained. Peas are fertility symbols which play a certain superstitious role particularly connected to nuptial customs. They therefore belong at least to the same sphere as these winged creatures which are doubtless to be seen as amorettes. B.B.

Schindler, n° A15

340 - Angels bearing the emblems of Christ - Cat. 240

Engraving.
Signed. Dated 1511, later changed to 1533
Inscription on the picture: QUI PETIS AEGRA/MEMBRA LEVARE/HIC TIBI DULCES/COLLIGE FLORES.
132×94 mm. LoBnitzer 7,1, Schindler All. 1.
Stuttgart, Staatsgalerie, Graphische Sammlung A8821.

Raised up on a flat pedestal, three angels are carrying a vase on a frame decorated with rugs and garlands, along with a purse, the cross and its nails, a ladder, a spear with the crown of thorns, the sponge with vinegar, the martyr's column, the whip and the bundle of rods. Two angels seen from behind serve as carriers, the third with his mouth open in a groan, is steadying the pile of objects.

The transportation of the instruments of the Passion is portrayed here exactly as a triumphal procession of classical times, during which trophies were carried upon such frames (fercula).

This idea indubitably refers back to the series of triumphal pictures engraved in the style of Mantegna (Hind 14,15). The technique of using a direct frontal view seen from floor-level succeeds in creating a

worm's eye view; the human ideal is strongly highlighted, the body and head being given their full plasticity, always slightly angular; a marked preference for oblique angle views; all elements which frequently occur in Mantegna's work. The Italian's influence on HL is nowhere as obvious as in this print. Reference is made to a "Mantegna Period", yet these influence persist. B.B.

Sommer, 1936, p. 250. — Baxandal, 1980, p. 141. — Schindler, 1981, n° A 11, p. 7ff, 95, 98. — Liebmann, 1982, p. 388.

341 - Saint George Standing - Cat. 241

Engraving.
Initialed, c. 1520. Dated 1533 on a later print.
120×68 mm. B. 3, H. 15, LoBnitzer 13,1.
Schindler A 12, 11.
Berlin, Kupferstichkabinett, SMPK.

This picture of the saint contains many features which make it a highly original work. Dressed in classical armour of a somewhat fantastical nature, the helmet decorated with a variety of feathers, the handle of the broken spear in his left hand, a sword in his right hand which is raised as if ready to strike, his head bent upwards towards the right, his face twisted in a grimace, St. George stands in front of the slain dragon, its head still pierced by the end of the spear, its entrails spilling from its abdomen. The overall impression is of a dance celebrating the adversary's corpse (Sommer). The impession of triumph is accentuated by the presence of a drape of honour hanging behind the figure.
Whereas the form of the light figure standing out against a dark background of forest landscape recalls the earliest prints, the structure of the torso is comparable to the man of sorrows, the bent head, the compact proportions and the stability of the main motif recalls Saint Sebastian. A drawing conserved at Basel may be a study for the head. B.B.

Sommer, 1936, p. 265 ff. Schindler, n° A 12, p. 57-60, 95, 98.

Angels bearing the emblems of Christ - Cat. 240

341 - St. George standing - Cat. 241

342 - Two amorettes with the pea-pod - Cat. 242.
343 - Cupid standing on a sphere brandishing a bow - Cat. 243
344 - Enraged amor on the snail - Cat. 244

344 - Enraged amor on the snail - Cat. 244

Copper engraving.
With monogram. Ca. 1520.
In a later state dated 1533.
B.7, H.33, Loßnitzer 22, I, Schindler A16,1
Paris, Bibliothèque Nationale, Cabinet des Estampes.
ECN 2627

A winged putto sits on the house of a large snail which is crawling across a piece of pasture-land. The violent gestures of the naked boy betray great agitation obviously caused by the fact that the string of his bow which he is holding above his head is broken. In his left hand he holds a snapped arrow and in his quiver there are other arrows which are bent although at least apparently intact. The boy's eye-bandage has slipped into his forehead.
Although there is no specific interpretation of this allegory it is possible to outline a circle of themes from which it originates: the disarming of Amor, his ineffectiveness and powerlessness which enemy forces seek to bring about, whether they be Death or Platonic Love (cf. E. Panofsky, Blind Cupid, in: E.P., Studies in Iconology, New York 1939, etc.). It seems plausible that the impotence which here enrages Amor could come from the slowness with which humans act - represented by the proverbial slowness of the snail.
In formal terms the figure of the putto presupposes Italian influences; it is considerably foreshortened (e.g. the right foot) and seen from below. Yet by this time there was already a certain assimilation of Italian forms and contents north of the Alps. This is shown by parallels between this print and Barthel Beham's approximately contemporaneous engraving "Putto riding through the air on a ball" (B.32).

B.B

Schindler, 1981, no.A16, p.8,95,98. - Liebmann, 1982, p.388.

338 Bis - Christ, the man of sorrows - Cat. 238 Bis

Engraving.
Initialed, c. 1520. Dated 1533 on a later print.
118×70 mm. LoBnitzer 6, I Schindler A 14, 1.
Berlin, Kupferstichkabinett, SMPK.

The man of sorrows is portrayed in an almost mannered attitude in front of an enormous tree trunk (a symbol perhaps of the trunk of the cross). In the background to the right, seen at an oblique angle, stands a large cross built out of halved tree trunks and against which a ladder has been placed. The figures entire body is caught up in a twisting movement which carries down to include the right leg on which he is standing. The only counter-movement is created by the head, which is turned to the left, bearing a crown of thorns made from newly cut branches, the mouth is open and wailing.
The composition as a whole creates an impression of nervous tension which has been captured in the moment itself. In its style this print closely ressembles that of St. Peter (cat. 237), as far as the moment, the diverse proportions and the rendering of the garment is concerned. With regard to the subject, this print calls to mind Dürer's engraving B 20. One should also take into account that it may have been inspired by the motif of ressusitation from the altar at Isenheim by Grünewald (1512-1515, Colmar, Unterlindenmuseum). B.B.

Schindler, 1981, n° A 14, p. 95 f, 98

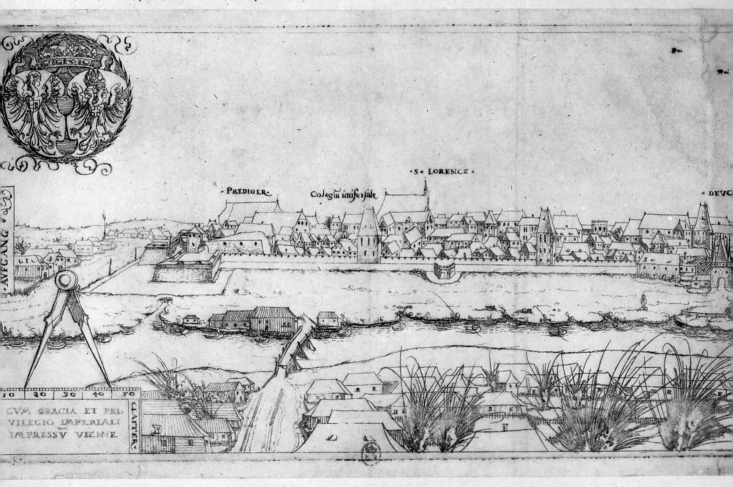

346 - Landscape with two pine trees - Cat. 246
Pen and black ink.
Free copy from Altdorfer's etching Wz. 178. Ca. 1517/20
140×210 mm.
Paris, Bibliothèque Nationale, Cabinet des Estampes.
ECN 7977

The artist has made several significant changes to his model: he has diminushed the section and presents the objects more in close-up; thus, for example, the town in the background and the group of trees behind the rock on the right are brought more into the foreground. Elements of perspective such as those between this group of trees and the pines on the edge of the picture, lose their effect. As a result the drawing gains in density which is further increased by broader and more generous strockes as in the tree tops or in the bushes for example. The line thus becomes less important in terms of giving form and illusion and more important for its ornamental content; one need only compare the contours of the chain of mountains in the background. B.B.

F. Winzinger, Neue Zeichnungen Albrecht und Erhard Altdorfers, in: Wiener Jahrbuch für Kunstgeschichte 18 (22), 1960, p. 13f.

346 - Landscape with two pine trees - Cat. 246

AUGUSTIN HIRSCHVOGEL

Born in 1503 in Nuremberg, from about 1543 in Vienna where he died in 1553. Active as glass painter, ceramicist, mathematician, and later primarily as cartographer. His 150 or so surviving landscape etchings date from his stay in Weimar.

345 - View of the town of Vienna from the North - Cat. 245.
Etching.
With monogram, dated 1547 and with title: WARE CON-
TERFETVG DER STAT WIEN DURCH AVG: HIRS:
187×1020 mm. B.81, Schwarz 81
Paris, Bibliothèque Nationale, Cabinet des Estampes.
ECN 1542

Apart from this depiction Hirschvogel also did a view of the town from the South and a town plan (Schwarz 80, 143). They were commissioned by the Vienna city council; this shows that the versatile artist's principal professional activities in his Vienna period were those of cartographer and mathematician. Only the foreground, in which he had a relatively free hand beyond topographical restrictions, brings Wolf Huber to mind. B.B.

Schwarz, 1917, n° 81, p.19, 185.

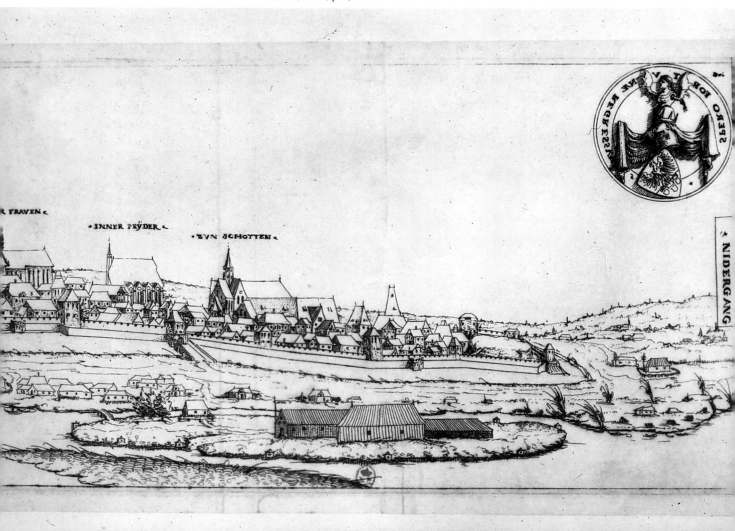

343 - Cupid standing on a sphere brandishing a bow - Cat. 243

Engraving B. 6.
Stuttgart - Staatsgalerie, Graphische Sammlung A. 8823

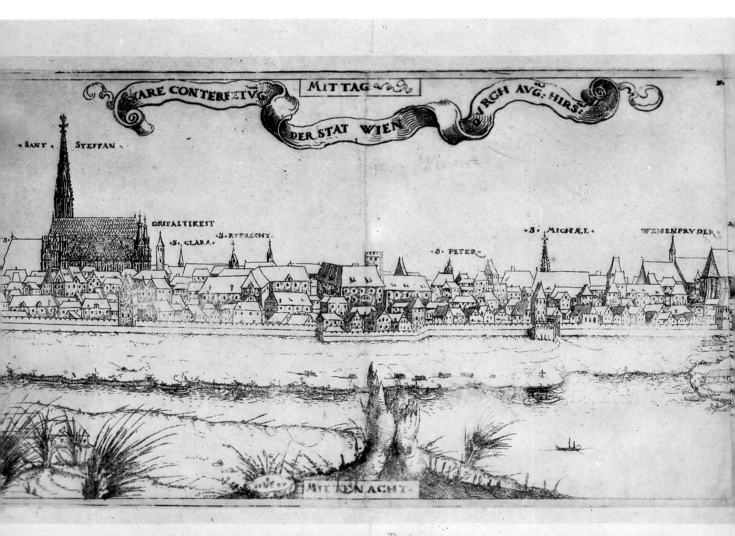

345 - View of the town of Vienna from the North - Cat. 245

347 River Landscape with wooden bridge - Cat. 247.

Etching.
With monogram and dated 1546.
143×214 mm. B.76, Schwarz 76.
Paris, Bibliothèque Nationale, Cabinet des Estampes.
ECN 1540

As in cat. 246 fig. 346 this landscape opens up in two diametrical directions: on the one had by means of a path and a bridge which wind away to the background on the left in analogous curves and form a unity owing to the similarity of the fence and the railings on the bridge, and on the other hand by means of the river which flows diagonally across towards the background. The path and bridge are optically connected to the village in the middle of the picture while the wide river leads rapidly to the background, heading for the castle on the hill. On the left the path and the river go right up to the front border of the picture ; the bridge is extended towards it by the rowe of three willows so that the landscape seems to be continued right up to the position of the beholder. This bold experiment which is particularly successful in this drawing could have been stimulated by Wolf Huber's landscape drawings.

On the other hand the ornamental rigidity of the line is completely obvious, as, for example, in the tree-top on the left where there is no longer any difference between the lines of the bent branches and the thread on which the plaque is hung. B.B.

Schwarz, 1917, n° 76, p.99, 183 f. - cat. The Danube School, 1969/70, n° 101.

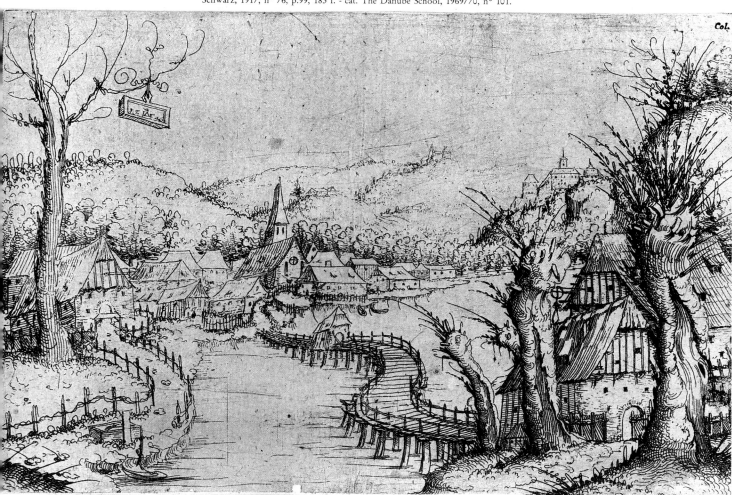

347 - River Landscape with wooden bridge - Cat. 247

348 - Landscape with a church - Cat. 248.

> Etching.
> With monogram and dated 1543.
> 153×185 mm. B.68. Schwarz 68.
> Paris, Bibliothèque Nationale, Cabinet des Estampes.
> ECN 1537

Hircshvogel was the first artist after Altdorfer to produce pure landscape etchings again. Stylistically his debt to the latter is evident in the way in which he draws trees, though with a degree of abstraction going

tension. It is not so much a case of developing a general view behind the trees which are arranged like a fence in the foreground, but rather of opening three different sorts of views of varying depth which do not even accord plausibly with the dimensions of the buildings. They are opened up by the way in which the river branches off, giving perspectives in two main directions, supported by the parallel adjustment of objects such as the church and the bridge. The most likely influence on this technique probably comes from the Netherlands. B.B .

Schwarz, 1917, n° 88. - cat. The Danube School, 1969/70. n° 96.

beyond that of Altdorfer and even Huber. Further evidence of this debt is to be found in his re-use of Altdorfer's leitmotifs, such as the double positioning of trees or views through arches. However, these leitmotifs do not dominate the print as individual elements but are used to compile an artificial composition which is not altogether free of

349 - The death of Cleopatra - Cat. 249.

Etching.
With monogram and dated 1547.
89×154 mm. Considerably cut at the top. B.5, Schwarz 5,II.
Paris, Bibliothèque Nationale, Cabinet des Estampes.
ECN 1533.

The female nude lies propped up against a tree-trunk on a piece of raised ground behind which a hilly river landscape unfolds itself. The woman, no longer bearing the insignia of a ruler, supports herself with her right fore-arm; with her left hand she brings to her breast the head of the snake whose bite is to kill her. The representation of the recumbent body in natural surroundings, which departs completely from the iconography, has a parallel in the theme of the resting nymph of the water spring seen in, among others, several paintings by Granach (cf. Koepplin/Falk, 1976, n° 543 ff.).
Nevertheless, the human body was not exactly Hirschvogel's strong point as this almost badly drawn nude demonstrates: one need only look at her left hand or the crossed legs. This could be a copy of an unknown model. This is also suggested by the odd technique, the use of stipple in the centre of the drawing and the contours traced with one stroke, features which do not appear in the landscape and which are reminiscent of works by the Italian engraver Giulio Campagnola. B.B.

Schwarz, 1917, n° 5, p.60, 164.

350 Landscape with castle on a-rock and a fir tree - Cat. 250.

Etching.
With monogram and dated 1546.
144×215 mm. B. 74, Schwarz 74.
Paris, Bibliothèque Nationale, Cabinet des Estampes.
ECN 1539.

On the right an isolated fir-tree takes up the whole of the picture from top to bottom. Some distance away on the left there is a building with an enclosed piece of land in front of it. Behind it a hill with a large castle. In the middle the view opens up over a river and further into a broad landscape. A bridge connects the town on the opposite bank behind which wooded ranges of hills with another castle stretch away to the horizon.
The fascination of this drawing lies in the diversity of picturesque motifs which the artist has not always been able to connect to one another, as in the fork in the path front left. B.B.

Schwarz, 1917, n° 74.

352 - King Christian II of Denmark - Cat. 252

Etching.
With monogram and dated 1546.
From Sigmund Baron of Herberstain's Rerum moscoviticarum commentarii, Vienna 1549.
202×100 mm. B. 15, Schwarz 15.
Paris, Bibliothèque Nationale, Cabinet des Estampes. ECN 1534.

349 - The death of Cleopatra - Cat. 249

The king stands in full armour facing obliquely to the left. His left hand holds a halberd, his right hand grasps a strap to which an empty escutcheon is fastened.

The subject can only be identified from the de luxe copy in Vienna which is provided with a coat of arms coloured by hand and has the name appended to it. It is probably the presentation copy for King Ferdinand I.

The figure of the knight, on which it is hardly possible to recognise any personal features, shows a close affinity to Burgkmaier's rulers from the Genealogy of Emperor Maximilian (H. 324-415). In fact Hirschvogel literally copied the figures for portraits of four other regents. B.B.

Schwarz, 1917, n° 15, p. 29-34, 166 - Cat. The Danube School, n° 103, p. 92 f.

CHRISTVS & IN FAMEM BAIVLAT IPSE CRVCEM / HVNC DECANTATA CELEBREMVS LAVDE SEQVENTES / ET SIBI QVISQVE SVAM BAIVLAT IPSE CRVCEM.

190×159 mm. B.3, Schwarz 3,1.
Paris, Bibliothèque Nationale, Cabinet des Estampes.
ECN 1532.

Two passages with ogival arches are traced with light strokes. The procession comes out of them and moves towards the left of the picture, with Christ at the head sinking to his knees under the weight of the cross. On the outer left a man who could be Simon of Cyrene supports the crossbeam of the cross. A horseman appears in the crowd behind

351 - Christ carrying the cross - Cat. 251
Etching.

With monogram and dated 1545. Four-lined poem on top edge of picture: *CONSVLIT HIC NOSTRAE SVDORE QVIETI/*

350 - Landscape with castle on a rock and a fir tree - Cat. 250

Christ; on the right stands a man with his back to us, preparing to strike a blow with a mighty swing of both arms which, however, has not been well thought out by the artist. All the figures move rather stiffly and have disproportionately large, snub-nosed heads.

This drawing is directly influenced by Sebald Beham's wood-cut (B.89) treating the same theme. The form of the arches is identical, as are the position of Christ, the group of man and child front right, etc. The ogival soffits seen in perspective giving space and forming a background for the group of figures, can be traced back further than Beham as fas as Altdorfer. B.B.

Schwarz, 1917, n° 61, 162

CONSVLIT HIC NOSTRÆ PROPRIO SVDORE QVIETI
CHRISTVS & IN FAMEM BAIVLAT IPSE CRVCEM
HVNC DECANTATA CELEBREMVS LAVDE SEQVENTES
ET SIBI QVISQVE SVAM BAIVLET IPSE CRVCEM
· 15 45 ·

351 - Christ carrying the cross - Cat. 251

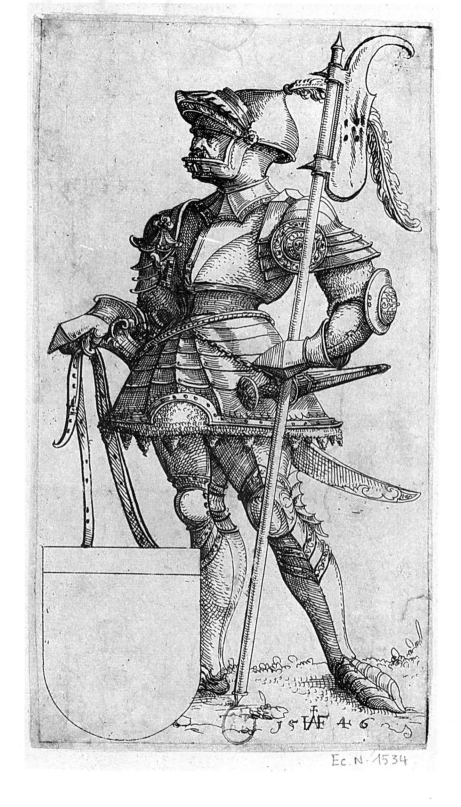

352 - King Christian II of Denmark - Cat. 252

MONOGRAMMIST HWG

He may have been working in Nuremberg towards the middle of the 16th century. Thus far, his known work comprises 6 woodcuts of which three may certainly be ascribed to him. A picture of Christ bearing the Cross (Munich, Bayerisches Nationalmuseum) has also been tentatively attributed to him.

353 - Stag hunt - Cat. 253

353 - Stag hunt - Cat. 253
Woodcut.
With 2 sets of initials, HWG and VS.
c. 1545.
97×216 mm.
Paris, Bibliothèque Nationale, Cabinet des Estampes.
ECN 1530.

354 - Christ and his disciples on the road to Emmaus - Cat. 254
Woodcut.
c. 1545.
106×212 mm.
Paris, Bibliothèque Nationale, Cabinet des Estampes.
ECN 1528.

The style clearly follows very closely that of Wolf Huber. The large areas of shading rendered by the vigorous parallel hatching, the fluidity of the lines and above all the impression of space in the lanscape all indicate this.
An acquaintance with Huber's style may have come not only from his few woodcuts but also from his much copied drawings. Here the cut is a little coarse and consequently the scene which is visible through the opening in the rocks is somewhat blurred. B.B.

Voss, 1907, pp. 47-50 — Voss, 1910, p. 37.

The them of stag hunting, as that of tournaments, is a courtly subject and has often been treated, for example in the woodcut (H 115) and various pictures (Vienna, Madrid, among others) by Cranach. In our print, a couple — princely? — in all their finery and a castle in the distance are likewise to be found. B.B.

Voss, 1909, p. 59 ff. Voss, 1910, p. 37 — Friedländer/Müle, 1970, p. 126 — I. O'Dell — Franke, Kupferstiche und Radierung aus der Werkstatt des Virgil Solis, Wiesbaden 1977, p. 21, 49.

354 - Christ and his disciples on the road to Emmaus - Cat. 254

HANNS LAUTENSACK

Born around 1520 in Bamberg, probably trained in Nuremberg. Etcher and medallist, he is also referred to as a painter. In 1554 he wen to Vienna by order of Ferdinand I. He must have died there between 1564 and 1566.

355 - Portrait of Ulrich Schwaiger - Cat. 255

Engraving and etching.
Initialed, dated 1554.
On the receptacle, the device G.M.H. — W. G.V.G.W., on the lid the inscription SVE XXX.
215×255 mm. B. 1, H. 69, Scmitt 10.
Paris, Bibliothèque Nationale, Cabinet des Estampes
ECN 1577.

This is most probably a portrait of Ulrich Schwaiger, goldsmith, stone engraver and sigillographer at Augsburg. The metal receptacle with its notched handles and the star-shaped lid would seem to be an allusion to his craft. B.B.

Schmitt, 1957, p. 66ff.

356 -Portrait of Leonhard Von Eckh - Cat. 256

Copper engraving, landscape etched.
With monogram and date 1553.
Inscription on the parapet: ANNO AEPATIS SVE LXXVII. OBDORMIVIT IN CHRISTO ANNO MDL DIE XVII MARTII.
344×242 mm. B.11, H.51, Schmitt 4.
Paris, Bibliothèque Nationale, Cabinet des Estampes. ECN 1572.

The half-figure facing to the right is behind a parapet in a room which looks out on to a landscape like a sort of loggia. The portrait is completed on the left by a curtain and a still life of carefully stacked books. A cartouche in the soffit of the wall holds the subject's coat of arms. The inscription shows that this is a posthumous portrait of the Bevarian chancellor. It goes back to a model by Barthel Beham. The details of his age are incorrect as Eckh, who was born in 1480, did not reach the age of 77. In addition, Lautensack follows his model and shows Eckh as a man at the height of his powers instead of as an old man. B.B.

Schmitt, 1957, n° 4, p.9f, 64.

357 -Portrait of Felicitas von Eckh, born Freyberg - Cat. 257.

Copper engraving, landscape etched.
With monogram and date 1553.
Inscription on the parapet: ANNO AETATIS SVE LXI.
352×247 mm. B.12, H.74, Schmitt 5.
Paris, Bibliothèque Nationale, Cabinet des Estampes. ECN 1573
This composition is built up out of exactly the same elements as in cat. 256, in reverse order which the artist stuck to right as far as transferring the monogram and date from the left to the right moulding of the parapet. This shows that the two prints belong together as companion pieces. In place of the book still life in the portrait of the man there are objects appropriate to the functions of a married woman - receptacles and bottles, one of which is marked "rose water".
The age of 61 given on the inscription concurs with the dating of the engraving and fits the person portrayed who, moreover, is dressed in widow's clothes. It is likely that the widow commissioned a sort of memorial picture in 1553 in which she herself could be reproduced from life whereas for the portrait of her late husband an already existing portrait had to be copied. B.B.

Schmitt, 1957, n° 5, p.9, 64.

355 - Portrait of Ulrich Schwaiger - Cat. 255

ANNO ÆTATIS SVE LXXVII

OBDORMIVIT IN CHRISTO ANNO
M.D.L. DIE XVII MARTII.

1553.

ISL

356 - Portrait of Leonhard Von Eckh - Cat. 256

ANNO ÆTATIS SVE. LXI.

1553

357 - Portrait of Felicitas von Eckh, born Freyberg - Cat. 257.

358 -The tournament - Cat. 258.

Etching.
With monogram and title : PRIMVS MARTIALIVM LVDOR-
VM PEDESTRIS CONFLICTVS 1560. From: Hans Francolin,
Rerum praeclare gestarum intra et extra moenia..., Vienna
(Raphaël Hofhalter) 1561.
385×500 mm. H.78, Schmitt 34.
Paris, Bibliothèque Nationale, Cabinet des Estampes. ECN 1570

This work contains detailed and illustrated depictions of the enter-
tainments put on in honour of Duke Albrecht V of Bavaria on the occasion of his visit to Vienna in May 1560. The author was the herald
to the emperor; different artists sent him wood-cuts and etchings. The
scene of the tournament represented is the old Hofburg (imperial
plalace) of Vienna with the Schweizertor which was erected in 1552.
B.B.

Schmitt, 1957, n° 34, p.7, 79.

359 -David - Cat. 259

Etching.
With monogram and date 1551.
172×231 mm. before being cut in half.
B.51, I, H.2, II, Schmitt 28,II.
Paris, Bibliothèque Nationale, Cabinet des Estampes. ECN 1545.

Print from the right half of a subsequently cut plate of David and
Goliath. Copies made from the intact plate are to be found in
Brunswick and London.
The sunbeams radially covering the whole sky could have been in-
fluenced by similar light phenomena in works of Wolf Huber or
Altdorfer. The figure of David as well as the whole composition are
taken from Holbein's Historiorum veteris instrumenti Icones, Lyon
(M.v. G. Trechsel) 1538, fol. E. IV v. The tree was added by Lauten-
sack. B.B.

Schmitt, 1957, n° 28, p. 28, 77.

358 - The tournament - Cat. 258.

359 - David - Cat. 259

360 - Town on the opposite bank of the river - Cat. 260.

Etching.
With monogram and date 1553.
120×175 mm. B.43, H.33, Schmitt 53.
Paris, Bibliothèque Nationale, Cabinet des Estampes. ECN 1561

This drawing is related to cat. n° 261 not only in its use of motifs but also with regard to its composition, as in the diagonal course of the river and the way in which the rocky mountain attracts the eye. However the view has an altogether greater sense of space and relaxation. The tree in the foreground gives space, an effect which Lautensack frequently re-used later. B.B.

Schmitt, 1957, n° 53, p. 24 f. 88.

361 - Landscape with mill - Cat. 261.

Etching.
With monogram and date 1553.
171×117 mm. B.27, H.17, Schmitt 59.
Paris, Bibliothèque Nationale, Cabinet des Estampes. ECN 1556

· 360   Town on the opposite bank of the river - Cat. 260.

477

In keeping with the high format the individual motifs are piled up on top of each other in this picture, rather than graded into the distance. The path in the foreground does not lead into the landscape but is led abruptly out of the picture after crossing the bridge. On the other hand the bridge is responsible for marking the course of the stream. Just a little upstream we come across the water-mill and a few more buildings. A massif of rock towers over it and its deep black shadow adds oppresive weight to it. On the left a view of wooded uplands. The print gives the impression of being both condensed and particularly haphazard, with a fragmentary nature as in Altdorfer's landscapes.

B.B.

Schmitt, 1957, n° 59.

361 - Landscape with mill - Cat. 261.

The Flight to Egypt, Baptism of Christ, Healing of a Blind man.

Etchings.

From a sequence of the Vita Christi of which 6 sheets are known so far. 3 of them are dated 1554 and 3 others 1555.

Subsequently changed on all the plates in 1559.

Paris, Bibliothèque Nationale, Cabinet des Estampes. ECN 1548, 1549, 1552.

Unlike the thematically specified sequences by, for example, Dürer, such as the life of Mary or the Passion of our Lord, this is simply a number of unconnected episodes from the life of Christ. In addition to those shown here there are the "Temptation of Christ", "Christ listening to the women from Cana" and "Christ cursing the fig-tree". A common feature of all these scenes is that they are set in open landscapes.

362 - The Baptism of Christ - Cat. 262.

With monogram and date 1554.

Tittle : CHRISTVS BAPTISATVR A IOANNE IN IORDANE LVCAE. III.

155×320 mm. B.46,I, H.35, Schmitt 69,I.

Paris, Bibliothèque Nationale, Cabinet des Estampes. ECN 1549

362 - The Baptism of Christ - Cat. 262.

On the right the baptism group on a stretch of the river-bank which is not connected to the rest of the landscape and out of scale withe the principal motif of the picture, a rocky island with extensive fortifications. Behind this a big town can be seen, lightly drawn on the opposite bank. Some distance away a bridge crosses the river. The emphatic contrast between striking individual motifs and the landscape in the background which creates an effect of depth is reminiscent of Dutch landscapes such as those of Patinir, Herri met de Bles or Cornelis Massys. The same applies to the way in which the figures are isolated in front of the landscape. B.B.

363 - The flight to Egypt - Cat. 263.

With monogram and date 1555.
Title : IOSEPH CVM IESU ET MARIA IN AEGYPTUM FVGIT MATTHAEI,II.
160×222 mm. B.45, H.34, Schmitt 68,I.
Paris, Bibliothèque Nationale, Cabinet des Estampes. ECN 1848

The group of Mary on the ass and Joseph is borrowed from Dürer's Life of Mary (B.89). They are placed on a plateau with a fir-tree and bushes, with a river below winding its way into the distance through bizarre rock formations.

363 - The flight to Egypt - Cat. 263.

364 -The healing of a Blind man - Cat. 264.

With monogram and date 1555.
Title : CAECVS SECVS VIAM SEDENS SANATVR LVCAE
XXVIII (sic!) MAT:XX. MAR: X.
156×221 mm. B.49, H.38, Schmitt 72,1.
Paris, Bibliothèque Nationale, Cabinet des Estampes. ECN 1552

The blind man calls out tu Jesus as he hears him walking past.
Thereupon the crowd tries to silence him, but Jesus listens to his sup-
plication and heals him. B.B.

Voss 1909, p.58f - Schmitt, 1957, n° 68-73, p. 26-28, 92-94.

365 -The flight to Egypt in a river Landscape - Cat. 265

Etching.
With monogram and date 1558.
192×289 mm. B.56, H.42, Schmitt 74.
Paris, Bibliothèque Nationale, Cabinet des Estampes. ECN 1554

364 - The healing of a Blind man - Cat. 264.

481

Almost identical format and compositional similarities ling this sheet to the Bileam and 3 further landscapes with biblical scenes which possibly all originate from one cycle.

In comparison with the earlier Flight the figures are less important, they are no more than accessories in the landscape which opens out into the distance. The most modern elements of this landscape are without doubt the way in which the river disappears into the distance and the graded effect of the mountains on the sides. Both come from the Netherlands, probably via the first landscape etchings of the Antwerpen graphic artist and publisher Hieronymus Cock which date from 1551 and 1558 (H.1,8-21). On the other hand the foreground seems more familiar: views through bridges as an opening to the picture occur very frequently in Wolf Huber's works, as do oversized conifers with intertwined branches. Willows, ferns and rocks come from the general repertoire of motifs of the Danube School.

In this respect the drawing has something of the character of an experiment. Here we find extension into depth and a sense of space on the one hand answering on the other hand the need for a composition which fills the whole surface. But this does not take place consistently, as one can see in the changing dimensions of the path on the left and the strength of the current which had to be "built in" to make the course of the river in the foreground more plausible. B.B.

Schmitt, 1957, n° 74, p. 30, 94.

365 - The flight to Egypt in a river Landscape - Cat. 265

366 -Landscape with workers in the vineyard - Cat. 266.
Etching.
With monogram and date 1559.
194×295 mm. B.53, I, H.10, I, Schmitt 75,I.
Paris, Bibliothèque Nationale, Cabinet des Estampes. ECN 1567

A path leads round the slope of a vineyard. There is a stationary cart on it. Workers are unloading stakes and putting them on both sides of the path. At the foot of the vineyard there are fields, farms surrounded by trees, a village around a church. A castle on a rock closes the middle distance. Behind it a hilly coast is unfolded with a town far away on the right. The surface of the water forms a piece of horizon on the right-hand edge.
Different plans for landscapes have been joined together in a superior way. The foreground also seems to bear witness to fresh observation.
B.B.

Schmitt, 1957, n° 75, p.30. 94 f.

367 -River Landscape with three figures - Cat. 267.
Etching.
Ca 1559.
190×288 mm. H.12, Schmitt 77.
Paris, Bibliothèque Nationale, Cabinet des Estampes. ECN 1569

366 - Landscape with workers in the vineyard - Cat. 266.

367 - River Landscape with three figures - Cat. 267.

In the near distance a tree on a hillock marks the middle axis of the composition. On the right a wide path leads past the hillock and goes deeper into the picture passing through a gate until it finally disappears behind the mound of rock on the edge of the picture. A horseman and a wanderer show that the path can be used, and third figure lies in the shade at the foot of the hillock in the foreground. Deeper in the landscape the bank of a powerful river comes into sight beyond the rock, bordered by a chain of mountains. The deep line of escape is interspersed with boats, a church, a fortress on a rock and several towns. For reasons of perspective the bank and mountain features are foreshortened and run right the way across the picture until they reach a narrow section of the horizon line on the left. The latter, giving a strong contrast between proximity and distance, is intersected by a rock which indicates the opposite bank. Between this rock and the elevated foreground the river describes a curve in order to flow out of the picture in the bottom left-hand corner. In the middle of the bend lies a flat wooded island with a stronghold on it.

Some of the motifs are reminiscent of those in earlier etchings, for example the island, the tree in the middle, the wooded rocky slope; however, in formal terms the composition shows itself to be one of the most mature of Lautensack's œuvre, by the unconstrained way in which a great range of depth is produced and the view is kept free of interruptions in spite of the differences of relief. The diagonal view of the riverbank escaping towards the horizon and the way in which the eye is led from an elevated viewpoint would have been inconceivable without an acquaintance and understanding of Cock's work. In fact this etching gives an even greater sense of space and can be compared with the series of landscapes later produced by Breughel. B.B.

Schmitt, 1957, n° 77, p.31, 95 - cat. The Danube School, 1969/70, n° 108.

368 -Bileam's encounter with the angel - Cat. 268.

Etching.
Ca. 1558/59.
187×285 mm B.55, H.41, Schmitt 80.
Paris, Bibliothèque Nationale, Cabinet des Estampes. ECN 1546

On the orders of the Moabite king Balak the prophet Bileam is supposed to have laid a curse on the Israelites who had moved out of Egypt.
Initially God commanded him to refuse but then let him go with the
king's emissaries, though he also sent an angel to meet him. At the
sight of the angel Bileam's ass draws back three times, whereupon its
rider tries to bring it under control more and more forcefully. The
third time the animal falls to its knees in front of the angel and defends
itself with human tongue. Bileam's eyes are opened so that he too
recongises the angel and admits his sin (4. Moses 22).
The motif of the gate of rock with a tree in front of it appears in
another Lautensack landscape etching which dates from 1544 and is
very similar in its general composition (Schmitt 46). It also appears in
a high format adaptation dating from 1554 (Schmitt 66). In one sense
it might go back to the Danube School, in another sense it could go
back to Dutch painting of the early 16th century (cf. Joos van Cleve,
Rest on the Flight to Egypt, Brussels). B.B.

Schmitt, 1957, n° 80, p. 28f, 94, 96.

368 - Bileam's encounter with the angel - Cat. 268.

NIKLAUS MANUEL DEUTSCH

Probably born and died at Berne (1484-1530). Painter, draughtsman, craftsman, poet and politician. Town councellor at Berne in 1523 he is put in charge of the bailiwick of Erlach. Convinced supporter of the Reformation, whose ideas he defended in his political writings.

369 - The Wise Virgin - Cat. 269
>Woodcut.
>Initialed, 1518.
>184×106 mm. B. 1, H. 3.
>Berlin, Kupferstichkabinett, SMPK.

Taken from a series of ten illustrations on the theme of the wise and the foolish virgins, some of which are dated 1518.
This parable, from Matthew 25, 1-13, was to be found most often decorating the portals of German gothic churches. Niklaus could have seen this on the main door of Berne cathedral, which was completed in about 1495. Unlike Cranach's apostles, his female figure is presented in a full landscape, standing in a meadow with a mountain range in the background. The sky behind the upper part of her body structures the hatched lines and clouds, giving the picture as a whole a well-balanced decorative aspect. The costume as well as the hairstyle, both surprisingly modern and opulent for a wise virgin, also contribute to this. B.B.

Cat. *Niklaus Manuel Deutsch,* 1979, n° 243

370 - The Foolish Virgin - Cat. 270
>Woodcut.
>Initialed, c. 1518.
>186×105 mm. B. 9, H. 9.
>Berlin Kupferstichkabinett, SMPK.

With an affected gesture the young virgin, turning towards the left, holds out her extinguished oil lamp thereby demonstrating that its contents have been used up. The landscape on either side, with the mountain chain stretching into the distance on the left and the mountain topped with buildings on the right, is reminiscent of Altdorfer's background scenes. B.B.

Cat. *Niklaus Manuel Deutsch,* n° 249

369 - The Wise Virgin - Cat. 269

370 - The Foolish Virgin - Cat. 270

URS GRAF

Born in 1485 in Solothurn. Trained as a glodsmith in his father's workshop. In addition he was active as a painter, glass painter, and designer of wood-cuts and engravings. During his years of travel he appeared in Strasbourg and Basel; he frequently travelled to Italy as a mercenary. In 1509 he settled in Basel where he died in 1527 or 1528

371 - Eight men in conversation - Cat. 271.
    Copper engraving.
    With monogram. Ca. 1506/07.
    317×222 mm. H. 27.
    Paris, Bibliothèque Nationale, Cabinet des Estampes.
    ECN 1237

Graf based this print on different models. Thus the architectural framework is probably inspired by Dürer's "Prodigal son" (B.28). The figure with his back turned to us is copied from a wood-cut from an edition of Virgil (Strasbourg, Johann Grüninger, 1502; the figure of Ascanius in the combat between Dares and Entelius, V,362-467). Graf changed the spiral scroll above this figure into a hat-feather.
This detail is characteristic of the flowing lines in this wood-cut which are able to give a structure to large areas by means of short strokes of considerably varied strength as well as creating a certain material content, as, for example, in the grain of the wooden gable in the front of the house on the left. B.B.

E. Major/E. Gradmann. Urs Graf, Basel o.J., n° 128, p.37.

372 - 373 The Passion - Cat. 272 - 273
    Fourteen small figures from the life of Christ.
    420×330 mm.
    Paris, Bibliothèque Nationale, Cabinet des Estampes.
    ECN 1240-1253.

Ec. N. 1240

Ec. N. 1241

Ec. N. 1242

Ec. N. 1243

Ec. N. 1244

Ec. N. 1245

Ec. N. 1246

Ec N. 1247

Ec N. 1248

Ec N. 1249

Ec N. 1250

Ec N. 1251

Ec N. 1252

Ec N. 1253

THE MASTER OF THE MARIAZELL MIRACLES

The painter of this series of woodcuts of the Mariazell Miracles comprising 25 prints cans probably be identified with a painter originating from Augsburg. Between 1512 and 1517 he was working in Lower Austria. In 1519 he was summoned by the Abbot Valentin Pierer to Mariazell in Steiemark in order to execute the paintings of the miracle of the Virgin Mary for a large altar, and to work on a project for this series of woodcuts.

374 to 376 - Three prints taken from the series of the Mariazell Miracles - Cat. 274 to 276

Woodcut.
c. 1519/20 (?)
Berlin, Kupferstichkabinett. SMPK. Inv. n° 243, 1889.

The influence of the Danube School extended into Styria. The great centres were the powerful monasteries of the region, the most important being the Benedictine abbey in Upper Styria, the Abbey of Saint Lambrecht where the holy place of Mariazell was to be found. The paintings of the miracles of the mother of God were undertaken in order to attract an increasing number of pilgrims to the place and to this end the execution of the altars was entrusted to artists of talent. The first altar piece dates from 1512 and constiues the small Marizell altar. It comprises six miracle scenes which clearly show to what extent the landscape painting, reminiscent of the atmosphere found in the Danube School, corresponded to the popular style of the miracle theme. Following this were two more extensive cycles, the first of which comprises fifty different scenes. Many indications would lead to believe that, shortly after the completion of the large Mariazell miracle altar towards 1519/20, the abbot of the monastery, Valentin Pierer, commissioned a series of woodcuts in order to make his place of pilgrimage known to the outside world thereby countering the competition engendered by the pilgrimage to the "Schöne Maria" at Regensburg (cat. 84-85 ill. 106-107). In this series of woodcuts portraying different miracles, 25 prints are to be found in Berlin and 22 in Vienna. One of the Vienna prints, however, did not find its way to Berlin and it can therefore be supposed that the original set included even more prints. The wishes granted by the famous holy image of Mariazell are represented. The unquestionable influence of Cranach's early Vienna work is apparent; but the artist also borrowed from Huber's drawings, so much so that one may surmise an intermittent activity in his studio over a period of twenty years. R.B.

Cat. Kunst der Donauschule, 1965, p. 164 ff and n° 412. — Cat. The Danube School, 1969/70, p. 67 ff — Winzinger, 1979, n° 170.

374 to 376 - Three prints taken from the series of the Mariazell Miracles - Cat. 274 to 276

Ain Man schöß seinen nagsten/den er vermainet ain Pern gewesen sein
mit ainem strall durch den hertzkasst bey dem denngken Tüttel ein. Und
als er Mariam anrüesset/vnnd sich gen Zell mit ainem opffer versprach.
ward im geholffen. Als er dañ nachmalln am plössen leib angezaigt hat.

Ein Priester wardt gefanngen von den vnglaubigen/selb dreyssigist/
vnd yn ain grüben zu vnnderist geworffen/vnnd mit puluer verströt.
Mariam zw Zell rüfft Er an/die halff ym aus aller not.

Ainer frawen von Stainenkirchen yn der gepurdt mißlang/das sy vnd
das khindt khain trost des lebens hetten. So pald sy yr man gen Zell
verhieß/wardt mütter vnd khindt von stundt gesundt.

BIBLIOGRAPHY

Further information may be obtained by consulting the following publications which have very frequently been referred to in this catalogue.

ANDERSON Christiane, Charles Talbot: From a Mighty Fortress, Prints, drawings and books in the age of Luther 1484-1546; Cat. Exh. Detroit, 1983.

ANZELEWSKI, Fedja: Dürer und seine Zeit, Meisterzeichnungen aus dem Berliner Kupferstichkabinett; Cat. Exh Berlin, 1967.

BALDASS Ludwig: Albrecht Altdorfer, Vienna, 1941.

BARTSCH Adam (B): Le Peintre-graveur; 21 Bde, Vienna, 1803-21.

BAXANDALL Michael: The Limewood Sculptors of Renaissance Germany; New Haven/London, 1980.

BENESCH Otto, Erwin Auer: Die Historia Friderici et Maxmiliani, Berlin, 1957.

BUCHNER Ernst: Albrecht Altdorfer und sein Kreis; Cat. Exh. Munich 1938.

FRIEDLANDER Max J.: Albrecht Altdorfer, Berlin 1923.

FRIEDLANDER Bock: Die Zeichnungen alter Meister im Kupferstichkabinett; pub. Max J. Friedländer, Die deutschen Meister: detailed description of a collection of drawings. Prepared by Elfried Bock; 2 Bde Staatliche Museen zu Berlin, Berlin 1921.

FRIEDLANDER and Möhle: Der Holzschnitt, new edition by Hans Möhle, Berlin, 1970.

GEISBERG Max (G): Der deutsche Einblattholzschnitt in der erste Hälfte des 16 Jhs, Munich, 1930.

ROTE Ludwig: Georg Lemberger, Leipzig 1933.

HEINZLE E: Wolf Huber, Innsbrück, 1953.

GEISBERG and Strauss: The German Single-Leaf Woodcut; 1500-1550, Rev. and edited by Walter L. Strauss, 4 Vol., New York, 1974.

GROTE Ludwig: Georg Lemberger, Leipzig, 1933.

HEINZLE E. Wolf Huber, Innsbrück, 1953.

HIND Arthur M.: Nielli, chiefly Italian, of the 15th century; Plates, Sulphur Casts and Prints preserved in the British Museum, London, 1936.

HOFMANN Werner: Luther und die Folgen für die Kunst: Cat. Exh. Hamburg, 1973.

HOLLSTEIN F.W.H.: German Engravings, Etchings and Woodcuts c. 1400-1700; Amsterdam 1954.

HOLLSTEIN F.W.H.: Dutch and Flemish Engravings, Etchings and Woodcuts c.1450-1700; Amsterdam, 1962.

JAHN Johannes: Lucas Cranach als Graphiker; Leipzig, 1955.

JAHN Johannes: Lucas Cranach d'A; das gesamte graphische Werk; Munich, 1972.

KOEPPLIN Dieter: Das Sonnengestirn der Donaumeister in Werden und Wandlung Studien z. Kunst d. Donauschule; Linz, 1967, pp 78-114.

KOEPPLIN and Falk: Lucas Cranach: Gemälde Zeichnungen, Druckgraphik. Dieter Koepplin/Tilman Falk; Kunstmuseum Basel, 2 Vol. Cat. Exh. Basel and Stuttgart, 1974-76.

KRUMMER-SCHROTT Ingeborg: Der Schnitzaltar in Niederrotweil am Kaiserstuhl. In: Jb. d. Staatl. Kunstslg. in Baden-Würtemberg 8 1971, pp 65-96.

Die Kunst der Donauschule 1490-1540. Stift St. Florian u. Schloss-museum. Cat. Exh. Linz, 1965.

Kunst der Reformationszeit. Altes Museum, Cat. Exh. Berlin DDR 1983.

LIEBMANN M.J.: die deutsche Plastik 1350-1550, Leipzig 1982.

LOSSNITZER Max: Hans Leinberger (Veröffentlichungen d. Graphischen Gesellsch. 18) Berlin, 1913.

Lucas Cranach: Gemälde-Zeichnungen-Druckgraphik. Cat. Exh. Berlin 1973.

Martin Luther und die Reformation in Deutschland, pub. Gerhard Bott, Cat. Exh. Nuremberg, 1983.

Meister um Albrecht Dürer, Germ. nat. Nuremberg. Cat. Exh. Nuremberg, 1961.

MINOTT Charles S.: Martin Schongauer. New York, 1971.

Nikolaus Manuel Deutsch Maler, Dichter, Staatsmann; Cat. Exh. Berne, 1979.

OETTINGER Karl: Zu Wolf Huber's Frühzeit. In: Jb. d. Kunsthist Slgn. in Wien, Vol 53, 1957, pp. 71.

OETTINGER Karl: Altdorferstudien. Erlanger Beitr. z. Sprach- u. Kunstwiss. III, Nuremberg, 1959.

PACKPFEIFFER Katharina: Studien zu Erhard Altdorfer. Diss. Wien, 1978.

Prints and Drawings of the Danube School; Cat. Exh. New Haven, 1969 (Yale, St. Louis, Philadelphia 1969/70).

ROSENBERG Jacob: Die Zeichnungen Lucas Cranachs d.A., Berlin, 1960.

SCHINDLER Herbert: Der Meister HL = Hans Loy? Werk und Wiederentdeckung Königstein i.T., 1981.

SCHMITT Annegrit: Hans Lautensack, Nuremberg, 1957 (Nürenberg Forschungen).

SCHRAMM Albert: Die Illustration der Lutherbibel. In: Luther und die Bibel, Leipzig, 1923.

SCHWARZ Karl: Augustin Hirschvogel, Berlin, 1917.

SOMMER Clemens: Der Meister der Breisacher Hochaltars. In: Zeitschr. d. deutschen Vereins f. Kunstwiss. 3, 1936, pp. 245-274.

STANGE Alfred: Malerei der Donauschule, Munich 1964.

The Book of Hours of the Emperor Maximillian the First, commentary by W.L. Strauss, publ. Abaris Books Inc., 1974.

TIETZE Hans: Albrecht Altdorfer, Leipzig, 1932.

VOSS Hermann: Der Ursprung des Donaustils, Leipzig, 1907 (Kunstgeschichtliche Monogr. 7).

VOSS Hermann: Aus der Umgebung Albrecht Altdorfers und Wolf Hubers. In: Mitteil. d. Ges. f. Vervielfältigende Kunst. Beil. d. "Graphischen Künste", 1909, pp. 52-60, 73-77.

VOSS Hermann: Wolf Huber, Leipzig, 1910. (Meister d.Graphik. 3).

WINKLER Friedrich: Die Zeichnungen Albrecht Dürers; 4 Vol, Berlin, 1936-39.

WINKLER Friedrich: Ein Tittelblatt und seine Wandlungen; In: Zeitschr. f. Kunstwiss. 15, 1961 pp. 149-163.

WINZINGER Franz: Albrecht Altdorfer: Zeichnungen (compl. coll.) Munich, 1952.

1963: Albrecht Altdorfer: Graphik, Holzschnitte, Kupferstiche, Radierungen (compl. coll.) Munich.

1964: Unbekannte Zeichnungen Georg Lembergers. In: Zeitschr. d. deutschen Vereins f. Kunstwiss. XVIII, pp. 81-90.

1973: die Miniaturen zum Triumphzug Kaiser Maxmillians I. Kommentardb. 2 Vol Graz.

1979: Albrecht Altdorfer: Gemälde, (compl. coll.), Munich.

1979: Wolf Huber: das Gesamtwerk, 2 Vol., Munich.

WYNEN Arnult: Michael Ostendorfer (um 1492-1559); Ein Regensburger Maler der Reformationszeit; Diss. Freiburg, 1961.

377 - The Danube at Sarmingstein - Budapest, Fine Arts Museum.

Catalogues. (Exh. Cat.)

Basel:

1974 - D. Koepplin/T. Falk, Lucas Cranach. Gemälde, Zeichnungen, Druckgraphik. Kunstmuseum Basel. 2 Bde, Basel u.Stuttg: 1974-76.

Berlin:

1967 - F. Anzelewsky, Dürer und seine Zeit. Meisterzeichnungen aus dem Berliner Kupferstichkabinett. Berlin: 1967.

1973 - Lucas Cranach. Gemälde- Zeichnungen - Druckgraphik. SMPK, Gemäldegalerie und Kupferstichkabinett. Berlin: 1973.

1983 - Kunst der Reformationzeit. Altes Museum, Berlin (Ost): 1983.

Bern:

1979 - Nikolaus Manuel Deutsch. Maler, Dichter, Staatsmann. Bern: 1979.

Detroit:

1983 - Christiane Anderson/Charles Talbot, From a Mighty Fortress. Prints, drawings and books in the age of Luther 1483-1546, Detroit: 1983.

Hamburg:

1983 - Luther und die Folgen für dei Kunst. Hrsg.v.W.Hofmann, Hamburg: 1983.

Linz:

1965 - Die Kunst der Donauschule 1490-1540. Stift St. Florian und Schloßmuseum. Linz: 1965.

Munich:

1938 - Albrecht Altdorfer und sein Kreis. Hrsg.v.E.Buchner, München²: 1938.

New Haven:

1969 - Prints and Drawings of the Danube School. Yale, St. Louis, Philadelphia, New Haven: 1969/70.

Nuremberg:

1961 - Meister um Albrecht Dürer. Germ. Nat. Museum Nürnberg, Nürnberg: 1961.

1983 - Martin Luther und die Reformation in Deutschland. Hrsg.v.G.Bott, Nürnberg: 1983.

ABBREVIATIONS

B.	BARTSCH Adam : Le peintre-graveur, 21 vol., Vienne, 1803-1821.
B.B.	BRINKMANN Bodo
F.A.	ANZELEWSKI Fedja
G.	GEISBERG Max : Der Deutsche Einblattholzschnitt in der ersten Hälfte des 16. Jahrhunderts, Munich, 1930.
G./St.	GEISBERG Max : The German Single-leaf Woodcut: 1500-1550. Revised and edited by Walter L. STRAUSS, 4 Vol., New York, 1974.
H.	1. HOLLSTEIN F.W.H.: German Engravings, Etchings and Woodcuts ca. 1400-1700; vol. 1-7, Amsterdam s.a. (1954-1968); vol. 8-11, Amsterdam 1968-1975; vol. 16-27, 1975-1980.
	2. HOLLSTEIN F.W.H.: Deutsch and Flemish Engravings, Etchings and Woodcuts ca. 1450-1700. 26 vol., Amsterdam s.a. 1969-1982.
K.	Kupferstichkabinett.
M.R.	ROTH Michael.
R.B.	Mme R. BRAIG.
SMPK.	Staatliche Museen Preussischer Kulturbesitz.
W.P.	PFEIFFER Wolfgang.
Wz.	WINZINGER Franz.

378 -The Crucifixion - Cat. 173

Lucas Cranach
Wood engraving.
Unsigned, before 1502.
398×284 mm. P. IV, P. 40, n° 2.
Berlin, Kupferstichkabinett, SMPK Inv n° 86-10.

The crucifixion, a recurring theme in the art of this period, was portrayed in different ways by Cranach. Cranach's very early engraving probably dates from his time in Vienna, directly preceding his protrayal of Calvary of 1502. It is similar to Albrecht Dürer's engraving from the "Grosse Passion" of approximately 1498 on which it is probably based. This engraving is particularly expressive, as is the later version, even if, unlike the later version, it lacks something in overall tension. In particular, the group of riders does not seem to be involved in the central action of the picture. However, if one considers the three massive posts of the crosses, the huge tree stumps, the expression of the thief nailed and bound to the cross and the form of the second thief, one can see that Cranach's passionately expressive style, which marked the birth of the Danube School, is apparent even in this early work.

R.B.

Koepplin/Falk, 1974, n° 63 — Cat. *Lucas Cranach* 1973, n° 64.

BEBA · 13, rue de l'Aude 75014 PARIS
Achevé d'imprimer en juillet 1985
N° 1615 · Imprimerie BOUCHY · Bagneux

Photogravure
DR GRAPHIC · Montreuil

Photocomposition
BDC · Paris

Dépôt légal mars 1984
ISBN : 2.904048.04.4
© JMG Paris

The layout of this volume was designed by Maurice Guillaud.

DATE DUE

GAYLORD   PRINTED IN U.S.A.